Contents

List of figures	*page*	vi
List of tables		viii
Contributors		x
Series editor's foreword		xiii

1   The role of economic analysis in supporting disability policy   1
John Cullinan, Seán Lyons and Brian Nolan

2   Disability, social inclusion and poverty   14
Brian Nolan

3   Disability and the labour market   38
Brian Nolan

4   The private economic costs of adult disability   58
John Cullinan and Seán Lyons

5   A socioeconomic profile of childhood disability   74
John Cullinan and Aine Roddy

6   Resource allocation for students with special educational needs
and disabilities   93
Denise Frawley, Joanne Banks and Selina McCoy

7   Ageing, disability and policy   110
Eamon O'Shea

8   The economics of dementia   123
Paddy Gillespie and Sheelah Connolly

9   The costs of community living for people with intellectual disabilities   142
Aoife Callan

10   The economics of mental health services   160
Brendan Kennelly

11   The socioeconomic determinants of mental stress   177
David Madden

Index   187

Figures

1.1 Employment rates of people with and without disabilities in the late 2000s *page* 5

1.2 Disability benefit recipients as a percentage of the population aged 20–64 in 28 OECD countries, 2010 or latest available year 6

1.3 Number and percentage of males and females with a disability in Ireland, 2011 7

1.4 Type of disability by age group, 2011 8

2.1 Highest level of education completed, by type of disability (%) 17

2.2 Level of education by age group for adults aged 25 to 64 (%) 18

2.3 Percentage of those identified as having a disability in both Census and NDS limited by disability before completion of full-time education, by age group and gender 19

2.4 Estimated relationship between chronic illness/disability and educational attainment, controlling for age and gender 20

2.5 Percentage of people with a disability who do not participate in social activities, by gender and age group 29

2.6 Percentage of people with a disability who do not participate in social activities, by type of disability 30

3.1 Principal economic status for all adults and for adults with a disability, by type of disability (%) 40

3.2 Main activity of adults with a disability, by sex and age group (%) 41

3.3 Main activity by main disability type (%) 42

3.4 Impact of disability on labour force participation, men 45

3.5 Disability onset and labour force participation 47

3.6 Features or aids required for work by sex and age group (%) 52

THE ECONOMICS OF DISABILITY

Manchester University Press

IRISH SOCIETY

The Irish Society series provides a critical, interdisciplinary and in-depth analysis of Ireland that reveals the processes and forces shaping social, economic, cultural and political life, and their outcomes for communities and social groups. The books seek to understand the evolution of social, economic and spatial relations from a broad range of perspectives, and explore the challenges facing Irish society in the future given present conditions and policy instruments.

SERIES EDITOR
Rob Kitchin

ALREADY PUBLISHED

Public private partnerships in Ireland: Failed experiment or the way forward for the state? *Rory Hearne*

Migrations: Ireland in a global world
Edited by Mary Gilmartin and Allen White

The domestic, moral and political economies of post-Celtic tiger Ireland: What rough beast? *Kieran Keohane and Carmen Kuhling*

Challenging times, challenging administration:
The role of public administration in producing social justice in Ireland
Chris McInerney

Management and gender in higher education
Pat O'Connor

THE ECONOMICS OF DISABILITY

Insights from Irish research

Edited by John Cullinan,
Seán Lyons and Brian Nolan

MANCHESTER UNIVERSITY PRESS

Published by Manchester University Press
Altrincham Street, Manchester M1 7JA, UK
www.manchesteruniversitypress.co.uk

British Library Cataloguing-in-Publication Data is available

Library of Congress Cataloging-in-Publication Data is available

ISBN 978 1 5261 0730 5 *paperback*

First published by Manchester University Press in hardback 2014

This edition first published 2016

Printed by Lightning Source

3.7	Reasons for not being interested in work for those with disability, by gender and age group (%)	53
4.1	The standard of living approach	61
6.1	Funding models	98
6.2	Overview of GAM at primary and post-primary	99

Tables

1.1 Self-perceived long-standing limitations in usual activities due to health problem, shares of population, EU countries, 2011   *page* 9

2.1 Ordered probit model of educational qualifications by degree hampered, estimated marginal effects   21

2.2 At risk of poverty rate and consistent poverty rate for adults aged 16 and over in 2006, 2007 and 2008, by disability status (%)   23

2.3 The probability of being at risk of poverty, estimated marginal effects   25

2.4 The probability of being consistently poor, estimated marginal effects   26

2.5 Onset of chronic illness/disability and household income, estimated marginal effects   27

2.6 Results for models predicting social participation, estimated marginal effects   32

3.1 Probit model of labour force participation, men aged 15–64, estimated marginal effects   44

3.2 Probit model of labour force participation, women aged 15–64, estimated marginal effects   46

3.3 Onset of chronic illness/disability and probability of stopping work, age 15–65   48

3.4 Persistent chronic illness/disability and probability of being in work, age 15–65   49

3.5 Results of estimated wage equation, men   50

3.6 Results of estimated wage equation for employees with versus without hampering illness/disability with selection bias correction, men   51

4.1 Breakdown of SILC 2011 sample households by disability status   67

4.2   Estimated economic cost of disability in 2011 – all disabled
      households   68
4.3   Estimated economic cost of disability in 2011, by number of
      persons with a disability, severity and condition   70
5.1   Children with a disability classified by gender and age group, 2011   75
5.2   Children with a disability classified by type of disability and
      age group, 2011   76
5.3   Logit models of primary carers' labour force participation,
      estimated marginal effects   84
5.4   Summary of main econometric results – comparisons relative
      to households with children without a disability   86
6.1   Criteria for additional teaching posts under the GAM
      (primary level)   100
6.2   Logistic regression model of the association between high
      SEN prevalence and school characteristics at primary level   102
6.3   Logistic regression models of the association between high
      SEN prevalence and school characteristics at post-primary level   103
8.1   Estimating the costs of dementia in Ireland for 2010   127
8.2   Estimating the costs of dementia in Ireland for 2021, 2031
      and 2041   131
8.3   Econometric modelling of the costs of dementia in Ireland   135
9.1   Cost typology   147
9.2   Characteristics of individuals by type of care setting   149
9.3   Outcomes across residential type   151
9.4   Raw average weekly cost of residential support   152
9.5   Results of GLMs, estimated coefficients   153
10.1 Mental health expenditure, 2011   164
10.2 Mental health care per capita allocation, 2007 (€m)   167
10.3 HSE mental health budget by super catchment area, 2010 (€)   167
10.4 Overall distribution of the cost of mental health problems in
      Ireland, 2006   169

Contributors

Editors

John Cullinan is a Lecturer in Economics at the National University of Ireland (NUI), Galway. He completed his doctoral studies at NUI Galway and holds Masters degrees in econometrics and economics from the London School of Economics and Political Science and University College Dublin (UCD), respectively. John previously worked as a Lecturer in Economics at the University of Limerick, NUI Maynooth and UCD, as a Consultant with Indecon Economic Consultants and he was a Visiting Scholar at the University of California, Berkeley in 2008. John's research interests lie in the application of econometric and spatial modelling techniques in the fields of health economics and spatial economics. He has a long-held interest in the economics of disability.

Seán Lyons is an Associate Research Professor at the Economic and Social Research Institute and an Adjunct Associate Professor in the Department of Economics at Trinity College Dublin (TCD). Formerly he was a partner at Indecon Economic Consultants, a senior adviser for Ireland's telecoms regulator and a Managing Consultant at London Economics. Seán holds a PhD in Economics (TCD), an MPhil in Economics (University of Cambridge) and a BA in History (TCD). He specialises in applied microeconomics, with a particular focus on regulation, consumer demand analysis and policy modelling and he has a long-standing research interest in the cost of disability and the economics of long-term care. Seán is Honorary Secretary of the Statistical and Social Inquiry Society of Ireland.

Brian Nolan is currently Principal of the College of Human Sciences in University College Dublin and has been Professor of Public Policy there since 2007. He previously worked at the Economic and Social Research Institute and the Central Bank of Ireland. He has a BA in Economics and History from UCD, an MA in Economics from McMaster University (Ontario) and a doctorate in economics from the London School of Economics and Political Science. His main areas of research are poverty, income inequality, the economics of social policy and health economics. He co-edited the *Handbook of Economic Inequality* (2008) and *The Great Recession and the Distribution of Household Income* (2013) for Oxford University Press, which also published *Poverty and Deprivation in Europe*, co-authored with Christopher T. Whelan (2011).

Contributors

Joanne Banks works in research on special educational needs at the Economic and Social Research Institute. She is particularly interested in the experiences of students with special needs in mainstream education, special needs identification and the ways in which resources are assigned to children with special needs.

Aoife Callan is a Health Research Board-funded Health Economics Postgraduate Research Fellow based at the Discipline of General Practice and Discipline of Economics at National University of Ireland, Galway. Her research interests include health and social care economics, health technology assessment, non-market valuation techniques and applied microeconometrics.

Sheelah Connolly is a Research Fellow within the Academic Unit of Neurology, Trinity College Dublin. She was awarded a PhD in Epidemiology from Queen's University Belfast and an MSc in Health Economics from the University of York. Her research interests lie in the social determinants of health and the economics of ageing.

Denise Frawley is a Research Assistant at the Economic and Social Research Institute. She is currently working on a longitudinal project that will track the experiences, progress and outcomes for a cohort of students with special educational needs in primary and post-primary schools in Ireland.

Paddy Gillespie is a Lecturer in Economics at the School of Business and Economics, National University of Ireland, Galway. His research interests focus on the area of health economics and his work to date has explored a variety of questions in relation to heart disease, diabetes, dementia and infectious disease.

Brendan Kennelly is a Lecturer in Economics and Director of the MSc (Health Economics) programme at National University of Ireland, Galway. His main research interest is health economics, particularly in relation to mental health and suicide and he also does research on economics education. He has published papers on these and other topics in a number of leading journals.

David Madden is an Associate Professor of Economics at University College Dublin, where he has worked since 1991. His research interests lie in the areas of health inequality and poverty, obesity and taxation. His previous work experience includes AIB Investment Managers, the Central Bank of Ireland, the Ministry of Health, Kaduna, Nigeria, National University of Ireland, Maynooth and the Economic and Social Research Institute.

Selina McCoy is joint Education Programme Co-ordinator at the Economic and Social Research Institute and Adjunct Professor at Trinity College Dublin. She has published extensively on Irish education, addressing a range of policy-relevant topics spanning primary and second-level education, post-school transitions and higher education.

Eamon O'Shea is a personal Professor in the Discipline of Economics at National University of Ireland, Galway. He has published numerous papers in leading international journals and has authored/co-authored 14 books and monographs, mainly in the field of ageing and social policy. He is a former Chair of the National Economic and Social Forum Expert Group on Care of the Elderly.

Aine Roddy is an Irish Research Council Scholar and PhD student in Economics at National University of Ireland, Galway. Her doctoral research focuses on the economics of childhood disability, in particular the economic costs associated with childhood disability.

Series editor's foreword

Over the past twenty years Ireland has undergone enormous social, cultural and economic change. From a poor, peripheral country on the edge of Europe with a conservative culture dominated by tradition and Church, Ireland transformed into a global, cosmopolitan country with a dynamic economy. At the heart of the processes of change was a new kind of political economic model of development that ushered in the so-called Celtic Tiger years, accompanied by renewed optimism in the wake of the ceasefires in Northern Ireland and the peace dividend of the Good Friday Agreement. As Ireland emerged from decades of economic stagnation and The Troubles came to a peaceful end, the island became the focus of attention for countries seeking to emulate its economic and political miracles. Every other country, it seemed, wanted to be the next Tiger, modelled on Ireland's successes. And then came the financial collapse of 2008, the bursting of the property bubble, bank bailouts, austerity plans, rising unemployment and a return to emigration. From being the paradigm case of successful economic transformation, Ireland has become an internationally important case study of what happens when an economic model goes disastrously wrong.

The Irish Society series provides a critical, interdisciplinary and in-depth analysis of Ireland that reveals the processes and forces shaping social, economic, cultural and political life, and their outcomes for communities and social groups. The books seek to understand the evolution of social, economic and spatial relations from a broad range of perspectives, and explore the challenges facing Irish society in the future given present conditions and policy instruments. The series examines all aspects of Irish society including, but not limited to: social exclusion, identity, health, welfare, life cycle, family life and structures, labour and work cultures, spatial and sectoral economy, local and regional development, politics and the political system, government and governance, environment, migration and spatial planning. The series is supported by the Irish Social Sciences Platform (ISSP), an all-island platform of integrated social science research and graduate education focusing on the social, cultural and economic transformations shaping Ireland in the twenty-first century. Funded by the Programme for Research in Third Level Institutions, the ISSP brings together leading social science academics from all of Ireland's universities and other third-level institutions.

Given the marked changes in Ireland's fortunes over the past two decades it is important that rigorous scholarship is applied to understand the forces at work, how they have affected different people and places in uneven and unequal ways, and what needs to happen to create a fairer and prosperous society. The Irish Society series provides such scholarship.

Rob Kitchin

1

The role of economic analysis in supporting disability policy

John Cullinan, Seán Lyons and Brian Nolan

Disability policy

A broad measure of consensus has emerged in Ireland and internationally on the nature of disability and the principles that should guide disability policy. Disability is now seen as a socioeconomic phenomenon, whereby disabled people are prevented from participating fully in social and economic activities due to the presence of various barriers. These barriers arise in many domains including societal attitudes, public and private infrastructures and institutions, and disability results from the adverse interactions that they may have with individual characteristics such as 'enduring physical, sensory mental health or intellectual impairment[s]', as the Disability Act (2005) characterises them. Moreover, there is a broad recognition that disability leads to 'high levels of social, economic and cultural disadvantage' (Disability Federation of Ireland, 2008).

In this context, disability policy now emphasises the need for services to be offered on a common basis for those with and without disabilities as far as possible (known as 'mainstreaming'), for supports to be flexible enough to cater for the changing profile of individuals' needs and preferences over the life course (the 'life cycle approach'), for supports to be provided on a bespoke basis that takes account of needs and available resources and for disabled people to be involved in decisions about the supports they receive. We outline each of these elements below.

Historically, most disability services were standardised, focused on deficits and often delivered in segregated group settings. The aim now is to 'mainstream' services where possible, delivering supports that allow recipients to stay in the same communities, educational establishments and workplaces as those without impairments. This has advantages over segregated provision of services, since it allows people to remain connected to natural, informal community supports and to exert more control over their lives. There are, however, challenges to implementing this approach. One is to avoid essential services and supports becoming diluted or inaccessible to those in settings where few people are using them (e.g. rural areas, small schools or workplaces). The effect on cost of changing service provision in this way may also vary; mainstream provision may lead to economies of scale or scope in some cases, but it may also lead to diseconomies if there is deadweight or low utilisation.

Related to the notion of mainstreaming is the life cycle approach. This recognises that the supports required by an individual are best viewed as defined by a changing set of preferences and barriers, not as static requirements by their disability, but rather related to their position in the life course. This implies a need to revisit an individual's supports over time and to assess preferences for services with reference to the wider population at a given point in the life course, as well as disabled groups per se.

The socioeconomic factors contributing to disability can bear very differently on individuals, depending on their exact circumstances. For example, societal attitudes towards disabled people can differ by the type of impairment, as documented in surveys by Ireland's National Disability Authority (2011). Opportunities for employment, education, social engagement and many other activities may differ among individuals, not just because of their impairments per se but because of their differing networks of families, friends and neighbours and their personal preferences. In addition, the nature of supports needed to help individuals live in their own communities can vary widely. While much public funding is focused on formal programmes, many people get some support from co-funded voluntary bodies. This has advantages for some people, because it can allow flexible supports to be delivered; for example, in cases where specialised but occasional services are required.

Because each individual faces a unique context, policy has shifted towards a more individualised or person-centred model. The idea is to craft a set of personalised supports based on an understanding of each person's needs and preferences. There is also a related goal to increase the level of control individuals have over the services they receive. These objectives imply a requirement to assess needs and consult with individuals on an individual basis, to fund and deliver personalised packages of supports and to ensure that access to supports is coordinated if different elements are provided by more than one agency. Ultimately, it should be possible to provide individualised budgets based on needs-based support plans, which would offer additional benefits in promoting efficient allocation of resources (ERGDP, 2011).

This approach stands in contrast to the traditional model whereby relatively standard packages of services were provided to specific groups, often by single providers. It thus represents a considerable challenge both to agencies involved in delivering services, many of which are in the voluntary sector, and to public sector bodies that plan and manage disability programme funding. However, better information and communication technologies are available to help with tracking and assessment of needs and resources, and it is increasingly commonplace in the private sector to see such technologies used to manage highly complex and flexible individual profiles.

Policy implementation

Yet, in practice, many disability services and the institutions that organise, fund and deliver them in Ireland fall a long way short of satisfying these objectives. In part this is due to resource limitations. Ireland's deteriorating fiscal position, culminating in the 2010 EU–IMF Economic Adjustment Programme (European Commission, 2011), led to postponement of some planned reform measures. Nevertheless, there were substantial increases in the public resources allocated to disability services prior to this. Health Service Executive (HSE) expenditure on disability services rose by more than a third between 2005 and 2009, before falling by about 5% in the two years to 2011 (Department of Health, 2012). Some of the rise related to increased pay rates, but staff numbers increased by about a quarter from 2005 to 2009 before falling by about 5% up to 2011 (Department of Health, 2012).

These increases allowed improvements in the provision of many services, and there has been some movement towards a more person-centred approach, but a recent review found that 'the pace of change has been slow and uneven' (Department of Health, 2012). Further reforms are planned, including improvements to the data infrastructure, accountability and transparency measures for agencies delivering services, development of a national resource planning model and piloting of person-centred services and supports. These reforms will be implemented against a backdrop of continuing limitations on resources, while it is likely that demand for services and supports will increase. Demographic projections indicate that (all else equal) there will be rising numbers of persons with the sorts of impairments that lead to disability: the population is living longer, leading to more age-related impairments; disabled people are living longer, potentially affecting severity; and informal caregivers are ageing too, which may affect the supply of care (ERGDP, 2011). Efficient resource allocation and delivery will be paramount in the face of limited funding and rising demand.

The economics of disability

Although the outlines of the reform programme are fairly clear, a lot of details remain to be filled in. Economic methods can make a significant contribution to understanding, measuring and addressing disability. Indeed, we see this as the primary motivation for this book: to provide evidence that can help to improve disability policies, services and supports.

Economic tools are relevant to studying disability and disability policy at several levels. First, applied economics is built on causal analysis. Because disability is now understood to be a consequence of how individuals' characteristics interact with their social, economic and cultural environments, economic methods can help to trace out and quantify the causes and extent of disability. Meeting the goal of individualising disability services will require a much richer understanding of how different sets of individual characteristics lead to varying levels of social, economic and cultural disadvantage. For example, to what extent does disability manifest itself as social disadvantage? How high are the barriers to employment of disabled people and what additional costs of living do they bear?

Second, economics offers tools for examining patterns of preferences and outcomes among different groups in a systematic way. Economic models can help us to understand changes in preferences over the life course. This is particularly relevant to the goal of mainstreaming services. Third, the ultimate focus of economics is on allocating scarce resources. Particularly in the current difficult economic circumstances in Ireland, it is important to maximise the efficiency with which services and supports are provided, as well as to put the right incentives in place to drive future efficiency gains. How do costs vary across different modes of service provision? Are there better ways to allocate resources?

Disability in Ireland

Like many other countries, Ireland has been working to reform its disability policies. This reform process was recently surveyed in Power *et al.* (2013). While Ireland historically shared the tendencies towards 'paternalism, medicalisation and segregation' prevalent in other jurisdictions, it also had specific local characteristics, including significant reliance on religious organisations to provide disability services and a very high degree of institutionalisation (Power *et al.*, 2013, pp. 343–4). By the 1990s, policy and legislative reforms were gathering pace. Equality legislation was enacted and supporting institutions were established, to be followed in the early 2000s by bodies empowered to coordinate development of disability policy and to perform information and advocacy roles. An explicit National Disability Strategy and related legislation were enacted in 2004–5.

Disability policy in Ireland has been characterised as 'highly centralised' by the OECD, and disability benefit claims are assessed at a national level (OECD, 2008). Over time, the funding model for disability supports has incorporated elements of formal contracting in the form of service agreements.

Most funding in Ireland is directed to service providers rather than linked to supported individuals as in some other jurisdictions (Power *et al.*, 2013).

In 2008, the OECD published a comparative study of disability policies in Ireland and three other European countries (OECD, 2008). This report emphasised the need to improve the rate of employment for disabled people in Ireland, which had been falling despite the country's strong rate of economic growth at that time. This problem was attributed partly to relatively low rates of educational attainment for disabled people (see also OECD, 2010). Low education and employment participation in turn were seen to contribute to low incomes and high incidence of poverty among this group. The OECD also emphasised the need for Ireland to 'strengthen coordination between actors and systems' (OECD, 2008, p. 14), particularly with respect to employment and social welfare policies, and to improve methods of performance management.

Ireland's low rate of employment among disabled people is illustrated in Figure 1.1. This is accompanied by high rates of income poverty (earning less than 60% of median equivalised income) among the disabled in Ireland, as compared to those in other developed countries (OECD, 2010).

The share of the population in Ireland receiving disability benefits is slightly above average for a developed country (Figure 1.2), and the share

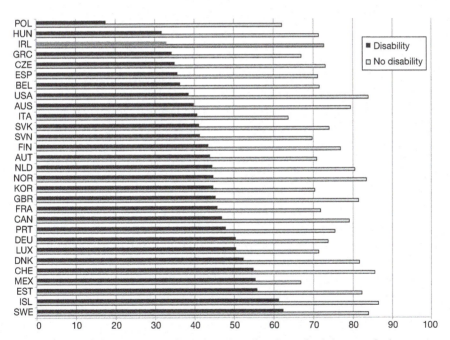

Figure 1.1 Employment rates of people with and without disabilities in the late 2000s
Source: OECD (2012).

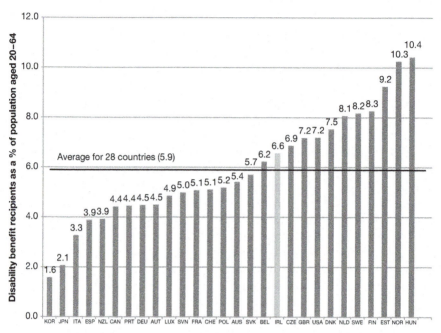

Figure 1.2 Disability benefit recipients as a percentage of the population aged 20–64 in 28 OECD countries, 2010 or latest available year
Source: OECD (2013).

of Irish GDP devoted to incapacity-related public spending is equal to the OECD average of 2.4% (OECD, 2013). Thus, Ireland spends much less than Scandinavian countries (e.g. Sweden or Denmark, which spend about 5% of GDP), but much more than other jurisdictions (e.g. Korea, 0.6% or Canada, 0.9%).

The most recent data on the prevalence of disability in Ireland are from *Profile 8: Our Bill of Health* from the 2011 Census of Population by the Central Statistics Office (CSO, 2012). Estimates of the prevalence of disability can vary widely, depending upon the definitions used. In the 2011 Census, disability was self-reported and based on questions related to whether an individual had one of seven long-standing conditions and whether they had difficulties doing any of four specified activities (CSO, 2012). According to the profile, there were 595,335 persons, accounting for 13.0% of the population, who had a disability as of April 2011. The Census data also show considerable variation in reported disability across a range of dimensions, including gender and age. For example, 13.2% of females had a disability, while the percentage was lower for males, at 12.7%. However, the differences were much more pronounced by age. Indeed, while 6.6% of boys and 4.1% of girls aged 0–14 years were reported as having a disability, the corresponding proportions for adult males and females were 14.5% and 15.6%, respectively.

Figure 1.3 presents more detailed information in relation to gender and age-specific disability rates for Ireland, revealing important patterns in reported disability across these dimensions. The absolute numbers and percentages of males with a disability were higher than for females for all ages until around 25 years of age. Thereafter, the numbers and percentages of adult males and females reporting a disability were broadly similar and increased steadily with age, until around 60 years of age. For older adults, the number of males reporting a disability declined significantly after age 60, though the corresponding number of females levelled off before increasing significantly after age 85. The proportions of males and females with a disability rose sharply at older ages.

The CSO (2012) report provides detailed information in relation to disability across a number of other dimensions, including location, family status, education, labour force participation etc., and interested readers are directed there. It also includes important information in relation to the 'types' of disabilities in Ireland, based on CSO definitions, and data on the number of individuals by type of disability are presented in Figure 1.4 by age

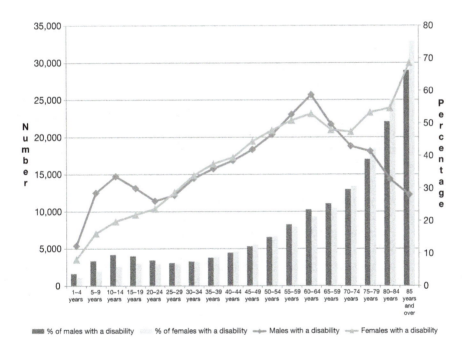

Figure 1.3 Number and percentage of males and females with a disability in Ireland, 2011

Source: CSO (2012).

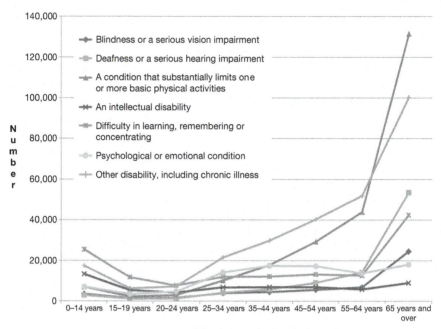

Figure 1.4 Type of disability by age group, 2011
Source: CSO (2012).

group. It shows that some disabilities are clearly more age related than others, while the most common disability overall was 'a condition that substantially limits one or more basic physical activities'. The category 'other disability, including chronic illness' was also highly reported and also strongly age related. According to the CSO data, 'difficulty in learning, remembering or concentrating' was most common among children, before falling sharply and then re-emerging amongst older people. The incidence of 'deafness or a serious hearing impairment' was relatively low until around age 55, before rising steadily with age, while 'blindness or a serious vision impairment' was less age related. 'Psychological or emotional conditions' were most prevalent in the years from age 30 to 60, while 'intellectual disability' peaked for those aged 10 to 14 years.

It is difficult to compare disability prevalence across countries, due to differences in definitions and measurement. However, based on a survey that has been collected on a consistent basis, Ireland has low rates of self-reported disability, as compared to other European countries (see Table 1.1). This metric may be influenced both by cultural factors and by Ireland's demographic composition. In particular, the country has a relatively young population and disability prevalence tends to increase with age. It is important to note, though, that this sort of comparison depends heavily on the group of comparators

Table 1.1 Self-perceived long-standing limitations in usual activities due to health problem, shares of population, EU countries, 2011

Some limitations (%)		Severe limitations (%)	
EU28 average	17.3	EU28 average	7.9
Iceland	6.8	Malta	3.6
Malta	8.2	Bulgaria	3.9
Sweden	9.3	Spain	3.9
Greece	11.0	Ireland	4.7
Ireland	11.7	Luxembourg	5.9
United Kingdom	12.4	Czech Republic	6.0
Luxembourg	12.7	Sweden	6.1
Cyprus	13.1	Netherlands	6.2
Bulgaria	13.2	Latvia	6.4
Spain	15.0	Switzerland	6.4
Belgium	15.2	Portugal	6.7
France	15.5	Poland	7.2
Lithuania	15.7	Lithuania	7.3
Switzerland	15.7	Denmark	7.5
Poland	15.8	Croatia	7.7
Czech Republic	17.4	Italy	7.7
Portugal	17.9	Romania	7.7
Denmark	18.1	Finland	7.7
Romania	18.8	Hungary	7.9
Italy	18.9	Greece	8.0
Austria	18.9	Belgium	8.4
Hungary	19.4	Estonia	8.5
Netherlands	21.1	Cyprus	8.9
Germany	22.3	United Kingdom	8.9
Estonia	22.6	France	9.1
Slovenia	22.8	Austria	9.3
Slovakia	24.1	Germany	10.0
Finland	24.3	Slovakia	10.0
Croatia	24.9	Iceland	10.4
Latvia	24.9	Slovenia	12.9

Source: Eurostat, EU-SILC, URL: http://appsso.eurostat.ec.europa.eu/nui/show. do?dataset=hlth_silc_07&lang=en.

chosen. For example, Ireland's rate of self-reported disability would be closer to the middle of the table if compared to other OECD countries rather than a European sample (see e.g. OECD, 2010).

About this book

This book brings together research relating to the economics of disability in Ireland. As stated earlier, the principal motivation is to provide evidence that can help to improve disability policies, services and supports. In doing so, the book addresses a number of key questions of relevance to the economic circumstances of people with disabilities, with particular emphasis on the relationship between disability and social inclusion, poverty, the labour market, living standards and public policy. Importantly, it also incorporates a life cycle perspective on disability, considering issues of specific relevance to children, working-age adults and older people with disabilities. There is also a focus on issues relating to resource allocation and to wider society, while the book also presents a number of contributions focusing on mental health.

A second motivation for this book is to fill a significant gap in the literature concerning the economics of disability, both in Ireland and internationally. We adopt a relatively broad perspective, in common with authors such as Haveman and Wolfe (2000) who use economic data and tools to identify the disabled, examine policies affecting children and address questions about the effects of disability and related policy measures on incomes, poverty, labour force participation and employment. Previous works by Berthoud *et al.* (1993), Stancliffe and Lakin (2005) and Salkever and Sorkin (2000) either are dated, relate to other jurisdictions or focus on very specific disability-related issues. In contrast, this book explores a range of issues and debates of relevance to the economics of disability using recently available data and new, up-to-date research. Moreover, while there has been a substantial amount of research on the economics of disability in Ireland published in a number of leading academic journals, this research tends to be disconnected from, and often remains inaccessible to, a wider audience of interested parties. Thus, the third motivation for this book is to provide an update and overview of the key findings from this wide range of economics-related research, presenting it in a single volume. Each chapter presents a clear and relatively non-technical treatment of the specific topic under consideration, making it accessible to a greater number of interested readers. In doing so, it aims to provide an important addition to our knowledge and understanding of the economics of disability and will serve as a useful and up-to-date resource for policymakers, advocates, researchers, academics and students, across a range of disciplines, both in Ireland and internationally.

Outline of the book

In a speech to the World Bank in 2004, the Nobel Prize winning economist Amartya Sen made a distinction between two types of economic issues, or what he called 'handicaps', that tend to be associated with disability (Sen, 2004). First, according to Sen, individuals with disabilities face lower human capital accumulation possibilities, are less likely to be employed and are likely to have lower earnings. This he called an 'earning handicap'. Second, because individuals with disabilities tend to have extra needs, they face greater difficulties in achieving utility or economic well-being from a given level of resources, i.e. they face what Sen calls a 'conversion handicap'.

This book starts with three chapters that consider issues that are closely linked to Sen's classification. In Chapter 2, Brian Nolan examines the associations between disability and a variety of measures of social inclusion, including education, poverty and social participation. In Chapter 3, he examines the relationship between disability and a number of key labour market variables, including participation, earnings and barriers to work. John Cullinan and Seán Lyons, in Chapter 4, switch the focus from Sen's earning handicap towards his notion of a conversion handicap. They provide top-down estimates of the additional economic costs faced by disabled adults, as signalled through their households' lower average standard of living. The focus is on estimating the additional income required to achieve the same standard of living as an otherwise equivalent household with no disability.

The next four chapters are motivated by the life cycle perspective on disability policy, since, as discussed earlier, the supports required by an individual are likely to be related to their position in the life course. With this in mind, John Cullinan and Aine Roddy construct a socioeconomic profile of childhood disability in Chapter 5 and examine the association between the childhood disability status of households and a range of socioeconomic outcome measures, including parental labour market outcomes, levels of parental education, household income, social class and economic hardship. Given the importance of human capital accumulation for children and throughout the life course, Chapter 6, by Denise Frawley, Joanne Banks and Selina McCoy, discusses resource allocation for students with special educational needs and disabilities. The aim is to provide empirical evidence to inform how special educational needs can be best resourced in Ireland.

The subsequent two chapters continue with the life cycle theme, considering issues of relevance to older people with disabilities. In Chapter 7, Eamon O'Shea considers some policy aspects of ageing and disability. The focus is on whether there exists the possibility of a common approach to thinking about policy questions in relation to ageing and disability and their various interfaces. This is important, since, as shown earlier, there exists a strong association between disability and increasing age. One area of particular importance in this context is that of dementia, and in Chapter 8 Paddy Gillespie and Sheelah Connolly present a detailed economic analysis of dementia in Ireland.

About 90% of specialist disability services are provided through the voluntary sector, and the majority of this budget is devoted to people with intellectual disabilities in residential programmes and adult day services (ERGDP, 2011). The final three chapters of this book start with a contribution on the services provided to these people, before widening the focus to the broader area of mental health services and other issues relating to mental health. Aoife Callan, in Chapter 9, discusses evidence on the costs of community living for people with intellectual disabilities, including an exploration of the costs associated with different types of residential support settings and the relationship between costs and respondent characteristics. Chapter 10, by Brendan Kennelly, examines the economics of mental health services and presents a broad overview of key economic issues facing the provision of such services in Ireland. A number of issues are addressed, including the nature and extent of mental illnesses in Ireland, the resources spent on care provided to people with mental illnesses, as well as the economic cost of mental illness in Ireland. In Chapter 11, David Madden examines the socioeconomic determinants of mental stress. The focus is on socioeconomic factors which are most closely associated with mental stress, but the chapter also considers the socioeconomic determinants of subjective well-being.

References

Berthoud R., Lakey J., McKay S. (1993) *The Economic Problems of Disabled People*, London: Policy Studies Institute.

CSO (2012) *Profile 8: Our Bill of Health*, Dublin: Stationery Office.

Department of Health (2012) *Value for Money and Policy Review of Disability Services*, Dublin: Department of Health.

DFI (Disability Federation of Ireland) (2008) *Guide to Government Policy on Disability for Voluntary Disability Organisations*, Dublin: DFI.

ERGDP (Expert Reference Group on Disability Policy) (2011) *Report of Disability Policy Review*, accessed April 2013 at www.dohc.ie/publications/ disability_policy_review.html.

European Commission (2011) *The Economic Adjustment Programme for Ireland*, European Economy, Occasional Papers 76, Brussels: DG for Economic and Financial Affairs.

Haveman R., Wolfe B. (2000) The economics of disability and disability policy, in Culyer A.J., Newhouse J.P. (Eds) *Handbook of Health Economics*, Edition 1, Volume 1, Amsterdam: Elsevier.

National Disability Authority (2011) *A National Survey of Public Attitudes to Disability in Ireland*, Dublin: NDA.

OECD (Organisation for Economic Co-operation and Development) (2008) *Sickness, Disability and Work, Breaking the Barriers (Vol. 3): Denmark, Finland, Ireland and the Netherlands*, Paris: OECD Publishing.

OECD (2010) *Sickness, Disability and Work: Breaking the Barriers, A Synthesis of Findings Across OECD Countries*, Paris: OECD Publishing.

OECD (2012) *OECD Economic Surveys: Sweden 2012*, Paris: OECD Publishing.

OECD (2013) *OECD Economic Surveys: France 2013*, Paris: OECD Publishing.

Power A., Lord J.E., deFranco A.S. (2013) *Active Citizenship and Disability: Implementing the Personalisation of Support*, Cambridge: Cambridge University Press.

Salkever D., Sorkin A. (Eds) (2000) *Essays in the Economics of Disability*, Bingley, UK: Emerald Group Publishing Limited.

Sen A. (2004) *Disability and Justice*, keynote speech at the Disability and Inclusive Development Conference, World Bank, Washington, DC, 30 November to 1 December.

Stancliffe R., Lakin K. (Eds) (2005) *Costs and Outcomes of Community Services for People with Intellectual Disabilities*, Baltimore, MD: Paul H. Brookes Publishing.

2

Disability, social inclusion and poverty

Brian Nolan

Introduction

Social inclusion is generally taken to mean being in a position to participate fully in the life of the society one lives in, while conversely social exclusion entails being prevented from doing so. While the precise difference between the concepts of poverty and social exclusion is much discussed in the extensive research literature on these topics, poverty is widely seen as inability to participate fully in the life of one's society due to lack of resources – as formulated for example in Peter Townsend's influential *Poverty in the United Kingdom* (1979) and subsequently adopted at European Union level. People with disabilities face many barriers to full participation in society and are thus likely to face a heightened risk of social exclusion across various dimensions; they are likely to face barriers in the labour market in particular, which may result in reduced incomes and an increase in the likelihood of poverty. Indeed, consideration of disability serves to highlight important aspects of social inclusion as a concept, as well as related concepts that feature in the research literature, such as Sen's capability approach – see, for example, Mitra (2006).

The impact of disability on the likelihood of experiencing poverty and exclusion has been investigated in many countries, often in the context of analysis of the role of social transfers. Typically these show that the social protection system has a very substantial impact in reducing measured income poverty among those affected by disability, but that their poverty rates after transfers are well above average. Examples include Ben-Shalom *et al.* (2011) for the USA, Townsend (1979) and Burchardt (2000; 2003) for the UK, Dunn (2003) for Canada, Gleeson (1998) and Saunders (2005; 2007) for Australia, as well as Parodi and Sciulli (2008) for Italy. Comparative analysis is complicated by difficulties in capturing disability empirically in a consistent fashion across countries, but significant advances have been made in those terms in an EU context in particular (see, for example, Grammenos, (2013)). There is an extensive research literature on the economics of disability and disability policy, as reviewed in Haveman and Wolfe (2000), highlighting the role of incentives facing individuals as a consequence of the way income support and the labour market are structured. It is striking that until the recent recession disability was much more prevalent than unemployment across the OECD countries, and spending on disability benefits was typically twice as high as spending on unemployment benefits (OECD, 2010). Much of the emphasis in policy-related research has thus been on disability and the labour market, to which we turn in Chapter 3. Poverty and inclusion have also, however, been a major focus for disability policy more generally, as exemplified by the introduction to the European Union's *European Disability Strategy 2010–2020*, which highlights the fact that the rate of poverty for people with disabilities is 70% higher than the average (EC, 2010).

The extent and nature of this poverty and exclusion, and how they vary across the very diverse set of persons being categorised as affected by disability, is central to the impact of disability, and understanding the factors and barriers at work is key to designing policy to effectively promote inclusion. While comparative studies have much to offer in this regard, so too do in-depth analyses of a particular case. In this chapter we look at various aspects of inclusion and exclusion for people with disabilities in Ireland, using available data from key statistical sources and studies based on them, focusing on education, poverty and deprivation, and social life and social participation. Unusually, these studies allow us to go beyond the description of the overall poverty risk faced by those with disabilities, to probe the extent to which that reflects factors such as age, education, gender, region and household composition, and also the degree of disability experienced. We also discuss the policy issues that arise in seeking to address poverty, notably the level and structuring of income support which plays a central role in Ireland, as in other rich countries. The next chapter then deals with disability and the labour market, which both is of central importance in itself and helps in understanding the patterns of poverty and social exclusion described here.

Data and measures

As discussed in Chapter 1, the term 'disability' can mean different things depending on the context, and the way this complex concept is captured in available statistics also varies across sources. The 'biopsychosocial model' advocated by the World Health Organization (WHO), in which disability is understood as emerging from an interaction between the individual and the physical and social environment (NESC, 2009), underlies the International Classification of Functioning, Disability and Health (ICF; WHO, 2001). The ICF in turn provided the framework for Ireland's National Disability Survey (NDS), which followed up a large sample of those identified in the

Census of Population of April 2006 as having a disability, together with a smaller sub-sample of other people. This provided a basis for the estimation of the prevalence of disability in the population and for the examination of the living circumstances and needs of people with disabilities. Published reports from the NDS detail the nature, severity and cause of the disability and a broad range of characteristics of people with disability, including education, work and important aspects of the social and physical environment (Central Statistics Office, 2008; 2010).

Unfortunately, the Census of Population and the NDS report different estimates of the prevalence of disability, because a significant number of the NDS sub-sample selected as not reporting a disability in the Census were then identified in the NDS as actually having a disability. (A much smaller number identified in the Census as having a disability turned out not to be identified as such in the more detailed NDS.) About 9% of the population were identified as having a disability in the 2006 Census (Central Statistics Office, 2007), and statistics from the published 2006 Census reports and analysis of the sample of anonymised records from that source relate to this group. About 8% of the population were identified as having a disability in both the 2006 Census and the NDS; this group is of particular interest, as it includes the majority of those with more severe disabilities, and the published reports from the NDS focus on this group in looking at disability prevalence etc. Adding in the 'false negatives' from the Census picked up in the NDS, who tend to have less severe levels of disability and fewer different types of disability than this group, suggests that a total of about 18.5% of the population have a long-term disability (see CSO, 2010; Watson and Nolan, 2011). However, the small size of the sub-sample not reporting a disability in the Census on which this is based limits the scope for meaningful disaggregation and analysis.

Both the Census and the NDS include people living in communal establishments as well as those in private households, which is not the case with the household surveys that represent another important source of information and base for research, including in particular the Living in Ireland survey carried out annually by the Economic and Social Research Institute from 1994 to 2001, the Survey of Income and Living Conditions (SILC) carried out annually by the Central Statistics Office (CSO) from 2003 on (e.g. CSO, 2013), and the Quarterly National Household Survey (QNHS) carried out by the CSO, which has had occasional special modules of relevance to disability (see Russell et al., 2008). Capturing disability in such general household surveys poses considerable definitional and methodological difficulties. In the surveys in question, adults reporting chronic or long-standing illness or disability in the surveys can be distinguished and there is some additional information about the nature of the condition involved and how much it limits or hampers the person.[1] This cannot serve as a substitute for the in-depth information on disability prevalence obtained in a dedicated exercise such as the NDS. However, it does allow analysis of the relationship between the presence of disability and core aspects of social inclusion, complementing what can be learned from the NDS and the Census. It is of particular value, for example, that rather than interviewing a new sample each year, the Living in Ireland surveys sought to track the same individuals over time. This allows the overall experience of disability over a number of years and the onset of disability to be captured, which is helpful in trying to pin down the impact of disability. The fact that studies such as EU-SILC were carried out across the EU also very valuably allows the poverty risk faced by Irish people with a disability to be placed in comparative context.

Disability and education

In assessing the impact of disability on inclusion it makes sense to start with education, which has such a major influence on subsequent outcomes in the life course across all dimensions. The relationship between disability and educational attainment is a complex one: disability may have a negative impact on educational attainment, but low level of education is also associated with an enhanced risk of becoming disabled. Figure 2.1 shows data from the 2006 Census on the highest level of education achieved by the general adult

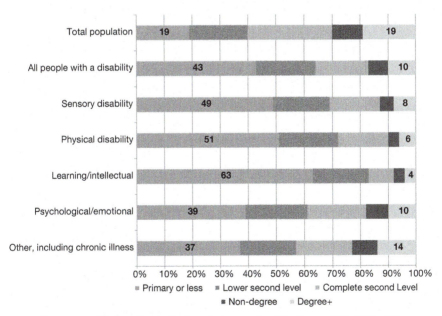

Figure 2.1 Highest level of education completed, by type of disability (%)
Source: CSO (2007, Table 21).
Notes: Age of adults is 15 years and over. Census of Population definition of disability.

population and those who have a disability, which makes clear that the latter are very disadvantaged in terms of educational level. Among adults with disabilities, 43% have not progressed beyond primary education, compared to 19% of all adults, while only 10% of people with disabilities have a third-level degree, compared to 19% of all adults. As might be expected, those with an intellectual and learning disability are the most disadvantaged, with 63% not having progressed to second level, whereas 37% of those with a chronic illness left school before second level.

These differences reflect both age and disability effects, since older adults are more likely to have a disability and the level of education completed by older cohorts is lower than for younger ones. However, even if we control for the fact that people with disabilities belong to a cohort that typically left education sooner, they remain significantly disadvantaged. Figure 2.2 shows the highest level of education achieved, broken down by age group (based on the 5% anonymised sample from Census 2006 produced by the CSO), and for each group those with disabilities have lower levels of education than people without. For instance, among those in the 25–29 year age group, 19% of people with a disability finished schooling with primary education or less and 36% completed third level, compared to 3% and 52%, respectively, for those

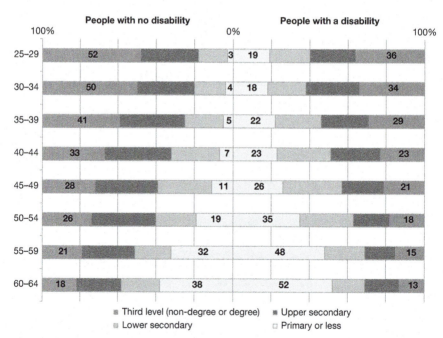

Figure 2.2 Level of education by age group for adults aged 25 to 64 (%)
Source: Watson and Nolan (2011, Figure 3.3), based on analysis of Census 2006 COPSAR data.

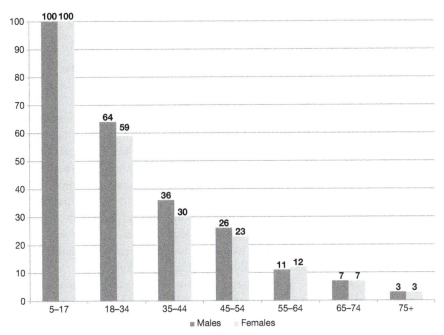

Figure 2.3 Percentage of those identified as having a disability in both Census and NDS limited by disability before completion of full-time education, by age group and gender
Source: CSO (2010, Table 6.4).

without a disability. Similarly, in the age group 60–64 years, 52% of people with disabilities have only primary education or less, compared with 38% for those without a disability.

Much of the disability experienced by older adults develops through the life course, rather than being present from birth, and low levels of education, with associated disadvantages in the labour market and in living standards, appear to increase the risk of developing a disability as a person gets older. However, the causation also clearly goes in the other direction for some. The NDS shows that about 1 in 8 people with a disability have had the disability from birth, and a further 1 in 10 acquired the disability between then and age 18. Figure 2.3 shows the proportion of people with a disability whose disability limited them before the completion of full-time education. Among those aged 18–34 with a disability, about 60% had been affected by it before the completion of full-time education, but this is true of only about 7% of adults aged 65–74 with a disability.

The NDS provides further detail on the experiences of people whose disability affected them in their school years. In order to complete their education, people with disabilities who were affected during their schooling needed additional supports. These included accessible transport (16%), accessible or adapted classrooms and equipment (14%), a teacher's aide or learning support assistant (14%), a personal assistant (11%) and accessible buildings and facilities (10%). While most people with a disability were able to access these necessary supports, about one third of people left education before they intended to because of their disability (CSO, 2010).

Econometric analysis of the relationship between long-term illness or disability and educational attainment has been carried out using microdata from the Living in Ireland surveys (Gannon and Nolan, 2005). They estimated ordered probit models relating the individual's educational attainment to whether they report a chronic illness or disability and the degree to which that hampers them, with and without controlling for a range of other characteristics that may be associated with level of education. Without taking age and gender into account, those reporting a chronic illness or disability that hampered them 'severely' or 'to some extent' were much more likely to have no educational qualifications than those with no illness or disability, and much less likely to have attained a third-level qualification. As illustrated in Figure 2.4, this gap is reduced, but by no means eliminated, when controls for age and gender are introduced.

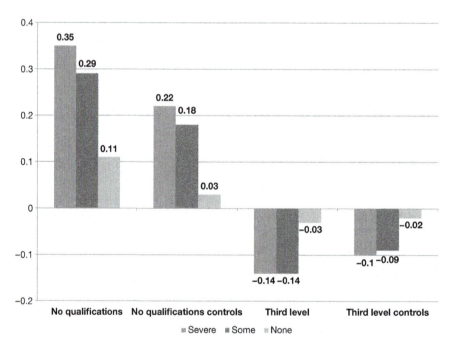

Figure 2.4 Estimated relationship between chronic illness/disability and educational attainment, controlling for age and gender

Source: Gannon and Nolan (2005), based on analysis of Living in Ireland surveys.

The estimated results for the full model presented in Table 2.1 show that, compared to the reference category (no disability, male, living in the East/ South region and aged under 25), the probability of having no educational qualifications was 22 percentage points higher for someone severely hampered in their daily activities, about 18 percentage points higher if hampered to some extent, about 3 percentage points higher if not hampered by their illness or disability, about 4 percentage points lower if aged 25–34 and so on. Those who were hampered severely or to some extent in their daily activities were still much less likely to have any educational qualifications than those with no chronic illness or disability. They were also less likely to have a Leaving Certificate or third-level education than those reporting no chronic illness or disability. After correcting for the influences of age, gender and region on educational attainment, those reporting an illness or disability which did not hamper them in their daily activities were now seen to be statistically indistinguishable from those with no illness or disability.

It was also possible to distinguish between those who had the illness or disability they were reporting in the survey from before the age of 25 – when an impact on educational attainment might be expected – and those affected only after 25, when such a direct impact would be unlikely. Illness or disability

Table 2.1 Ordered probit model of educational qualifications by degree hampered, estimated marginal effects

	No qualifications	Intermediate/ junior	Leaving	Third level
Ill/disabled and severely hampered	0.221**	−0.004	−0.123**	−0.094**
Ill/disabled and hampered to some extent	0.178**	0.007**	−0.099**	−0.086**
Ill/disabled and not hampered	0.029	0.005	−0.016	−0.018
Age 25–34	−0.043**	−0.010**	0.022**	0.030**
35–44	0.071**	0.010**	−0.039**	−0.042**
45–54	0.155**	0.012**	−0.086**	−0.081**
55–64	0.315**	−0.011**	−0.173**	−0.131**
65+	0.448**	−0.036**	−0.237**	−0.174**
Female	−0.036**	−0.007**	0.020**	0.024**
Border Midlands Western Region	0.056**	0.009**	−0.030**	−0.035**

Source: Gannon and Nolan (2005, Table 3.6), based on analysis of Living in Ireland survey for 2001.
Notes: Pseudo R^2=0.0873.
** Statistically significant at 5% level.
Reference category: not ill/disabled, age under 25, male, South East region.

present before 25 and where the respondents were hampered in their daily lives was indeed associated with a substantially increased likelihood of having no qualifications and a reduced chance of having a third-level qualification. However, illness or disability that affected the person only after age 25, where the individuals were hampered in their daily lives, was also estimated to have a negative (though more modest) impact. This is probably because the chances of being affected by disability or illness later in life are related to a range of background individual and household disadvantages that increase the likelihood of low levels of educational attainment, and the disability measures are picking up their effects. This might well also be the case, to some extent, for those affected by illness or disability from before age 25, of course, and means that the scale of the underlying effect of illness or disability per se may not be as great as the raw estimates suggest. Even taking this into account, however, disabilities acquired early in life are seen to have substantial direct effects on educational attainment. A similar pattern of results was found when analysing data from the special module on disability included with the QNHS in 2002, which had a much larger sample than the Living in Ireland survey, though it was confined to those of working age.

Comparative data from EU-SILC also allow educational outcomes in Ireland for those with a disability to be compared with elsewhere in the EU. The percentage of early school-leavers among those aged 18–24 with disability in Ireland is above the EU average and the corresponding figure for those without disability is below the EU average, so the gap between them is particularly wide in the Irish case (see Grammenos, 2013, Table 19, p. 73). By contrast, the percentage of those aged 30–34 who have completed tertiary education is particularly high in Ireland, both for those with and without disability, and the gap between them is narrower than in the EU, on average (see Grammenos, 2013, Table 23, p. 86).

Disability and poverty

Given the various constraints that arise for those with a disability in seeking to participate in the everyday life of society, and in the labour force in particular, as well as the additional costs that may be associated with disability, disability in itself could be expected to represent a 'risk factor' in terms of low income and poverty. Since neither the Census nor the NDS obtain data on income, analysis of the relationship between disability and poverty relies on the large-scale household surveys already mentioned, which do gather income data in considerable detail. In the EU-SILC surveys on which we draw here, respondents were asked if they suffered from any 'chronic (longstanding) illness or condition (health problem)'[2] and separately whether in the last 6 months they were limited in activities people usually do because of a health problem, to which they could reply that they were 'strongly limited', 'limited', or 'not limited'.

Whereas education, labour force participation and earnings vary across individuals, poverty is generally assessed at the level of the household, assuming that the people living in a given household share their resources and have a similar standard of living. A number of different indicators of poverty will be the focus here. The first, based purely on income, is what is termed the 'at risk of poverty' rate: the percentage falling below a poverty threshold set at 60% of the median equivalised (i.e. adjusted for household size) household income in the country at the time. This is widely used in comparative research and in the monitoring of poverty across the European Union (EU), being one of the central indicators in the EU's agreed set of social inclusion indicators. The second is the 'consistent poverty' rate, where, as well as having an income below the 60% threshold, the household reports a significant level of deprivation; this deprivation is currently measured in terms of the lack of 2 or more of 11 basic items.[3] Such a 'consistent poverty' measure was originally developed in Irish poverty research in the late 1980s/early 1990s and subsequently refined (see Callan *et al.*, 1993; Nolan and Whelan, 1996; Whelan *et al.*, 2006) and has been a major focus of anti-poverty policy nationally since the mid-1990s.

Table 2.2 shows the relationship between chronic illness, limited physical activity and these two poverty measures for adults in EU-SILC for 2006, 2007 and 2008. It brings out the heightened poverty risk and experience of consistent poverty for people who had a chronic illness or health problem, or who were limited in their activities. The 'at risk of poverty' rate was higher in each year for those reporting a chronic illness or health problem than for other adults, and highest for those whose activities were severely limited where it reached over one quarter in 2006 and 2007. The 'consistent poverty' rate was about twice as

Table 2.2 At risk of poverty rate and consistent poverty rate for adults aged 16 and over in 2006, 2007 and 2008, by disability status (%)

		Chronic illness or health problem		Limited activity in last 6 months		
		No	Yes	Not limited	Limited	Strongly limited
2006	At risk of poverty rate	14.4	20.9	14.3	21.7	27.5
	Consistent poverty rate	4.7	8.8	4.5	10.2	12.8
2007	At risk of poverty rate	14.1	22.0	13.8	24.9	27.7
	Consistent poverty rate	4.1	8.5	4.0	8.9	13.1
2008	At risk of poverty rate	12.7	16.0	12.6	16.5	18.7
	Consistent poverty rate	3.2	6.4	3.2	6.8	7.9

Source: CSO (2009, Table 2.7 and Table 4.4).

high for those reporting a chronic illness or health problem as it was for other adults, and was higher still for those whose activities were severely limited.

Microdata analysis by Gannon and Nolan (2005) using the Living in Ireland surveys for 2000–1 explored these relationships in some depth. They found that the 'at risk of poverty' rate and the 'consistent poverty' rate were both about twice as high for adults reporting chronic illness or disability as for other adults. As in EU-SILC, those with a chronic illness or health problem that did not limit their activity had the same rates of poverty as persons not reporting an illness or health problem. On the other hand, almost half of those reporting a chronic illness or disability that severely hampered them in their daily activities were at risk of poverty, and about 16% were in consistent poverty at that point. Statistical analysis of the relationship between chronic illness or disability and poverty, controlling for other characteristics, identified lower and upper bounds for the estimated impact, reflecting whether educational attainment and current employment – which are both influenced by illness or disability – were controlled for in the models.

The estimation results for the equation relating to the risk of poverty are presented in Table 2.3. In the simple model without controls, the estimated impact of having a severely hampering chronic illness or disability on the likelihood of being below the income line was substantial, the impact was still large for those hampered to some extent and it was much smaller but still statistically different from zero for those whose chronic illness or disability does not hamper them at all. The second column shows the results controlling for age, gender, region and household composition, but not for education level or whether the individual is working. All these control variables were statistically significant and their inclusion substantially reduced the estimated effect of having a chronic illness or disability. However, being hampered, whether severely or to some extent, was still associated with a significantly increased likelihood of being below the income line. For those who were severely hampered by their illness or disability, the proportion at risk of poverty was 22 percentage points higher than for those without an illness or disability – less than the 32-point increase in the model with no control variables but still very substantial. For the 'hampered to some extent' group, the proportion at risk of poverty was now increased by 12 percentage points. For the disabled but not hampered group, there was now no statistically significant increase in the likelihood of being at risk of poverty, compared to those with no illness or disability.

Finally, the third column of Table 2.3 shows the results when education level and whether the individual is working were also included. We see that these were both statistically significant. Their inclusion approximately halved the size of the estimated effects of having a hampering chronic illness/ disability, as compared with the second model, but those effects were still statistically significant. So the overall conclusion is that having a chronic illness

Table 2.3 The probability of being at risk of poverty, estimated marginal effects

	Model (a)	Model (b)	Model (c)
Ill/disabled and severely hampered	0.317**	0.223**	0.110**
Ill/disabled and hampered to some extent	0.206**	0.117**	0.050**
Ill/disabled and not hampered	0.060**	0.020	0.005
Female		0.013	−0.034**
Number of children		0.035	0.026**
Number of adults		−0.085	−0.083**
Age 25–34		−0.053**	−0.004
Age 35–44		−0.035*	0.013
Age 45–54		0.011	0.044**
Age 55–64		0.121**	0.082**
Age 65+		0.175**	0.045**
BMW		0.071**	0.067**
Married		−0.069**	−0.053**
Working			−0.231**
Secondary education			−0.022**
Tertiary education			−0.053**
Pseudo R^2	0.039	0.168	0.239

Source: Gannon and Nolan (2005, Table 5.8), based on analysis of Living in Ireland survey for 2001.
Notes: ** Statistically significant at 5% level.
* Statistically significant at 10% level.
Reference category: column (1): not ill/disabled; column (2): not ill/disabled, age under 25, male, East region; column (3): not ill/disabled, age under 25, male, South East region, primary education only, not working.

or disability and being hampered in one's daily activities was associated with a substantial increase in the probability of being below 60% of median income; the scale of that increase was somewhere between 11 and 22 percentage points where the individual was severely hampered, and between 5 and 12 percentage points where he or she was hampered to some extent.

The corresponding estimation results for the likelihood of being in consistent poverty are presented in Table 2.4. Before the inclusion of the control variables, both the hampering dummy variables were significant and had substantial effects but a non-hampering illness/disability was not significant. The variables added in model (b) made little difference, but, once again, when education and work status were added in model (c) they were significant and reduced the estimated impact of hampering illness/disability. Having a chronic illness or disability and being hampered to some extent still increased the likelihood of being in consistent poverty, but being severely hampered had a much more pronounced effect. While the consistent poverty rate was about 3% for someone without an illness or disability, an individual with a severely hampering illness/disability had a predicted rate that was between 6 and

Table 2.4 The probability of being consistently poor, estimated marginal effects

	Model (a)	Model (b)	Model (c)
Ill/disabled and severely hampered	0.118**	0.130**	0.057**
Ill/disabled and hampered to some extent	0.042**	0.040**	0.014**
Ill/disabled and not hampered	0.013	0.017*	0.009
Female		0.002	−0.006**
Number of children		0.012	0.008**
Number of adults		−0.011**	−0.009**
Age 25–34		−0.002	0.006
Age 35–44		0.001	0.007
Age 45–54		0.004	0.005
Age 55–64		0.028**	0.011
Age 65+		−0.006	−0.014**
BMW		0.003	0.001
Married		−0.024**	−0.015**
Working			−0.047**
Secondary education			−0.005
Tertiary education			−0.014**
Pseudo R²	0.039	0.109	0.185

Source: Gannon and Nolan (2005, Table 5.10), based on analysis of Living in Ireland survey for 2001.
Notes: ** Statistically significant at 5% level.
* Statistically significant at 10% level.
Reference category: column (1): not ill/disabled; column (2): not ill/disabled, age under 25, male, East region; column (3): not ill/disabled, age under 25, male, East region, primary education, not working.

13 percentage points higher, in other words consistent poverty rates of between 9% and 16%. Thus, someone with a severely hampering disability could be up to five times more likely to be in consistent poverty. Someone whose illness/disability hampers them to some extent was just 2–4 percentage points more likely to be in consistent poverty than a non-disabled person.

The Gannon and Nolan (2005) study also found that the number of persons in the household at work and the extent of social welfare dependence played a crucial, interlinked role in determining poverty risk. For ill or disabled persons under 65 years of age, being at risk of poverty was generally associated with there being noone in the household at work. For those aged 65 or over, the number at work in the household was less important but still had a role to play. The other side of the same coin was dependence on social welfare payments: among those with a long-term illness or disability and in households below the 60% of median income threshold (the 'at risk of poverty' threshold), only 10% of household income came from work and most of the rest came from social welfare payments.

The fact that the Living in Ireland surveys were longitudinal in design also allowed the impact on poverty of disability experience over time as well as the onset of disability to be studied, going beyond what is possible with cross-sectional data. Gannon and Nolan (2006) found that disability onset was associated with a very substantial increase in the probability of being below the 60% of median income threshold. Econometric analysis showed that the personal and household characteristics of those affected played some role in increasing this risk, but even when they were taken into account disability onset per se increased the 'at risk of poverty rate' substantially. Table 2.5 shows the results from a probit model explaining or predicting household income among those at risk of disability onset, first simply in terms of whether disability onset actually occurs, and then adding in the range of socioeconomic characteristics. When no other variables were included, disability onset was a significant predictor of a decline in weekly household income. When individual and household characteristics were included the

Table 2.5 Onset of chronic illness/disability and household income, estimated marginal effects

	Chronic illness or disability only	+ personal characteristics	+ household circumstances	+ education
Onset of chronic illness/disability	−0.238**	−0.201**	−0.186**	−0.149**
Female		−0.046**	−0.032	−0.045**
Age 25–34		0.075**	0.111**	0.148**
35–44		−0.0376	0.092**	0.156**
45–54		0.022	0.068*	0.183**
55–64		0.010	-0.064*	0.118**
65+		−0.245**	−0.330**	−0.085**
2 adults in household			0.256**	0.211**
3 or more adults in household			0.238**	0.215**
1 child in household			−0.177**	−0.166**
2 or more children in household			−0.332**	−0.323**
No education beyond primary				−0.378**
Year	0.058**	0.061**	0.062**	0.051**
Constant	4.724	4.755	4.665**	4.744**
R^2	0.019	0.051	0.105	0.185

Source: Gannon and Nolan (2006, Table 4.2).
Notes: ** Statistically significant at 5% level.
* Statistically significant at 10% level.
Reference category: no onset, male, aged 16–24, single adult household, no children, post-primary education qualification.

estimated effect of onset on income was reduced by about one third but was still highly significant. Predicted household income in the year of onset was about 15% lower than it would otherwise be, taking the characteristics of the individual and his or her household into account.

Distinguishing amongst those experiencing onset by the severity of the disability they report, onset of a severely hampering disability was seen to have a much more substantial impact than one that was hampering 'to some extent', but the latter was still associated with a decline in household income, whereas onset of a non-hampering disability was not accompanied by such a decline, as compared with those who did not experience onset. Those experiencing onset of a disability that hampered them to some extent faced a predicted reduction of about 15% in income, as compared with those with no onset, whereas for those severely hampered the predicted scale of the reduction was about twice that size.

Persistent disability over the life of the panel survey from 1994 to 2001 was also seen to be strongly linked to lower household income in Gannon and Nolan (2006). Even when the personal and household characteristics, including education level, of the individual were taken into account, the predicted household income of someone reporting persistent disability was 20% lower than for someone who was otherwise similar but had no experience of disability over the period. Persistent chronic illness or disability thus substantially increased the probability of being below the relative income poverty threshold. When other individual and household characteristics were taken into account, the predicted 'at risk of poverty' rate was 13 percentage points higher for someone who experienced persistent disability, compared with those who experienced no disability over the panel period. Once again, reduced employment appeared to be the key channel through which disability increased poverty risk.

These results apply to the period before the onset of the economic crisis and recession, when levels of relative and consistent poverty have risen for the general population. Data for Ireland do not suggest that this was particularly pronounced among those affected by disability. Comparative data from EU-SILC also allow Ireland to be put in comparative perspective. Data for 2009 show that the percentage of those reporting disability who fell below the 60% of median relative poverty line in Ireland was very close to the overall EU-27 average, but the corresponding income poverty rate for those not reporting disability in Ireland was slightly below the EU average, so the gap between those reporting versus not reporting disability in Ireland was wider than in the EU on average (see Grammenos, 2013, Table 31, p. 115). At EU level a measure of severe material deprivation is also employed as a social inclusion indicator, and it is striking that with this indicator the gap between those with and without disability is particularly wide for Ireland, well above the average gap for the

EU-27; 17.5% of those with a disability were deprived on this basis in Ireland, as compared with 11% in the EU (see Grammenos, 2013, Table 37, p. 129).

Disability and social participation

The impact of disability on broader aspects of participation in the life of the community is also of central relevance to its effects on social inclusion broadly conceived. Here the NDS has a good deal of relevant information that helps to dispel what may be some common presumptions and provide a nuanced picture. Results from the NDS show that most people with a disability in all age groups participate in some social activities: 96% of women and 95% of men do so. There is some age gradient but it is modest: 97% of adults under the age of 35 with a disability participate in social activities, as compared with 91% of adults aged 75 and over (CSO, 2010).

Exploring these data in more detail, Figure 2.5 shows the percentage of people with a disability who do not participate in social activities, broken down by gender and age group. For both men and women, non-participation is

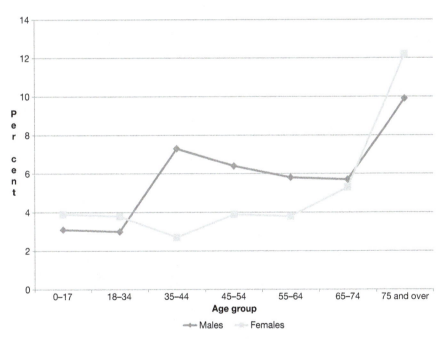

Figure 2.5 Percentage of people with a disability who do not participate in social activities, by gender and age group

Source: CSO (2010, Table 8.1a).

Notes: Private households only. Census/NDS definition of disability.

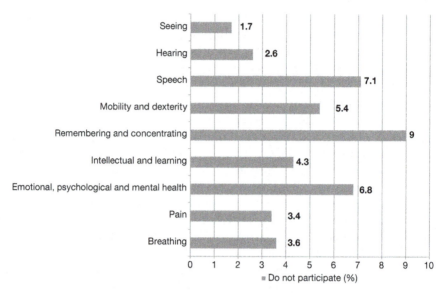

Figure 2.6 Percentage of people with a disability who do not participate in social activities, by type of disability

Source: CSO (2010, Table 8.2a).

Notes: Private households only. Census/NDS definition of disability.

highest among those over the age of 75. Among younger adults, men are more likely than women not to participate in any social activities, particularly in the 35–44 and 45–54 age groups.

Figure 2.6 shows how the proportion of people with a disability who do not participate in social activities varies by the type of disability. This is highest for people whose main disability is remembering and concentrating, speech, or emotional, psychological and mental health.

Other forms of participation are also affected by disability. Results from the NDS show that people with a disability were less likely to have participated in sports or physical exercise in the previous 12 months (38%, compared to 67% of people without a disability). They were also more likely to report reasons related to their health or disability for non-participation (54% of inactive people with a disability attributed this as the reason for non-participation, compared to 3% of inactive adults without a disability). Nonetheless, 45% of men and 36% of women with a disability participated in sports or physical exercise in the previous four weeks, with the percentage participating strongly related to age. For example, 83% of boys and 79% of girls with a disability under the age of 18 participated in sports over the four weeks prior to the survey. This decreased to 24% of men and 16% of women aged 75 and over (CSO, 2010).

The detailed information on participation provided in the NDS also shows the importance of different modes of communication for people with particular types of disability. For instance, using the internet was relatively more important to people with hearing disability (32%) and to people with intellectual and learning disability (37%) than for all other people with a disability (25%). While almost 80% of all people with a disability communicated by telephone, email, text or writing, this figure dropped to 67% for people with intellectual and learning disability.

Drawing on social participation data from specially designed modules attached to the Quarterly National Survey and the Survey of Income and Living Conditions in 2006, CSO (2009) reported that people with a disability were somewhat less likely than other adults to be involved in community and voluntary groups (23% of people with a disability, compared to 29% of other adults). However, it found no significant difference in civic participation. While most people with a disability had at least weekly contact with relatives (82%) and friends (78%), the figures were slightly lower than those for other adults (85% had weekly contact with relatives and 89% with friends). On the other hand, people with a disability were more likely to speak to neighbours at least once a week (83% versus 77%). A telephone survey of a nationally representative sample, commissioned by the National Disability Authority (NDA) and carried out in 2004, found that those with a disability were substantially less likely than others to have had a social outing or a visit to friends or family in the previous week.

Finally, microdata on social participation and involvement in the community from the 2001 Living in Ireland survey were also analysed by Gannon and Nolan (2005). The available indicators covered whether the respondent was a member of a club or organisation, how often he or she talked to neighbours, how often he or she met friends or relatives (living outside the household), whether he or she had an afternoon or evening out in the last fortnight that cost money and whether he or she intended to vote in the next general election. Analysis of these responses showed that those with a chronic illness or disability that hampered them severely in their daily activities were much less likely than others to be a member of a club or association, to talk to their neighbours most days, to meet friends or relatives most days or to have had an afternoon or evening out for entertainment in the last fortnight, and also slightly less likely to say they would vote in a general election. For those with a chronic illness or disability that hampered them only 'to some extent' the picture was more mixed: they had a below-average percentage in clubs/associations and were also less likely than average to have had an afternoon or evening out in the last fortnight, but, in terms of frequency of contact with neighbours, relatives or friends and voting intentions, looked little different to those with no illness or disability. Those with chronic illness or disability that did not hamper them at

Table 2.6 Results for models predicting social participation, estimated marginal effects

	Club member	Meet people most days or once/twice a week	Talk to neighbours most days, or once/twice a week	Evening out in last fortnight
Ill/disabled and severely hampered	−0.199**	−0.071**	−0.153**	−0.244**
Ill/disabled and hampered to some extent	−0.089**	−0.015*	−0.022*	−0.077**
Ill/disabled and not hampered	−0.010	−0.004	0.003	−0.043**
Female	−0.153**	0.001	−0.009	−0.031**
Number of children	−0.013**	−0.004*	0.007**	−0.025**
Number of adults	0.010*	−0.002	−0.002	0.007*
Age 25–34	−0.086**	−0.027*	0.002	−0.040**
35–44	−0.045**	−0.061**	0.037**	−0.146**
45–54	−0.028	−0.082**	0.059**	−0.202**
55–64	−0.008	−0.074**	0.076**	−0.236**
65+	−0.096**	−0.083**	0.074**	−0.342**
BMW region	−0.067**	0.023**	0.014*	−0.007
Married	0.039**	−0.001	0.003	0.020*
Working	0.065**	−0.001	−0.028**	0.077**
Secondary education	0.015	0.003	0.052**	0.026**
Third level education	0.094**	−0.004	0.038**	0.066**
R^2	0.049	0.044	0.040	0.128

Source: Gannon and Nolan (2005, Table 6.7), based on analysis of Living in Ireland survey for 2001.
Notes: ** Statistically significant at 5% level.
* Statistically significant at 10% level.
Reference category: not ill/disabled, age under 25, male, single, East region, single, not working, primary education only.

all were indistinguishable from those with no chronic illness or disability, on these indicators.

Logistic regression models were estimated in order to control for differences between the groups being compared in terms of, for example, age and gender, which could affect their levels of social participation. The results, presented in Table 2.6, showed that having controlled for those other characteristics, the presence of a severely hampering chronic illness or disability significantly reduced the probability of participation in terms of club membership, frequency of contact with neighbours and with friends or relatives, and having an evening out. The presence of an illness or disability that hampered the individual to some extent was now seen to also be associated with a reduced level of participation on all of the indicators, although the scale of the estimated impact was a good deal less than for severely hampering illness or disability. Individuals reporting chronic illness or disability that did not affect them in their daily activities had predicted participation similar to someone without an illness or disability.

Drawing on the longitudinal aspect of the Living in Ireland survey, Gannon and Nolan (2006; 2007) also found that levels of social participation were significantly related to having a chronic illness or disability throughout the life of the panel survey. After controlling for personal and household characteristics, the predicted rate of participation (in all four aspects measured) for those reporting disability throughout the panel was 9 percentage points lower than for those with no experience of disability over the period.

Social inclusion policies and disability

Policy perspectives with respect to social inclusion and to disability have developed substantially in the Irish case over a relatively short period. Ireland was one of the first European countries to develop a structured anti-poverty strategy in the early/mid-1990s, and this evolved post-2000 into the social inclusion plans that formed part of the EU-wide Social Inclusion strategy that became embedded at that time. At around the same time disability also came to the forefront of the political/policy agenda, with the publication in 1996 of the *Report of the Commission on the Status of People with Disabilities*, arguing for a rights-based approach, generally seen as an important landmark. This was followed by the establishment of the National Disability Authority in 1999 to provide policy advice to government and public bodies, promote relevant research and advise on standards and guidelines in services to people with disabilities.

Social inclusion, broadly conceived, can be seen as the focus of disability-related policies covering such areas as building standards and the built environment, transport, access to public services and access to health services and education. The provision of and basis for access to disability-related services has proved particularly contentious, in the context of the framing and subsequent implementation of the 2005 Disability Act. From a narrower poverty perspective, though, the main emphasis in the Irish case as elsewhere has been on income support policy and on employment. Employment and labour market participation is the subject of Chapter 3, where the interaction between income support and labour market participation for those with disability will also be discussed. Here it is worth emphasising the centrality of the level of income support provided, through a variety of social transfer programmes for those affected by illness and disability, in the living standards and income poverty risk of the recipient households. As examined in a series of studies carried out by the Economic and Social Research Institute, the level of support provided through the main social welfare schemes (those related to unemployment and pensions as well as to disability) has varied substantially over time relative to median income, and this – rather than changes in the way those programmes are structured – has been a key influence on the way relative income poverty rates have evolved (see Callan *et al.*, 1996; Nolan *et al.*, 2002; 2005; Watson and Maître, 2013).

Debates about changing income support structures in the disability field, on the other hand, have centred on whether the costs associated with disability should be covered by the introduction of a separate payment, not catered for in the mainstream social insurance and assistance payments. Several studies based on survey data have sought to estimate the likely scale of such additional costs in the Irish case (Cullinan *et al.*, 2011; NDA, 2004), and the National Disability Agency has argued on that basis that a Cost of Disability Payment should be introduced. Cullinan *et al.* (2011) have also argued for disability-adjusted poverty and inequality estimates and equivalence scales that take such additional costs into account, as have Jones and O'Donnell (1995) and Zaidi and Burchardt (2005).

Conclusions

People with disabilities face many barriers to full participation in Irish society and are seriously disadvantaged in terms of educational outcomes, poverty and social inclusion more broadly. Social inclusion is generally taken to mean being in a position to participate fully in the life of the society one lives in, while poverty is widely seen as inability to participate fully in the life of one's society due to lack of resources. This chapter has drawn on available data from key statistical sources and studies based on them for Ireland, and comparative data to put this in context. The evidence makes clear that, in terms of education, poverty and social participation, people with disabilities that seriously hamper them fared significantly worse than others. Importantly, in-depth analysis of micro-data demonstrates that this remains the case when one controls for factors such as age, gender and region account. The situation for people with disabilities in Ireland is in some respects similar to that in other European countries, but levels of non-employment and of deprivation compared with those not affected by disability are considerably higher than in the EU-27 on average.

This poses major challenges to the structures in place in central pillars of the welfare state: education, social protection, social services and training and activation. Social transfers play the major role in addressing low income and deprivation among those affected by disability, and variation in the level of support provided relative to other incomes is a key influence on relative income poverty rates over time. However, the limited success of the social protection system in keeping those reliant on cash transfers out of poverty makes it all the more important that opportunities for gainful employment be available for those affected by disability to the greatest extent possible, and it is on the labour market that the next chapter focuses.

Notes

1 For example, about 20% of adults in the Living in Ireland surveys in a particular year responded that they had a chronic illness or disability; about one quarter of these said they were not restricted at all in their daily life as a result, while about 55% were restricted to some extent and one fifth were severely restricted.
2 From 2010 the term 'disability' is employed in this EU-SILC survey question, as it was in the Living in Ireland surveys.
3 These are: going without heating, or being unable to afford any of the following: a morning, afternoon or evening out in the last fortnight, two pairs of strong shoes, a roast once a week, a meal with meat, chicken or fish every second day, new (not second-hand) clothes, a warm waterproof coat, to replace any worn out furniture, to keep the home adequately warm, to have family or friends for a drink or meal once a month, to buy presents for family or friends at least once a year.

References

Ben-Shalom Y., Moffitt R., Scholz J.K. (2011) *An Assessment of the Effectiveness of Anti-Poverty Programs in the United States*, Institute for Research on Poverty Discussion Paper no. 1392-11, Madison, Wisconsin.

Burchardt T. (2000) *Enduring Economic Exclusion: Disabled People, Income and Work*, York: York Publishing Services.

Burchardt T. (2003) *Being and Becoming: Social Exclusion and the Onset of Disability*, CASE Report 21, ESRC Centre for Analysis of Social Exclusion, London: London School of Economics.

Callan T., Nolan B., Whelan C. (1993) Resources, deprivation and the measurement of poverty, *Journal of Social Policy* 22, 141–72.

Callan T., Nolan B., Whelan B.J., Whelan C.T., Williams J. (1996) *Poverty in the 1990s: Evidence from the 1994 Living in Ireland Survey*, General Research Series Paper 170, Dublin: Economic and Social Research Institute/Oak Tree Press.

CSO (Central Statistics Office) (2007) *Census of Population 2006 Volume 11 Disability, Carers and Voluntary Activities*, Dublin: Stationery Office.

CSO (2008) *National Disability Survey 2006 – First Results*, Dublin: Stationery Office.

CSO (2009) *Community Involvement and Social Networks, 2006: Results from the Social Capital Module of the Quarterly National Survey Q3 2006 and the Social and Cultural Participation Module of the Survey of Income and Living Conditions 2006*, Dublin: Stationery Office.

CSO (2010) *National Disability Survey 2006 Volume 2*, Dublin: Stationery Office.

CSO (2013) *Survey on Income and Living Conditions (SILC)*, Dublin: Stationery Office.

Cullinan J., Gannon B., Lyons S. (2011) Estimating the extra cost of living for people with disabilities, *Health Economics* 20, 582–99.

Dunn P.A. (2003) Canadians with disabilities, in Westheus A. (Ed.) *Canadian Social Policy: Issues and Perspectives,* Waterloo: Wilfrid Laurier University Press.

EC (European Commission) (2010) *European Disability Strategy 2010–2020: A Renewed Commitment to a Barrier-Free Europe*, COM(2010) 636 Final, Brussels: European Commission, http://ec.europa.eu/justice/discrimination/disabilities/disability-strategy/index_en.htm.

Gannon B., Nolan B. (2005) *Disability and Social Inclusion in Ireland*, Dublin: The Equality Authority and the National Disability Authority.

Gannon B., Nolan B. (2006) *The Dynamics of Disability and Social Inclusion in Ireland*, Dublin: The Equality Authority and the National Disability Authority.

Gannon B., Nolan B. (2007) The impact of disability transitions on social inclusion, *Social Science and Medicine* 64, 1425–37.

Gleeson B. (1998) Disability and poverty, in Fincher R., Niewenhuysen J. (Eds) *Australian Poverty: Then and Now*, Melbourne: Melbourne University Press.

Grammenos S. (2013) *European Comparative Data on Europe 2020 and Housing Conditions*, Final report prepared by the Centre for European Social and Economic Policy on behalf of the Academic Network of European Disability Experts, University of Leeds.

Haveman R., Wolfe B. (2000) The economics of disability and disability policy, in Culyer A.J., Newhouse J.P. (Eds) *Handbook of Health Economics*, Edition 1, Volume 1, Amsterdam: Elsevier.

Jones A., O'Donnell O. (1995) Equivalence scales and the costs of disability, *Journal of Public Economics* 56, 273–89.

Mitra S. (2006) The capability approach and disability, *Journal of Disability Policy Studies* 16, 236–47.

NDA (National Disability Authority) (2004) *Indecon Report on the Cost of Disability*, Dublin: National Disability Authority.

NESC (National Economic and Social Council) (2009) *Well-Being Matters: A Social Report for Ireland,* Dublin: NESC.

Nolan B., Gannon B., Layte R., Watson D., Whelan C.T., Williams J. (2002) *Monitoring Poverty Trends in Ireland: Results from the 2000 Living in Ireland Survey*, Policy Research Series Paper No. 45, Dublin: The Economic and Social Research Institute.

Nolan B., Whelan C.T. (1996) *Resources, Deprivation and Poverty*, Oxford: Oxford University Press.

Nolan B., Whelan C.T., Maître B. (2005) *Trends in Welfare for Vulnerable Groups, Ireland 1994–2001*, Policy Research Series Paper No. 56, Dublin: The Economic and Social Research Institute.

OECD (Organisation for Economic Co-operation and Development) (2010) *Sickness, Disability and Work: Breaking the Barriers*, Paris: OECD.

Parodi G., Sciulli D. (2008) Disability in Italian households: Income, poverty and labour market participation, *Applied Economics* 40, 2615–30.

Russell H., Quinn E., King O'Riain R., McGinnity F. (2008) *The Experience of Discrimination in Ireland: Analysis of the QNHS Equality Module*, Dublin: The Economic and Social Research Institute and The Equality Authority.

Saunders P. (2005) *Disability, Poverty and Living Standards: Reviewing Australian Evidence and Policies*, SPRC Discussion Paper No. 145.

Saunders P. (2007) The costs of disability and the incidence of poverty, *Australian Journal of Social Issues* 42, 461–80.

Townsend P. (1979) *Poverty in the United Kingdom*, Harmondsworth: Penguin.

Watson D., Maître B. (2013) *Social Transfers and Poverty Alleviation in Ireland, An Analysis of the Survey on Income and Living Conditions 2004 – 2011*, Dublin: Economic and Social Research Institute and Department of Social Protection.

Watson D., Nolan B. (2011) *A Social Portrait of People with Disabilities in Ireland*, Dublin: Department of Social Protection and The Economic and Social Research Institute.

Whelan C., Nolan B., Maitre B. (2006) *Reconfiguring the measurement of deprivation and consistent poverty in Ireland*, Policy Research Series Paper No. 58, Dublin: The Economic and Social Research Institute.

WHO (World Health Organization) (2001) *International Classification of Functioning, Disability and Health*, Geneva: WHO.

Zaidi A., Burchardt T. (2005) Comparing incomes when needs differ: Equivalization for the extra costs of disability in the UK, *Review of Income and Wealth* 51, 89–114.

3

Disability and the labour market

Brian Nolan

Introduction

People with disabilities face many barriers to full participation in society, not least in the labour market. The extent and nature of participation in the labour market has a multitude of direct and indirect effects on living standards and quality of life, underpinning the patterns of poverty and exclusion discussed in the previous chapter. Major differences in labour market outcomes are observed between those affected by disability and others across the industrialised countries – see Acemoglu and Angrist (2001) and DeLeire (2000) for US evidence and Jones *et al.* (2006) for evidence from the UK. Before the economic crisis the employment rate of the disabled was only about three-fifths of that for the non-disabled on average across the OECD (OECD, 2003), and expenditure on disability-related benefits represents a substantial proportion of overall social transfers. The labour market situation of the disabled has thus been the focus of a range of institutional reforms and policy interventions in many countries, and employment is widely seen by policymakers as the primary route out of poverty and disadvantage for people with disabilities.

The labour market is also at the centre of economic research in the disability domain (Haveman and Wolfe, 2000). The impact of disability on employment, and on earnings for those who are employed, has been widely studied, including a relatively recent emphasis on dynamic effects making use of longitudinal data that captures the onset of disability. A significant emphasis has been on exploration of the observed earnings gap and the extent to which it is attributable to productivity-related differences between those with disabilities and others, and the difficulties faced in seeking to identify the impact of discrimination (see, for example, DeLeire, 2001; Jones *et al.*, 2006). The effects of disability-related benefits and other aspects of tax-transfer systems on financial incentives is also a major theme, with an extensive literature studying the relationship between disability benefits and labour supply – see Bound and Burkhauser (1999) for a review. Active labour market interventions aimed at promoting employment among those with disabilities are widely studied (OECD, 2003; 2010), and the impact of anti-discrimination legislation, such as the 1990 Americans with Disabilities Act in the USA and the 1995 Disability Discrimination Act in the UK, has also received significant attention – see Jones (2008) for a review.

Ireland represents a valuable case-study of disability and the labour market against this background, with a particularly low employment rate for those with disabilities, substantial expenditure on disability-related income support and high-quality microdata, including some that is longitudinal in nature, allowing for investigation of the issues that have dominated the international research literature and policy debate. In this chapter we first describe the extent to which people with disabilities are in paid work in Ireland and put that in comparative context. We then present the findings from analysis of the available microdata to tease out the extent to which the observed employment gap is related to observable factors. We then turn to the earnings of those with disabilities who are in work, and whether these appear to be distinctive. Finally, the barriers to achieving a higher level of labour force participation for those with disability and the policies aimed at addressing them are discussed.

Data

The previous chapter described the core statistical sources for the analysis of the position of people with disabilities in Ireland with respect to poverty as the Census of Population, the National Disability Survey (NDS) and a number of large-scale household surveys: these are also the key sources for the examination of labour force participation and earnings. The Census of Population 2006 included a number of questions relating to disability (CSO, 2007), while the NDS followed up a large sample of those identified in that Census as having a disability, together with a smaller sub-sample of other people. Published reports from the NDS include important work-related information on which we draw here (CSO, 2008; 2010). As noted in the previous chapter, the Census of Population and the NDS report different estimates of the prevalence of disability, because a significant number of the NDS sub-sample selected as not reporting a disability in the Census were then identified as actually having a disability in the NDS. About 8% of the population were identified as having a disability in both the Census and the NDS, and it is this group on which the published reports from the NDS primarily focus.

Household surveys represent the other key source of information and base for research on disability and the labour force, in particular the Living in Ireland survey (LII) carried out annually by the Economic and Social Research Institute from 1994 to 2001, the Survey of Income and Living Conditions (SILC) carried out annually by the Central Statistics Office (CSO) from 2003 onwards (e.g. CSO, 2013), and the Quarterly National Household Survey (QNHS) carried out by the CSO, which has had occasional special modules of relevance to disability (e.g. Russell *et al.*, 2008; Watson *et al.*, 2013). In these surveys, adults reporting chronic or long-standing illness or disability can be distinguished, with some additional information about the nature of the condition involved and how much it limits or hampers the person. Valuably, a wealth of other information about the individual and the household in which they live is also sought, including labour force status of household members and, in the case of LII and SILC, income from different sources including earnings and social transfers. The longitudinal nature of the LII surveys, tracking the same individuals from one year to the next, also allows the overall experience of disability over a number of years and the onset of disability to be captured.

Disability and labour force participation

The Census of Population is the natural starting point in examining the labour force situation of people with disabilities in Ireland, and this section analyses data from the 2006 Census. Focusing on persons in the 25–64 age group, Figure 3.1 shows the labour force status of people with disabilities (as captured

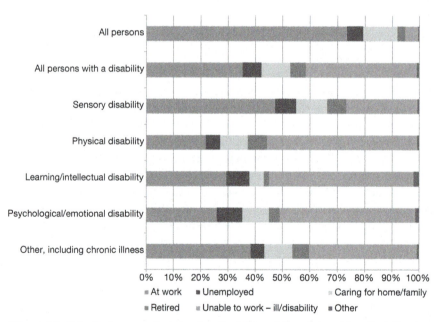

Figure 3.1 Principal economic status for all adults and for adults with a disability, by type of disability (age 25–64, %)

Source: CSO (2007, Table 9).

Notes: Census of Population definition of disability. Adults aged 25 to 64, students are excluded.

by the Census questions on disability), as compared to the total population. Overall, 35% of people with a disability were in work at that point, compared with 73% of all adults in that age range. The year 2006 was close to the peak of Ireland's economic boom, and it is striking that the gap between people with a disability and the overall adult population was so large at that point. The percentage at work was particularly low for those with a physical, psychological or emotional disability, while those with a sensory disability were more likely to be in employment.

Turning to the National Disability Survey, the percentage at work is even lower than in the Census. This is because the survey's severity threshold is higher (including only those reporting 'moderate' or greater restrictions for most disability types), which means that some people with less severe disabilities are excluded. Data from the survey show that among adults aged 18–64 years (excluding students) living in private households, 24% of people with a disability were at work, 7% were unemployed, 56% were unable to work because of their disability and a further 7% retired early because of their illness or disability.

In relation to employment, there was a clear age pattern, with 40% of men and 33% of women aged 18–34 and with a disability at work, whereas for the

Figure 3.2 Main activity of adults with a disability, by sex and age group (%)
Source: CSO (2010, Table 7.3).
Notes: Census/NDS definition of disability. Includes adults in private households aged 18 to 64 but excludes students, people who retired at normal age and 'other'.

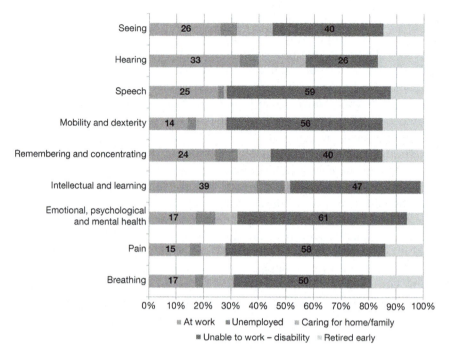

Figure 3.3 Main activity by main disability type (%)
Source: CSO (2010, Table 7.4).
Notes: Census/NDS definition of disability. Includes adults in private households aged 18 to 64,
excluding students, people who retired at normal age and 'other'.

55–64 age group the corresponding figures were only 10% for women and
12% for men (see Figure 3.2). The largest activity category for all age groups
for people with a disability, accounting for between half and to two-thirds
depending on age and gender, was 'unable to work due to illness or disability'.
In all age groups, men with a disability were more likely to be at work than
women. Men with a disability were also slightly more likely than women to be
unemployed and to have retired from work early, whereas women were much
more likely to be occupied in home or family care activities, with very few men
in that category.

Figure 3.3 shows the main activity by type of main disability from the NDS.
Those with an intellectual and learning disability were most likely to be at work
(39%); this group contains some very diverse types of disability, including conditions such as Attention Deficit Hyperactivity Disorder (ADHD) and dyslexia,
autistic spectrum disorders and intellectual disabilities. Those with a mobility
and dexterity disability and those with a pain disability were least likely to be
at work. Being 'retired early' was most common among people with breathing
difficulties or hearing difficulties. The proportion of people with a disability

who were unemployed was highest for those with intellectual and learning disability and those with difficulties in remembering and concentrating. People with emotional, psychological and mental health disability were most likely to describe themselves as 'unable to work due to disability or illness' (at 61%), while those with a hearing disability were least likely to do so.

The most recent available data on the labour force status of people with a disability is from the QNHS in 2010, which included a module on equality and discrimination. The study by Watson *et al.* (2013) based on these data reported that 36% of people with a disability were labour market participants at that point, with an unemployment rate of 22%; this compared with 77% and 16% respectively for working-age adults without a disability. Compared with corresponding results from the special module of the QNHS in 2004, unemployment had increased for people with a disability from 8% to 22%, whereas for those without a disability it rose from 5% to 16%, with that increase being greater for men than for women in both cases.

A comparative perspective on the impact of disability on labour market participation can be obtained from analysis of data from EU-SILC brought together at European level. Data for 2009 show that the employment rate for those of working age with disability in Ireland was substantially lower than in many other European countries, and was less than two-thirds of the EU-27 average (Grammenos, 2013, Table 7, p. 36). The activity rate (including those in employment and unemployed) for those with disability was also relatively low in Ireland, at about 70% of the EU-27 average (Grammenos, 2013, Table 15, p. 59). In a similar vein, analysis of labour force survey data by the OECD shows that employment rates of people with health problems or disability in Ireland are among the lowest in the OECD (OECD, 2010).

Econometric analysis of disability and labour force participation

In order to examine the factors affecting labour force participation and the impact of disability per se, over and above other influences, we draw on econometric analyses of the microdata from available large-scale household surveys containing the relevant information. In the Irish case, the key studies have employed data from the LII surveys and the special module included with the 2002 QNHS, already mentioned in the previous chapter. These studies (Gannon and Nolan, 2004a; 2004b) found that the labour market status of those reporting a long-standing or chronic illness or disability in these surveys differed systematically from the other respondents. About 40% of those reporting a long-standing/chronic illness or disability were in employment in 2000–2, with the remainder mostly counted as inactive rather than unemployed, compared with an employment rate of close to 70% for those not reporting such a condition.

Labour force participation also varied markedly with the extent of the restrictions in work or in daily activities associated with the illness or disability. For example, the QNHS 2002 special module on disability found the employment rate for men who said they were severely restricted in the kind of work they could do was only 18%, and for women it was only 15%. In the 2000 LII survey, the employment rate for those who said they were severely hampered in their daily activities by a chronic illness or disability was only 24%, compared with 64% for those who were not hampered.

Regression models were estimated to identify the influence of the presence of chronic illness or disability, and the extent to which it hampers or restricts the individual, controlling for other factors which are likely to influence labour force participation such as age, gender and education. A probit model was employed, the dependent variable being an indicator variable which took a value of 1 if the individual was either working or had been seeking work in the previous four weeks, and 0 otherwise. Because the patterns for men and women may be rather different, separate equations were estimated for each.

The results for men from the 2000 LII survey are presented in Table 3.1.

Table 3.1 Probit model of labour force participation, men aged 15–64, estimated marginal effects

	Marginal effect with no controls	Marginal effect with controls
Disabled with severe limitation in daily activities	−0.580**	−0.610**
Disabled with some limitation in daily activities	−0.360**	−0.295**
Disabled with no limitation in daily activities	−0.013	−0.012
Age 15–24		−0.015
25–34		0.114**
35–44		0.105**
45–54		0.086**
Married		0.074**
Unearned income/100		−0.0002
Secondary education		0.082**
Third level education		0.092**
Border, Midlands, West regions		0.003
Age youngest child <4		0.040
>=4 and <12		0.016
>=12 and <18		0.041**
McFadden Pseudo R^2	0.107	0.248
N observations	3315	3315

Source: Gannon and Nolan (2004b, Table 2), based on analysis of Living in Ireland survey for 2001.
Notes: ** Statistically significant at 5% level.
* Statistically significant at 10% level.

These show that when only the variables capturing chronic illness or disability were included as explanatory factors, men with a chronic illness or disability that limits them severely in their daily activities had on average a reduction of 58 percentage points in the probability of being in the labour force, relative to men without a chronic illness or disability. Those with a chronic illness which limited them in their daily activities 'to some extent' had that probability reduced by about 36 percentage points, and those with a chronic illness that did not limit them in their daily activities had a probability of being in the labour force that was not significantly different to those without such a condition. When the full set of explanatory variables was included in the estimated model, incorporating age, education, marital status and number of children, the effect of a severely limiting disability on labour force participation was little changed, fell somewhat for those who were ill/disabled with some limitation, while it remained insignificant for those reporting illness/disability with no limitation.

The key implications of those results are illustrated in Figure 3.4. Men who reported being severely hampered or restricted by long-standing/chronic illness or disability were 60 percentage points less likely to be in the labour force. For those who reported being hampered or restricted 'to some extent'

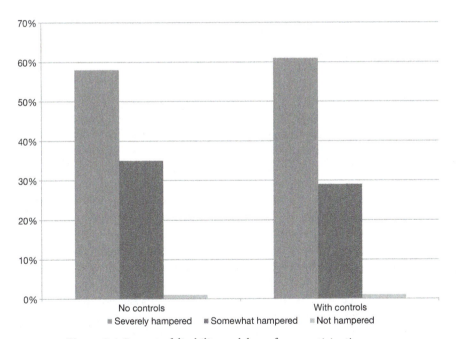

Figure 3.4 Impact of disability on labour force participation, men
Source: Based on Gannon and Nolan (2004b, Table 2).
Notes: Chart shows estimated reduction in probability of being in the labour force for those 'severely hampered', 'somewhat hampered' and 'not hampered' by this disability.

Table 3.2 Probit model of labour force participation, women aged 15–64, estimated marginal effects

	Marginal effect with no controls	Marginal effect with controls
Disabled with severe limitation in daily activities	−0.514**	−0.525**
Disabled with some limitation in daily activities	−0.260**	−0.216**
Disabled with no limitation in daily activities	−0.126**	−0.071*
Age 15–24		0.133**
25–34		0.365**
35–44		0.328**
45–54		0.263**
Married		−0.082**
Unearned income/100		−0.006
Secondary education		0.223**
Third level education		0.390**
Border, Midlands, West Regions		−0.046**
Age youngest child <4		−0.209**
>=4 and <12		−0.114**
>=12 and <18		−0.039
McFadden Pseudo R^2	0.031	0.148
N observations	3362	3362

Source: Gannon and Nolan (2004b, Table 3), based on analysis of Living in Ireland survey for 2000.
Notes: ** Statistically significant at 5% level.
* Statistically significant at 10% level.

by such a condition, that effect was about half as large – which was still very substantial. For men reporting a long-standing/chronic illness or disability that did not hamper or restrict them, the probability of being in the labour force was similar to others of the same age, gender and educational attainment who did not report any such condition.

Gannon and Nolan's (2004b) estimation results for women in the 2000 LII survey, presented in Table 3.2, show a similar pattern to those for men. Women with a condition that was limiting 'severely' or 'to some extent' had a reduction in their probability of labour force participation slightly smaller than for men in the same illness/disability situation. However, unlike for men, women with a chronic illness or disability that did not limit them in their daily activities were also less likely to be in the labour force (at the 10% significance level). The impact of having a chronic condition might vary not just with gender, taken into account by estimating separate models for men and women, but with the age or education level of the individual. This was tested by including in the statistical model a variety of interactions between each of the three illness/disability variables and other variables; this did not affect the overall pattern of the results.

As well as the LII-based results presented here, Gannon and Nolan (2004a; 2004b) carried out similar analysis with the larger sample from the 2002 QNHS special module, where the variables used to capture illness or disability reflect what the respondent said about the impact on their capacity to work as opposed to their daily activities, and this produced very similar results. Watson *et al.* (2013) undertook related econometric analyses with the microdata from the 2004 and 2010 special QNHS modules, and explored in detail changes over that period. Controlling for changes in the level of education and other characteristics, they found an increase in the labour market participation of men with a disability and a decrease for women with a disability, the opposite pattern to that observed for people without a disability, among whom the labour market participation of men fell slightly, while that of women increased slightly.

The longitudinal data obtained in the LII survey, following the same individuals from one year to the next, also allowed Gannon and Nolan (2006; 2007) to look at the impact on labour force participation of disability onset and overall experience of disability over a number of years. Tracking individuals from before the onset of disability through the period of onset and beyond, a substantial and sustained decline in their employment rate was seen. As Figure 3.5 shows, only about 60% of the individuals for whom disability onset was

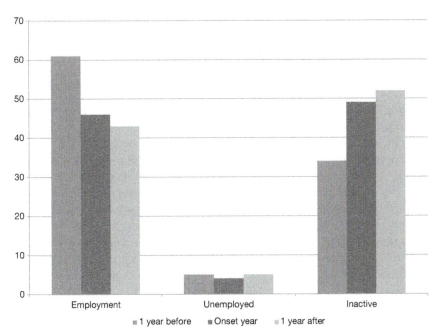

Figure 3.5 Disability onset and labour force participation
Source: Based on Gannon and Nolan (2006, Table 3.3).

Table 3.3 Onset of chronic illness/disability and probability of stopping work, age 15–65

	Onset of chronic illness/ disability only	+ personal characteristics	+ household circumstances	+ education
Onset of chronic illness/disability	0.231**	0.208**	0.204**	0.194**
Female		0.065**	0.065**	0.067**
Age 25–34		-0.023**	-0.022**	-0.025**
35–44		-0.029**	-0.035**	-0.039**
45–54		-0.029**	-0.031**	-0.037**
55–64		0.001	0.008	-0.006
2 adults in household			-0.004	-0.001
3 or more adults in household			0.006	0.006
1 child in household			0.009	0.008
2 or more children in household			0.031**	0.030**
No education qualifications				0.036**
Year	-0.003	-0.003	-0.003	-0.002
R^2	0.026	0.077	0.084	0.092
N observations	4802	4802	4802	4802

Source: Gannon and Nolan (2006, Table 3.3).
Notes: ** Statistically significant at 5% level.
* Statistically significant at 10% level.

observed were in employment prior to onset – they were already more prone to unemployment and inactivity than others. When disability onset occurred, their employment rate fell from 60% to 46%, and in the year after onset to 43%.

A probit model was estimated to look at the contribution which disability onset on its own made, controlling for other factors. The results in Table 3.3 show the implied marginal effects of each variable compared with someone who did not experience disability onset, is in the omitted under-25 age category, etc. If the only explanatory variable included in the model is disability onset, then we see that individuals with onset were 23 percentage points more likely to stop working than the omitted category, who were at risk but did not experience onset. (This means that about 28% of people with an onset stopped work, compared to only 5% of those without an onset.)

When controlling for age and gender, we see that women and older workers were more likely to stop working, and when this was taken into account the estimated effect of disability onset fell slightly, to 21 percentage points. In the third column some household characteristics are included as explanatory variables, and show that individuals in households with two or more children were more likely to stop working, but the estimated effect of disability was not affected. In the final column we introduce having no educational qualifications and this did increase the individual's probability of stopping work, but once again this made no difference to the impact of disability onset. So the results confirm the broad picture conveyed by the comparison of employment rates before and after disability onset, that a reduction of about 20 percentage points was associated with onset. This was more pronounced for those who were hampered severely or to some extent by that chronic illness or disability (though the very few cases where onset of a severely hampering disability was observed meant the effect of onset of a disability that hampers severely versus to some extent could not be reliably distinguished).

Over the eight-year life of the panel survey, individuals of working age reporting a chronic illness or disability throughout could also be identified.

Table 3.4 Persistent chronic illness/disability and probability of being in work, age 15–65

	Probability (working) base	Personal characteristics	Household circumstances	Education
Chronic illness/disability for entire panel	−0.419**	−0.470**	−0.439**	−0.414**
Disability onset	−0.262**	−0.220**	−0.203**	−0.187**
Disability exit	−0.142**	−0.104**	−0.069	−0.055
Other disability trajectory	−0.143**	−0.104**	−0.084**	−0.068**
Female		−0.355**	−0.372**	−0.381**
Age 25–34		0.098**	0.099**	0.118**
35–44		0.059**	0.079**	0.105**
44–54		−0.017	−0.012	0.035
55–65		−0.243**	−0.271**	−0.201**
Adult2			−0.018	−0.030
Adult3			−0.055	−0.056
Child1			−0.001	0.003
Child2			−0.057**	−0.052**
Poor in previous year			−0.386**	−0.356**
No education qualifications				−0.140**
Year	0.021**	0.0280**	0.028**	0.026**
R^2	0.042	0.178	0.237	0.246
N observations	15332	15332	15321	15321

Source: Gannon and Nolan (2006, Table 3.7).
Notes: ** Statistically significant at 5% level.
* Statistically significant at 10% level.

Over half of these individuals were not working in any of the survey waves, compared with 25% for those who reported disability onset during the period and 18% for those not reporting any chronic illness or disability throughout the panel. Results of a model estimated to look at the effect of persistent disability on the probability of being at work are shown in Table 3.4. We see in the first column that persistent disability reduced the probability of being in work by 42 percentage points, as compared with the reference category reporting no disability throughout the panel. Controlling for age and gender (in column 2) actually increased the estimated effect of persistent disability, but when household characteristics and the individual's education levels are included (in columns 3 and 4) that effect falls back again to about the level seen without any controls. So the impact of persistent disability throughout the panel survey on the likelihood of being in work was very substantial indeed. The results also show that those who reported disability onset, disability exit or other disability trajectories were less likely to be in employment in a given wave than those who reported no disability, but that gap was considerably less than for those persistently reporting disability.

Disability and earnings

While disability clearly substantially reduces the likelihood that an individual will be in work, the impact of disability may also continue to be felt by those in work, potentially affecting how much they earn. To investigate the relationship between disability and earnings, Gannon and Nolan (2006) analysed data from

Table 3.5 Results of estimated wage equation, men

	Coefficients
Ill/disabled and severely hampered	−0.168
Ill/disabled and hampered to some extent	−0.023
Ill/disabled and not hampered	0.151**
Years in work	0.0379**
Years in work squared/100	−0.058**
Years out of work	−0.031**
Years out of work squared/100	0.176**
Secondary education	0.221**
Third level education	0.621**
Constant	1.653**
R^2	0.348
N observations	2933

Source: Gannon and Nolan (2005, Table 4.5), based on analysis of Living in Ireland surveys for 2000 and 2001.
Notes: ** Statistically significant at 5% level.
Reference category: no disability, primary education.

the LII survey, which, unlike the Census, NDS or QNHS, obtained detailed data on earnings and other sources of income. In order to have sufficient cases for statistical analysis, the study concentrated on male employees and pooled results from the 2000 and 2001 LII surveys. A standard wage equation was estimated, with the hourly wage as the dependent variable and explanatory variables including years of experience, education and whether the individual is reporting a chronic illness or disability. The results in Table 3.5 show that having an illness or disability and being hampered severely or to some extent had no statistically significant impact on earnings, once education and experience had been taken into account. Illness or disability that does not hamper the person is actually seen to have a statistically significant positive effect, presumably picking up the effects of other characteristics not included in this simple model, which also fails to take into account that those in employment may also be distinctive in terms of their unobserved characteristics.

Disability may of course also have an impact on education and previous work experience that will feed through to influence earnings, and the previous chapter brought out the extent to which illness or disability affects educational attainment. As noted, another potentially important consideration is the fact that those with a disability and in employment may have particular unobserved characteristics that might affect the comparison, for example they may be more determined or more motivated on average, and these characteristics might well also affect their earnings, i.e. there could be 'selection bias'. The standard econometric estimation procedure to take this into account is to first estimate an equation capturing the factors influencing participation in employment, and using the results from that to 'correct' the wage equation. Estimated wage equations for those with and those without illness/disability corrected for potential

Table 3.6 Results of estimated wage equation for employees with versus without hampering illness/disability with selection bias correction, men

	No hampering illness/ disability	Hampering illness/disability
Years in work	0.026**	0.039**
Years in work squared/100	−0.034**	−0.073**
Years out of work	−0.010**	−0.062**
Years out of work squared/100	0.176**	0.203
Secondary education	0.262**	0.309**
Third level education	0.688**	0.651**
Constant	1.73**	1.444**
Lambda	−0.416**	0.228**

Source: Gannon and Nolan (2005, Table 4.7), based on analysis of LII surveys for 2000 and 2001.
Notes: ** Statistically significant at 5% level.
Reference category: primary education only.

selection bias in that way are shown in Table 3.6. The estimated constant term is now lower for those reporting a hampering chronic illness or disability, so the predicted hourly wage for an otherwise identical individual will be lower where he is reporting a chronic illness or disability and being hampered. The scale of the gap was of the order of £1 (€1.25) per hour, which is quite substantial. So, correcting the original estimates for potential selection bias had a substantial impact on the results, revealing a difference in hourly earnings between those with and those without disability that was not previously seen.

The reliability of this finding obviously depends on the robustness of the correction procedure itself, and this is not easy to assess. Experience in gender wage gap research, where it has been used extensively, suggests that different approaches to correcting for selection bias and, indeed, differences in the precise specification of equations can significantly influence the results. There is much less international experience to draw on in the disability context, but the effect we found from correcting for that bias does not appear out of line with what is available.

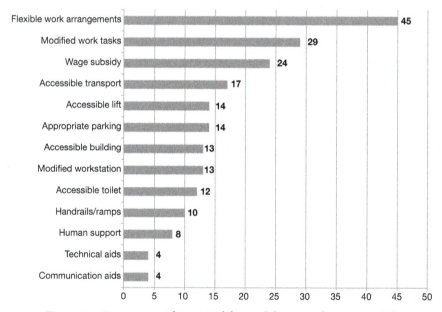

Figure 3.6 Features or aids required for work by sex and age group (%)
Source: CSO (2010, Table 7.29).
Notes: Census/NDS definition of disability. Adults in private households at work or who, if circumstances were right, would be interested in work. People who retire at normal age are not included. Multiple answers allowed.

Disability, barriers to work and policy

The barriers that people with a disability face in the world of work are central to their relatively low employment rate, and availability of specific supports as well as the broader environment can be key. The NDS found that, of those people with a disability who were not in a job, over one third (37%) would be interested in work if the circumstances were right, rising to almost two-thirds for younger people with a disability. These people, as well as those with a disability currently in work, were asked whether they required any of a list of 13 job features or aids to be able to work, and the responses are shown in Figure 3.6. Features of the job itself are by far the most important elements to enable people with a disability to work, including flexible work arrangements and modified job tasks. A wage subsidy was cited by about one quarter of respondents as being important. Issues related to accessibility were cited by a significant minority of respondents. These included accessible transport, appropriate lifts and parking, accessible buildings and modified workstations, accessible toilets and handrails or ramps. Human support is or would be needed by relatively small numbers of respondents, as would technical aids and communication aids.

The importance of work organisation in enabling people with a disability to work can also be seen in the considerable number working part time rather than full time. Of the people with a disability in the NDS who were at work, 28% work part time. In fact, 21% of men and 38% of women with a disability

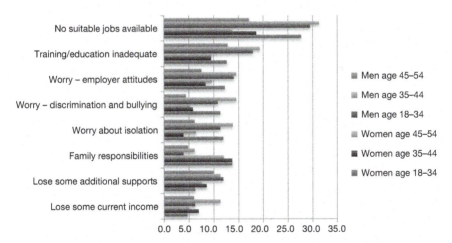

Figure 3.7 Reasons for not being interested in work for those with disability, by gender and age group (%)

Source: CSO (2010, Table 7.21).

Notes: Census/NDS definition of disability. Adults in private households not at work and who, even if circumstances were right, would not be interested in returning to work, excluding people who retired at normal age. Multiple answers allowed.

work part-time hours (that is, under 25 hours per week), compared to 6% of all men and 33% of all women in the labour force at that time.

The NDS also asked people with a disability who were not at work and said they were not interested in seeking work whether any of a set of reasons had discouraged them from looking for work over the previous six months. The responses, shown in Figure 3.7, revealed that the most common reason for discouragement among adults aged 18–54 years was the belief that there were no suitable jobs available. The second most common reason given by men was the belief that their skills or qualifications were inadequate, while for women the second most common reason given was family responsibilities. Concerns about discrimination or bullying, isolation and the attitudes of employers are reported by significant numbers of men and of younger women, less often by older men and women. People with a disability are also less likely to receive work-related training than others: 21% of adults with a disability of working age in the NDS received work-related training, compared with about 45% for the working-age population at the time.

Discrimination as a potential barrier to employment or advancement in the workplace for people with disabilities has been the subject of specific studies, including Watson *et al.* (2013), based on the 2004 and 2010 special modules with the QNHS. This was based on the person's self-report of discrimination and covered discrimination both in the workplace and when looking for work. The number of self-reports of work-related discrimination was considerably higher for people with a disability than for people without a disability in both 2004 and 2010, but the gap had narrowed significantly by 2010. There was a substantial fall in the reported prevalence of work-related discrimination among people with a disability between 2004 and 2010, from 26 to 19%, whereas there was little change in the prevalence of work-related discrimination among those without a disability, at about 13% in both years. Controlling for other factors, certain groups of people with a disability were seen to be at a higher risk of work-related discrimination, including lone parents with a disability, younger adults with a disability and people with a learning or intellectual disability. People with a disability living in the Dublin region are also more likely to report experiencing discrimination than those living elsewhere in Ireland.

The focus of policy in seeking to address barriers and promote employment for people with disabilities in Ireland has been on legislation to address discrimination, on the public sector as an employer, on active labour market policies, and on reforms in the tax/transfer system. The Employment Equality Acts 1998–2011 and the Equal Status Acts 2000–2011 outlaw discrimination in employment and vocational training (as well as more broadly in the provision of goods and services) based on any of nine distinct grounds, of which disability is one, and an enforcement structure is in place including the Equality Tribunal, which investigates or mediates claims of unlawful discrimination. Arising from the 2005 Disability Act, public sector organisations are obliged to promote and support the employment of people with disabilities and achieve a statutory minimum 3% target of staff with disabilities, and a statutory Sectoral Plan on employment and training matters for people with disabilities was prepared by the Department of Enterprise, Trade and Employment in 2006. As far as active labour market policy is concerned, people with disabilities have not been the primary focus, in good times or in bad, but will be affected by the major institutional changes recently implemented in the way these are delivered, which are intended to bring about much tighter integration with the benefit system. The benefit system itself remains particularly fragmented in the case of disability, and significant work disincentives appear to arise for some beneficiaries, in particular from the potential loss of entitlement to free health care upon moving into work. While a variety of structural reforms have been considered and analysed in recent years, the extent of change implemented in disability-related payments has been rather modest, though even these have proved politically contentious.

Conclusions

Ireland represents a valuable case-study of disability and the labour market. People with disabilities face many barriers to full participation in the labour market, and as a consequence their labour force participation rates and employment rates fall far below those for others of working age. In the 2006 Census of Population, among persons aged between 25 and 64 years only 35% of people with a disability were in work, compared with 73% of all adults. That was at the peak of Ireland's economic boom, and it is striking that the gap between people with a disability and the overall adult population was so large at that point – exceptionally wide compared with other EU or OECD countries. The percentage at work was particularly low for those with a physical, psychological or emotional disability, while those with a sensory disability were more likely to be in employment. Studies based on the analysis of survey microdata, which are able to take other characteristics into account in assessing the impact of disability per se, also bring out the very considerable impact of long-standing or chronic illness or disability on the likelihood of being in employment. Longitudinal data from surveys following the same sample over time show both the immediate impact of the onset of disability and the very substantial effects of disability that persists over a number of years.

Disability may also have an impact on earnings for those who are in work. Estimating these effects is complicated by the fact that those with a disability and in employment may have distinctive characteristics – for example, they may be particularly determined or motivated – and these characteristics that are unobserved in the surveys might well affect their earnings. Estimated wage equations for those with and those without disability corrected for this potential selection bias suggested a significantly lower predicted hourly wage for an otherwise identical individual reporting a hampering chronic illness or disability.

The barriers people with a disability face in the world of work were probed in the NDS, which found that features of the job itself are by far the most important elements to enable people with a disability to work, including flexible work arrangements and modified job tasks. A wage subsidy was cited by about one quarter of respondents as being important, and issues related to accessibility were cited by a significant minority of respondents, including accessible transport, appropriate lifts and parking, accessible buildings and modified workstations, accessible toilets and handrails or ramps. Discrimination as a potential barrier to employment or advancement in the workplace for people with disabilities has been the subject of a number of studies, finding a substantial fall in the reported prevalence of work-related discrimination among people with a disability between 2004 and 2010. Controlling for other factors, certain groups of people with a disability were seen to be at a higher risk of work-related discrimination, including lone parents, younger adults and people with a learning or intellectual disability.

In the current economic crisis employment rates have fallen sharply, for those with and without disabilities. The nature of the disadvantages faced by people with disabilities and the processes which underpin them are extremely complex and the design of policies to address the barriers to increased levels of employment is challenging. Nonetheless, experience elsewhere suggests that even in an unfavourable economic climate these barriers are not insurmountable.

Acknowledgements

This chapter draws heavily on joint work with Brenda Gannon (University of Leeds) and Dorothy Watson (ESRI).

References

Acemoglu D., Angrist J.D. (2001) Consequence of employment protection? The case of the Americans with Disabilities Act, *Journal of Political Economy* 19, 915–50.

Bound J., Burkhauser R.V. (1999) Economic analysis of transfer programs targeted on people with disabilities, in Ashenfelter O., Card D. (Eds) *Handbook of Labor Economics* Volume 3C, Elsevier, North Holland, 3417–528.

CSO (Central Statistics Office) (2007) *Census of Population 2006 Volume 11, Disability, Carers and Voluntary Activities*, Dublin: Stationery Office.

CSO (2008) *National Disability Survey 2006 – First Results*, Dublin: Stationery Office.

CSO (2010) *National Disability Survey 2006 Volume 2*, Dublin: Stationery Office.

CSO (2013) *Survey on Income and Living Conditions (SILC)*, Dublin: Stationery Office.

DeLeire T. (2000) The wage and employment effects of the Americans with Disabilities Act, *Journal of Human Resources* 35, 693–715.

DeLeire T. (2001) Changes in wage discrimination against people with disabilities: 1948–93, *Journal of Human Resources* 36, 144–58.

Gannon B., Nolan B. (2004a) *Disability and Labour Market Participation*, Dublin: The Equality Authority.

Gannon B., Nolan B. (2004b) Disability and labour force participation in Ireland, *Economic and Social Review* 35, 135–55.

Gannon B., Nolan B. (2006) *The Dynamics of Disability and Social Inclusion in Ireland*, Dublin: The Equality Authority and National Disability Authority.

Gannon B., Nolan B. (2007) The impact of disability transitions on social inclusion, *Social Science and Medicine* 64, 1425–37.

Grammenos S. (2013) *European Comparative Data on Europe 2020 and Housing Conditions*, Final report prepared by the Centre for European Social and Economic Policy on behalf of the Academic Network of European Disability Experts, Leeds: University of Leeds.

Haveman R., Wolfe B. (2000) The economics of disability and disability policy, in Culyer A.J., Newhouse J.P. (Eds) *Handbook of Health Economics*, Edition 1, Volume 1, Amsterdam: Elsevier.

Jones M.K. (2008) Disability and the labour market: A review of the empirical evidence, *Journal of Economic Studies* 35, 405–24.

Jones M.K., Latreille P.L., Sloane P.J. (2006) Disability, gender and the British labour market, *Oxford Economic Papers* 58, 407–59.

OECD (Organisation for Economic Co-operation and Development) (2003) *Transforming Disability into Ability: Policies to Promote Work and Income Security for Disabled People*, Paris: OECD.

OECD (2010) *Sickness, Disability and Work: Breaking the Barriers*, Paris: OECD.

Russell H., Quinn E., King O'Riain R., McGinnity F. (2008) *The Experience of Discrimination in Ireland: Analysis of the QNHS Equality Module*, Dublin: The Economic and Social Research Institute and The Equality Authority.

Watson D., Kingston G., McGinnity F. (2013) *Disability in the Irish Labour Market: Evidence from the QNHS Equality Module 2010*, Dublin: The Equality Authority.

4

The private economic costs of adult disability

John Cullinan and Seán Lyons

Introduction

There has been a protracted debate in Ireland concerning the possible introduction of a 'cost of disability payment', a cash payment that takes into account the extra and unavoidable expenditures that are incurred by individuals with a disability and their families. The importance of this issue has been acknowledged by, amongst others, the Commission on the Status of Disabilities in Ireland and the United Nations, since addressing the extra economic costs of disability seems a logical step towards alleviating elements of social exclusion for people with disabilities. For example, UN General Assembly Resolution 48/96 recommends that 'States should ensure that the provision of support takes into account the costs frequently incurred by persons with disabilities and their families as a result of their disability'. Indeed, interventions to promote the well-being and social inclusion of people with disabilities in many countries include policies to ensure adequate income for people living with disabilities or those caring for a person with a disability.

In considering the need for a cost of disability payment, or the level at which such a payment should be made, evidence on the extent of any extra costs faced by individuals with a disability and their families is required. While the level and nature of government assistance are ultimately determined by social and political choices, the design of the relevant policies should benefit from evidence on how disability affects the economic welfare of individuals and their families. Within this context, this chapter considers the economic cost of adult disability in Ireland. (Although we would prefer to include all households containing disabled persons, the available data restricts us to those with disabled persons over the age of 15). While there are a range of costs that are associated with disability, the focus here is on the direct private economic costs borne by households containing disabled persons when compared to the wider population. Thus, while the previous two chapters have examined issues that are clearly associated with Sen's notion of an 'earning handicap', the attention here is more closely related to his concept of a 'conversion handicap' (Sen, 2004). The analysis and estimates build on previous work by the authors (Cullinan *et al.*, 2011; Cullinan *et al.*, 2013), and present revised and up-to-date estimates of the economic costs of disability in Ireland, both in general and in the extent to which an individual is limited by their disability. It also presents, for the first time, cost estimates across a range of different disability conditions.

Our modelling framework is based on the standard of living (SoL) approach to estimating the economic cost of disability as developed in previous literature (Berthoud *et al.*, 1993; Zaidi and Burchardt, 2005), and is applied specifically to recent data for Ireland. The main advantage of this framework is that it allows us to formally test if individuals with a disability, especially those with more limiting disabilities, systematically have greater needs than non-disabled individuals and hence require higher disposable income to avoid poverty, or more generally reach the same level of well-being as those without disabilities. In this context, the SoL approach is well suited to estimating the cost of disability.

The chapter is structured as follows. The next section considers the different methodological approaches available for estimating the economic costs of disability and this is followed by a discussion of previous research and cost estimates. The data used and estimation approach followed are then set out, followed by a detailed discussion of the results and findings, as well as their implications.

Approaches to estimating the economic costs of disability

Previous research, both in Ireland and internationally, has drawn on four main approaches to quantifying the economic costs of disability. Below we briefly summarise three 'bottom-up' approaches before presenting a more detailed discussion of the fourth, the SoL approach, which is used in the remainder of this chapter. A detailed discussion of the various approaches can be found in Tibble (2005).

Three 'bottom-up' approaches

The direct survey approach (DSA) involves directly asking individuals with a disability (or their carer) how much extra they spend on specific expenditure items, with the implicit counterfactual being the same individual's expenditures, assuming they did not have a disability. The DSA is in practice the most straightforward and commonly used approach, since any additional costs identified can be aggregated to provide an estimate of total extra costs arising from a disability. However, there are some serious limitations associated with the DSA. First, it assumes that survey respondents are in a position to provide accurate estimates of current expenditures, which is often not the case. Second, it can be especially difficult for respondents to conceive of, and estimate, their expenditures in the counterfactual scenario. This means that the DSA may provide inaccurate estimates of the additional costs of disability (Berthoud *et al.*, 1993).

Expenditure diary approaches (EDAs) involve analysing the expenditures of a sample of persons with a disability, relative to corresponding expenditures for a sample of individuals without a disability. A comparison of expenditures is then used to identify areas in which individuals with disabilities tend to face additional expenditures. Once again, however, there are a number of drawbacks associated with the EDA. For example, the cost of data collection for DSAs tends to be large, while the interpretation of the results can be difficult. This is because the analysis of expenditure patterns tends to lose important variation through the effects of averaging. Another issue is that expenditure is an accurate indicator of consumption only if an individual with a disability and an individual without a disability buy at the same prices, which is often not the case.

The budget standard approach (BSA) is similar to the DSA in that individuals with a disability are asked directly to state what their additional needs are, but differs in that respondents do not answer in terms of their extra expenditures. Focus groups develop a list of items required for a reasonable standard of living and this list is then used to estimate the income needed to achieve a certain standard of living. In terms of problematic issues associated with BSAs, it is also necessary to develop 'control' budget standards for individuals without a disability in order to ascertain whether the needs identified differ for those with a disability. Furthermore, the standard of living required is not well defined and open to interpretation (Tibble, 2005).

The SoL approach

This chapter uses an indirect or 'top-down' approach known as the SoL approach to estimate the economic cost of disability. It assumes that a household's income determines its standard of living, so that for a given level of income there will be a reduction in standard of living where additional needs arise due to disability. This is because households with an individual with a disability divert scarce resources to purchase disability-related goods and services and thus suffer what Sen calls a 'conversion handicap'. Utilising this approach implies that the economic cost of disability is defined as the extra income required by a so-called 'disabled household' to achieve the same standard of living as an equivalent 'non-disabled household'. While the SoL approach does not take account of any foregone earnings or other potential opportunity costs of ill health or disability, it does have a number of advantages over direct attempts to measure the cost of disability. For example, no information is required in relation to the sources or levels of specific costs associated with disability, while it is also well suited to estimation using large-scale micro datasets collected for wider purposes. This

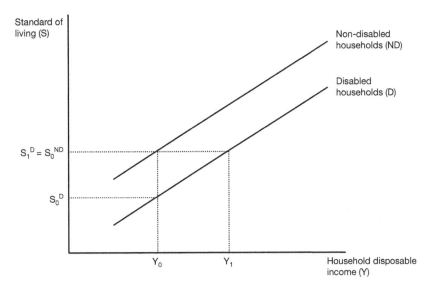

Figure 4.1 The standard of living approach
Source: Adapted from Zaidi and Burchardt (2005).

implies that it is unlikely to be vulnerable to strategic response behaviour among those surveyed, which is a danger with DSAs.

The SoL approach is illustrated in Figure 4.1. For a given level of income Y_0, a household containing an individual with a disability is predicted to have a standard of living of S_0^D. The corresponding standard of living for a comparable household without an individual with a disability is S_0^{ND}, and thus greater than for the disabled household. More specifically, the line in Figure 4.1 which illustrates the relationship between standard of living and income for disabled households lies below and to the right of the line for non-disabled households, implying that the former could enjoy the same standard of living as the latter, but would require a higher income to do so. For example, an income level of Y_1 would give the disabled household the same standard of living as the non-disabled household achieves at Y_0 i.e. $S_1^D = S_0^{ND}$. Thus, the implied economic cost of disability is the difference $Y_1 - Y_0$ and represents what we wish to estimate.

More formally, we can relate standard of living (S) to income and disability status as:

$$S = \alpha + \beta Y + \delta D \qquad [4.1]$$

where Y represents disposable household income, D is an indicator variable defining the disability status of the household and α, β and δ are the equation parameters. Thus, the additional cost of disability for a given standard of living is estimated as $dY/dD = Y_1 - Y_0 = -\delta/\beta$, assuming the linear relationship in

Equation [4.1]. In the simplified version presented in Figure 4.1, a household's standard of living is expressed only as a (linear) function of its income and disability status. In reality, other variables will also impact on standard of living and thus a range of control variables and a stochastic element are added to Equation [4.1] to form the econometric model for estimation. Furthermore, the relationship between standard of living and income may be non-linear and the most appropriate functional form can be tested for empirically. In practice most studies have adopted a log-linear specification, meaning that costs are estimated as a proportion of income, as opposed to an absolute amount. This is also the case in this chapter.

Previous research

A number of previous studies have assessed the additional economic costs of disability in Ireland using a variety of approaches, including the SoL approach. For example, the National Rehabilitation Board, using a DSA, surveyed 59 individuals with a disability in relation to the costs associated with disability and other disability-related issues (NRB, 1995). Additional costs were identified in a number of expenditure areas, including regular purchases such as food, medication, clothing and footwear, home heating, equipment, aids and furniture, as well as adaptations to homes. Indecon (2004) updated the NRB estimates to 2003 prices, implying that 'the extra cost associated with items specifically related to disability amounted to up to €48 per week'. A second study, Nexus Research (1996), focused on the extent and severity of disabilities faced by people with multiple sclerosis, and the implications for employment, income adequacy and other issues. A total of 260 persons interviewed reported relatively low levels of income as well as significant additional costs from their disabilities, further reducing the adequacy of their incomes.

A study by Indecon (2004) for the National Disability Authority used DSA, EDA and SoL approaches to estimate the economic cost of disability. Using the SoL approach, it estimated costs to be €143 per week for non-elderly households on average. However, the Indecon estimates were derived using data that used an imperfect measure of household disability status based on whether the household was in receipt of a disability-related payment, implying that the estimates may be subject to measurement error bias through the disability indicator variable. Furthermore, the data used did not allow for the direct estimation of the impact of severity of disability on the cost estimates, nor for differences in costs across conditions.

More recently, Cullinan et al. (2011) and Cullinan et al. (2013) have also employed the SoL approach to estimate the economic cost of disability in Ireland. Cullinan et al. (2011) used panel data from 1995 to 2001 to control for the effects of previous disability and income and correlated unobserved heterogeneity to quantify the additional long-run economic cost of disability. The findings suggested that the extra economic cost of disability in Ireland was large and varied by severity of disability, with important implications for poverty measures. In particular, since disability reduces the standard of living of households for a given level of income, poverty measures based solely on income will tend to underestimate the needs of households affected by disability. Cullinan *et al.* (2013) focused on disability-related costs for older people and again found them to be significant and to vary by severity of disability, as well as by household type. More specifically, the results suggested that the cost of disability increased in proportionate terms as the number of people in the household decreased.

A number of other studies have considered the economic cost of disability internationally, particularly in the UK and Australia – see Tibble (2005) for a good summary of the former. Overall, the international research has employed a variety of estimation techniques and consequently there has been considerable variation in estimates across studies. Four previous international studies have employed the SoL approach. The methodology was first proposed by Berthoud *et al.* (1993), who used 1985 survey data to estimate the cost of disability in the UK. The same approach was utilised by Zaidi and Burchardt (2005) in the context of an 'income equivilisation' study in the UK. They found that the 'extra costs associated with a low severity disability ranged from £18 (pensioner couple households, one disabled) to £96 (non-pensioner couple households, both disabled)'. The estimated costs rise significantly by severity, however, and 'for a high level of severity, extra costs for a household with mean income range from £104 to £546' per week. Saunders (2007) used the SoL approach for Australia and found that 'the costs of disability correspond to 29% of equivalised income', although this measure increased to 37% when a more realistic measure of disability was used. Finally, Burchardt and Zaidi (2008) find that social welfare payments in the UK are not sufficient to fully offset the extra costs experienced by families with children with a disability and that these families remain at considerably greater risk of poverty.

Data and estimation

The data analysed is from Ireland's Survey of Income and Living Conditions Research Microdata File (SILC). SILC is an annual survey conducted by the Central Statistics Office (CSO) to obtain information on the income and living conditions of households. It also collects information on poverty and social exclusion. A representative random sample of households throughout the country is approached to provide the required information and the survey is voluntary from a respondent's perspective. The first in the series commenced in 2003 and in this chapter we analyse microdata from 2011, the latest year for which the data is currently available. SILC is commonly used to construct material deprivation indicators and poverty measures, but also includes a wide range of additional individual-level (e.g. disability status) and household-level (e.g. disposable income) variables, making it ideal for applying the SoL approach. In total there were observations on 11,005 individuals in 4,307 households in the 2011 sample.

The dependent variable in the model is a proxy for each respondent household's unobservable standard of living. Following previous studies, a composite measure of SoL is generated comprising a set of relevant individual indicators. There are two desirable properties for each of the individual indicators that make up the composite measure. First, each individual indicator should be elastic with respect to income and, second, should not be systematically related to disability status – see Cullinan *et al.* (2011) for a discussion. Based on tests of the first desirable property of the individual indicators, as well as previous studies, we use a composite SoL indicator derived as a function of ownership of a number of 'household goods', as well as whether the household respondent was able to take a holiday in the previous year and had any savings. The household goods included are microwave, television, car, freezer, dishwasher, washing machine, computer and central heating. For each good, a household in the dataset is given a score of 1 if it owns the good, and similarly if the household took a holiday or had savings. These scores are then totalled for each household in order to derive the composite SoL indicator. Variants of this indicator using different subsets of individual indicators were also used to test the robustness of our findings, and further details can be found in Cullinan and Lyons (2014).

Once measured, standard of living is modelled as a function of a number of explanatory variables, with the main focus in this chapter on the 'disability status' of the household. The SILC dataset provides two possible measures of this key variable. The first disability status measure, which we call a 'condition-based disability measure', is constructed on the basis of responses to the following question, which is asked of all those aged 16 years or older in the household:

Do you have any of the following long-standing conditions?

1. Blindness, or a serious vision impairment.
2. Deafness, or a serious hearing impairment.
3. A difficulty with basic physical activities such as walking, climbing stairs, reaching, lifting or carrying.
4. An intellectual disability.
5. A difficulty with learning, remembering or concentrating.
6. A psychological or emotional condition.
7. A difficulty with pain, breathing or any other chronic illness or condition.
8. None of the above.

Based on responses to this question, an individual's disability status can be ascertained and also used to classify the disability status of his/her household, i.e. households with an individual over 16 with a disability based on this measure are classified as 'disabled', while households without an individual with a disability are classified as 'not disabled'. Using this question it is also possible to identify households with two or more individuals with a disability, or where individuals have multiple disabilities. Thus, a key feature of the SILC dataset is that it permits identification of the specific condition(s) that each individual with a disability in the dataset has and hence, for the first time, enables us to estimate the economic cost of disability by condition.

The condition-based disability definition is, however, restricted, to the extent that it defines disability on the basis of an existing and specified condition but does not consider whether the condition(s) has(have) a limiting effect on the individual. Thus, we also consider a second disability measure from the 2011 SILC dataset that is based on responses by the same subset of household members to the following question:

Do you have difficulty in doing any of the following activities [due to chronic illness]?

1. Dressing, bathing or getting around inside the home.
2. Going outside the home alone to shop or visit a doctor's surgery.
3. Working at a job or business or attending school or college.
4. Participating in other activities, for example leisure or using transport.
5. None of the above.

This question is asked only of people who indicated they had one or more of the specified conditions listed above. Thus, it allows us to derive a second alternative measure of disability, what is referred to subsequently as a 'limitation-based disability measure'.

However, it may well be that it is not only the presence of a disability/condition that is important in determining additional economic costs, but also the extent to which it limits or restricts a person in their day-to-day lives. The SILC dataset allows us to directly estimate the cost of disability in Ireland by 'severity of disability', using the following question:

For at least the last 6 months have you been limited in activities people usually do, because of a health problem? (If limited, specify whether strongly limited or limited)

to which individuals can respond (1) yes, strongly limited, (2) yes, limited, or (3) not limited. Thus, this question allows us to distinguish individuals in terms of those with either strong, some or no limitations in daily activities as a result of their disability/condition.

A profile of our sample by disability status based on the two separate measures is presented in Table 4.1 and all statistics reported here have been adjusted using sample weights. The condition-based measure suggests there are 1,836 (42.7%) households with an individual over 15 with a disability in the sample, while the limitation-based measure indicates 812 (18.9%) disabled households. The difference between the two numbers is likely to be driven by the presence of individuals whose disabilities/conditions are not severe enough to affect their activities or where individuals feel they have overcome the activity-limiting effects of their conditions. This might arise, for example, among older people who consider their activity limitation to be a natural consequence of ageing, rather than due to a specific disability. Conversely, some individuals report no specific condition but indicate that they are limited in undertaking their usual activities. This could happen in cases where people have some activity limitation but do not consider themselves to have a disability.

Table 4.1 also shows the numbers and proportions of households that report each of the specified conditions in the SILC survey. 'Difficulty with pain, breathing or any other chronic illness or condition' and 'difficulty with basic physical activities' are the highest represented conditions in our sample. Some other conditions are found in only a small number of households, which has implications for the subsequent analysis. It is worth noting that the numbers of households for each condition sum to more than the total number of disabled households, due to the presence of multiple disabilities in many cases. Indeed, the average numbers of conditions per individual and per household are also presented in Table 4.1 and show that for the sample, the average household has more conditions (0.54) than the average individual (0.33), while the average number of conditions for individuals with at least one condition is 1.27. This implies that most individuals with a disability report one condition, while most individuals reporting a condition are in mixed households that include people reporting no conditions.

Finally, Table 4.1 also presents the numbers of households disaggregated by the condition-based disability status and their reported degree of limitation. In this section of the table, we assign each household to the most 'severe' category reported by any of its members; a household in which someone reports a condition and a strong limitation to activities will be classified under the first heading, even if someone else in the household also reports they have a condition but no limitation. Most households containing a person with a disability also report some degree of activity limitation. A smaller number report activity limitation without a specific condition.

For the income variable, we include the natural log of net disposable household income, which is calculated by aggregating income from all sources and deducting income tax and social insurance contributions. The preferred log income specification can be represented graphically using Figure 4.1, where Y

Table 4.1 Breakdown of SILC 2011 sample households by disability status

Number of households by disability status – alternative disability measures

	Condition-based measure		Limitation-based measure	
	N	%	N	%
Disabled	1,836	42.7	812	18.9
Not disabled	2,459	57.3	3,483	81.1
Total	4,295	100.0	4,295	100.0

Number of households with at least one person with these conditions

	N	% of sample
Blindness, or a serious vision impairment	79	1.8
Deafness, or a serious hearing impairment	111	2.6
Difficulty with basic physical activities	608	14.2
Intellectual disability	61	1.4
Difficulty with learning, remembering or concentrating	114	2.7
Psychological or emotional condition	220	5.1
Difficulty with pain, breathing or any other chronic illness or condition	1,025	23.9
Other disability, not specified	407	9.5

Average number of conditions per individual and per household

	N	SD
All individuals	0.33	0.65
Individuals with at least one condition	1.27	0.63
All households	0.54	0.72
Households with at least one condition	1.27	0.53

Number of households by condition-based disability status and degree of limitation

	N	%
Condition present and strongly limited	232	6.0
Condition present and limited	573	14.8
Condition present and not limited	602	15.6
No condition present, but strongly limited	21	0.6
No condition present, but limited	86	2.2
No condition present and not limited	2,358	60.9
Total	3,872	100.0

Source: Analysis of SILC 2011 data.
Notes: All statistics use sample weights.
N denotes number of observations and SD denotes standard deviation.

is taken to denote the natural log of income. In this case, the estimated cost of disability as measured by the difference between Y_0 and Y_1 will be given as a percentage of household disposable income. We also include a number of other explanatory variables in modelling household standard of living. These include variables relating to household size, the tenure status of the household, the location and region of the household, as well as the age, gender and marital status of the head of household. Full details of these variables are available in Cullinan and Lyons (2014).

Based on the SoL framework and the available data, our econometric model for estimation is given by:

$$S_i = f(Y_i, D_i, \mathbf{X}_i^H, \mathbf{X}_i^{HoH}, \varepsilon_i) \qquad [4.2]$$

where S_i denotes the standard of living of household i, Y_i represents the disposable income of household i and D_i is an indicator variable defining the disability status of household i. $\mathbf{X}_i^H$ is a vector of household-level characteristics while $\mathbf{X}_i^{HoH}$ is a vector of characteristics relating to the head of the household. The error term is represented by ε_i and the model is estimated at the household level. Given the nature of the dependent variable, the preferred modelling approach is an ordered logit model, which is consistent with previous studies that have utilised the SoL approach. Once estimated, the model can be used to estimate the economic cost of disability as a percentage of income by dividing the estimated coefficient on the disability indicator variable by the estimated coefficient on log income. See Cullinan *et al.* (2013) for more details.

Results

Table 4.2 presents estimates of the economic cost of adult disability for Ireland in 2011 using the SILC data and the methods discussed above. Full details of the estimated econometric models used to derive these estimates are available in Cullinan and Lyons (2014) and the discussion below focuses on the main findings and estimates from the analysis. First, using parameter estimates from the econometric models, the cost of disability as a percentage of income

Table 4.2 Estimated economic cost of disability in 2011 – all disabled households

	Condition-based measure	Limitation-based measure
Estimated economic cost of disability as a percentage of income	35.4%	54.5%
Estimated median weekly disposable income for disabled households (€)	€584	€507
Estimated economic cost of disability per at median income level for disabled households (€)	€207	€276

Source: Analysis of SILC 2011 data.

is estimated to be 35.4% using the condition-based measure of disability and 54.5% using the limitation-based measure. The condition-based measure designates a much larger share of individuals as having a disability, and some of these individuals do not report significant limitations from their conditions. It seems reasonable that experiencing limitations to activities is more strongly associated with reduced standard of living than having a condition per se and this is consistent with our findings. Focusing on the condition-based measure, the results imply that at the median weekly disposable income for disabled households in 2011 of €584, the estimated economic cost of disability is €207 per week on average for these households. In terms of Figure 4.1, this is our estimate of the distance between Y_0 and Y_1, and is the estimated additional income that would be required for disabled households at the median income level to attain the same standard of living as an equivalent non-disabled household. Using the limitation-based measure of disability and the median weekly income for this group gives an estimated economic cost of disability of €276 per week on average.

As discussed previously, the economic cost of disability is likely to vary across different types of household, by severity of disability and by condition of disability. Hence, Table 4.3 presents estimates of the economic cost of disability (in percentage terms) across these dimensions. For example, the estimated economic cost of disability for a household using the condition-based measure is 27.7% of income on average for households with one person with a disability, but increases to an estimated cost of 63.6% of income where there are two or more individuals with a disability. (The difference in these estimates was found to be statistically significant.) This suggests that, as would be expected, the presence of more than one individual with a disability in a household leads to significantly higher economic costs. The same pattern is found if the limitation-based measure of disability is considered (47.5% versus 112.1%), and again the estimates are significantly higher than for the condition-based measure. Indeed, standard of living is found to be negatively related to the average number of conditions in the household in general when controlling for other factors (results not presented).

A number of previous studies have found that the economic cost of disability varies by severity of disability/condition and this is also found to be the case in Table 4.3. For those individuals who reported a specific condition and stated they were strongly limited in terms of undertaking regular/usual activities, the estimated economic cost of disability was 64.8%, higher than the average cost of 35.4% reported in Table 4.2. For those who reported a specific condition and were either limited or not limited, the corresponding estimated costs were 33.2% and 12.6%. Thus, a strong and (in most cases) statistically significant cost gradient is observed with respect to degree of limitation, with those most limited facing substantially higher economic costs. A small number

Table 4.3 Estimated economic cost of disability in 2011, by number of persons with a disability, severity and condition

	Condition-based measure	Limitation-based measure
By number of persons with a disability in household		
1 person with a disability only	27.7%	47.5%
More than 1 person with a disability	63.6%	112.1%
By condition-based disability status and degree of limitation, where no more than one person in household has a disability or limitation		
Condition present and strongly limited		64.8%
Condition present and limited		33.2%
Condition present and not limited		12.6%
No condition present, but limited or strongly limited		−13.3% NS
By condition, where only one person in household has a disability		
Blindness, deafness, or difficulty with basic physical activities		19.5%
Intellectual disability, difficulty with learning, remembering, concentrating, or psychological or emotional condition		40.4%
Pain, breathing or other condition		24.1%
Other disability, not specified		21.0%

Source: Analysis of SILC 2011 data.
Note: NS denotes not (statistically) significant.

of individuals reported that they did not have one of the specified conditions listed in SILC but that they were limited in terms of undertaking regular/usual activities by a health condition. However, no statistically significant effect on standard of living was observed for this group. In all instances the base case for comparison is a household where all individuals report no specific condition and also report no limitation to usual activities.

Finally, a range of estimated costs are presented in Table 4.3 by condition of disability. For purposes of comparability, we limited this analysis to households with only one individual with a disability who reported a single condition. Due to limitations in the sample size, it was necessary to group some of the conditions. Overall, the results show a substantial cost of disability for all five of the conditions or groups of conditions analysed, implying that all the conditions gave rise to significant additional economic costs. While there are some differences in the percentage cost estimates, these differences were generally not found to be statistically significant, although this may be a result of small sample sizes for some of the conditions. An extension of this analysis involved adding an extra category for households with one individual with a disability reporting multiple conditions but this term was, somewhat surprisingly, not found to be statistically significant (results not reported). Again, this could be a result of the relatively small sample sizes involved in this particular model.

Conclusions

This chapter presents revised and up-to-date estimates of the direct private economic costs of adult disability in Ireland using the standard of living approach. Regardless of the definition of disability considered, the results suggest that economic costs are significant, vary by the number of individuals within a household with a disability and also by the extent to which an individual is limited by their condition/disability. Overall the main finding is that the estimated economic cost of adult disability is 35.4% of income (or €207 per week) on average using a condition-based measure of disability and 54.5% (or €276 per week) on average using a limitation-based measure of disability. These are our central estimates of the additional income that would be required for households at the median income levels to attain the same standard of living as an equivalent non-disabled household.

These estimates can be compared to previous estimates generated using the SoL approach in Ireland. For example, Indecon (2004) estimated costs to be €143 per week for non-elderly households on average in 1999/2000. Cullinan *et al.* (2011) found that the estimated long-run cost of disability for households with members that are severely and somewhat limited by their disabilities was 32.7% and 30.3% of average weekly income, respectively, in 2001. In the short run, the corresponding proportions were estimated to be 37.3% and 20.3% of average weekly income. Cullinan *et al.* (2013) estimated the economic cost of disability for so-called older households (i.e. households containing only individuals aged 65 years and over) to be 40.4% of income, implying a cost of disability of €98.07 per week on average for these household at the median weekly income for older disabled households in 2001.

There are a number of possible reasons why the estimates in this chapter tend to be higher than previous estimates. Firstly, average household disposable incomes have increased significantly between 2001 and 2011, implying the average monetary estimate would be higher in any case, even for a fixed percentage cost estimate. However, it is also the case that the estimated economic cost of disability as a percentage of income is higher than in most previous studies. While this could be a result of differences in data sources, variable definitions and model specifications, it may also be indicative of an increase in the economic cost of disability over the period. Further time-series analysis is required to fully investigate this issue and is the subject of ongoing work.

Comparisons with estimates of the cost of disability in other countries are also complicated by a number of matters. First, as discussed, a range of different estimation techniques have been utilised internationally, including DSAs, EDAs and BSAs. While some previous international research has used the SoL approach, comparisons to these estimates are best viewed as tentative. This is because of differences in datasets used, definitions of disability, as well as model specifications. Notwithstanding this caveat, our estimates here do appear relatively large by international standards.

In terms of policy implications, the results in this chapter raise interesting and difficult choices for policymakers in these recessionary times for Ireland. Indeed, they are also important for considering the effectiveness of policies that aim to address the economic problems associated with disability more generally. They clearly suggest that current policy does not go far enough in addressing the extra costs faced by individuals with a disability in Ireland and support the case for the introduction of a cost of disability payment or a disability-adjusted poverty payment. The findings suggest that the additional costs of disability are significant and are borne most heavily by those individuals who suffer the most from their disability in their day-to-day lives, implying that policy interventions should be more closely targeted at this cohort.

Consistent with previous studies, the findings also have important implications for the measurement of poverty amongst those with a disability in Ireland. Since disability reduces the standard of living of individuals with a disability, poverty measures based on income will underestimate the needs of these individuals. This is because, for a given level of income, a very significant proportion is being directed away from goods and services typically associated with a higher standard of living. Thus, adjusting household data for disability would likely increase poverty rates in the country.

Before finishing, it is important to say a few words concerning the shortcomings of the analysis in this chapter. The omission of data on disabled persons aged under 16 years from the SILC dataset is an obvious limitation that could be addressed if a broader survey were available. Second, while the SoL approach has a number of advantages for estimating the economic cost of disability, it is not without its methodological limitations. Indeed, there are some important concerns relating to reverse causality, endogeneity and omitted variable bias that should be borne in mind. For example, if there is a 'vicious circle' between disability and poverty, then not only will disability impact on standard of living, but so too may standard of living impact on disability. This could lead to biased estimates of the economic cost of disability. Furthermore, if there exists some omitted variable that is correlated with both disability status and standard of living, then the SoL approach may lead to parameter estimates which suffer from omitted variable bias. While panel data can help to control for such issues, this is beyond the scope of the data and analysis used in this chapter and interested readers can refer to Cullinan *et al.* (2011) for more details.

Notwithstanding these caveats, it is worth stressing that the estimates and results from applying the SoL approach are superior to those based on the bottom-up approaches discussed earlier and that the general pattern of findings here is consistent with results from previous research. Overall they strongly suggest that the direct private economic costs of adult disability in Ireland are significant and need to be addressed.

References

Berthoud R., Lakey J., McKay S. (1993) *The Economic Problems of Disabled People*, London: Policy Studies Institute.

Burchardt T., Zaidi A. (2008) Disabled children, poverty and extra costs, in Sterlitz J., Lister R. (Eds) *Why Money Matters: Family Income, Poverty and Children's Lives*, UK: Save the Children.

Cullinan J., Gannon B., Lyons S. (2011) Estimating the extra cost of living for people with disabilities, *Health Economics* 20, 582–99.

Cullinan J., Gannon B., O'Shea E. (2013) The welfare implications of disability for older people in Ireland, *European Journal of Health Economics* 14, 171–83.

Cullinan J., Lyons S. (2014) Estimating the direct private economic costs of disability by condition, Discipline of Economics Working Paper Series, National University of Ireland, Galway.

Indecon (2004) *Cost of Disability Research Report*, Dublin: National Disability Authority.

NRB (National Rehabilitation Board) (1995) *Cost of Disability Study 1*, National Rehabilitation Board Occasional Paper Series, Dublin: National Rehabilitation Board.

Nexus Research (1996) *Multiple Sclerosis: Multiple Challenges for People in Ireland with MS and Service Providers*, Cork: The Multiple Sclerosis Society of Ireland.

Saunders P. (2007) The costs of disability and the incidence of poverty, *Australian Journal of Social Issues* 42, 461–80.

Sen A. (2004) *Disability and Justice*, keynote speech at the Disability and Inclusive Development Conference, World Bank, Washington DC, 30 November to 1 December.

Tibble M. (2005) Review of existing research on the extra costs of disability, Department for Work and Pensions Working Paper No. 21, London: Department for Work and Pensions.

Zaidi A., Burchardt T. (2005) Comparing incomes when needs differ: Equivalization for the extra costs of disability, *Review of Income and Wealth* 51, 89–114.

5

A socioeconomic profile of childhood disability

John Cullinan and Aine Roddy

Introduction

According to the most recent Census of Population for Ireland, there were 75,770 persons aged 19 years or less with a disability in Ireland in 2011, representing 6.0% of all persons in that cohort in the State (CSO, 2012). While it is widely acknowledged that children who experience an ongoing medical condition or disability face irreducible needs that must be met in order that they reach their full potential (Blackburn *et al.*, 2010; Petrenchik, 2008), less attention has been placed on the level of economic burden placed on families caring for a child with a disability, particularly in Ireland. According to EDCM (2007), such families face at least two specific challenges over and above those faced by all families which, taken together, increase their risk of living in poverty. These include the considerable additional and ongoing expenses associated with the cost of care for their disabled child, as well as an income penalty in the form of barriers to entering and sustaining employment. Indeed, evidence from the United Kingdom (UK) on the financial costs of childhood disability suggests that these additional costs leave families exposed to poverty and debt (Copps and Heady, 2007; Dobson and Middleton, 1998). Furthermore, a number of other international studies on the economics of childhood disability provide evidence that the direct and indirect costs associated with raising a child with a disability tend to lead to greater socioeconomic disadvantage at a household level (Petrenchik, 2008; Stabile and Allin, 2012).

To date, no research has comprehensively explored the socioeconomic circumstances of families caring for a child with a disability in Ireland. The purpose of this chapter is to fill this gap and to present, for the first time, a socioeconomic profile of childhood disability in an Irish context. Data from the Growing Up in Ireland survey are utilised and a range of dimensions are considered. These include an analysis of the associations between the childhood disability status of a household and a range of socioeconomic indicators relating to labour market outcomes, levels of parental education, social class, income and economic hardship. In doing so, the aim is to compare households with and without a child with a disability on the basis of these socioeconomic measures. Given the nature of the data that is available (i.e. cross-sectional), the analysis is necessarily descriptive and does not attempt to identify causal relationships and pathways.

The chapter is structured as follows. The next section presents a brief overview of childhood disability in Ireland, while the subsequent section reviews the international and Irish literature of relevance. The materials and methods used are then set out, followed by a discussion of the results and their implications. The final section concludes.

Childhood disability in Ireland

Comprehensive data in relation to the extent of childhood disability in Ireland is available from the Central Statistics Office's (CSO) most recent Census of Population (CSO, 2012). The data show that, as of 2011, there were 75,770 persons aged 19 years or under with a disability, accounting for 6.0% of that age cohort (Table 5.1). However, the proportions of younger persons with a disability vary by both age and gender, with higher prevalence rates for older males. For example, while the proportion of children aged less than one year with a disability is reported at 1.6% (1,156 children in total), this increases to 6.1% for children aged between 5 and 9 years and to 8.0% for those aged between 15 and 19 years. Similarly, reported disability is higher for boys (7.2%) than for girls (4.8%), with higher proportions of boys reported to have a disability in all of the age cohorts presented.

Although not reported in Table 5.1, the CSO data on childhood disability also shows that the number of children reported as having a disability has increased significantly since the previous Census in 2006. For example, the number of children with a disability aged one year or less increased by 549 (90.4%) over the period, with similarly large absolute and proportionate increases for children aged 1 to 4 years (4,237; 90.3%), aged 5 to 9 years

Table 5.1 Children with a disability classified by gender and age group, 2011

	Males	%	Females	%	Persons	%
Under 1 year	617	1.7	539	1.5	1,156	1.6
1–4 years	5,369	3.7	3,559	2.6	8,928	3.1
5–9 years	12,517	7.6	7,045	4.5	19,562	6.1
10–14 years	14,736	9.5	8,676	5.9	23,412	7.7
15–19 years	13,131	9.1	9,581	6.9	22,712	8.0
Total (0–19)	46,370	7.2	29,400	4.8	75,770	6.0

Source: CSO (2012).

(7,573; 63.2%), aged 10 to 14 years (7,443; 46.6%) and aged 15 to 19 years (8,364; 58.3%). This may be related to increases in the overall population of children over the period and could have important implications for the provision of services to children with disabilities, such as education, health and social care services.[1] It is also likely to have implications for the socioeconomic circumstances of many families.

Also of relevance in considering service provision and socioeconomic circumstances is the condition or type of disability that a child has, and Table 5.2 sets out data in relation to this for Ireland in 2011. It shows the number of children, by age group, with each of a range of specific conditions and limitations. For example, as of 2011, there were 5,008 children aged between 5 and 9 years with an intellectual disability, while 1,400 of the same cohort suffered from blindness or serious vision impairment. The most

Table 5.2 Children with a disability classified by type of disability and age group, 2011

	Under 1 year	1–4 years	5–9 years	10–14 years	15–19 years	Total
Blindness or a serious vision impairment	86	599	1,400	1,410	1,415	4,910
Deafness or a serious hearing impairment	60	533	1,183	1,174	1,170	4,120
A condition that substantially limits one or more basic physical activities	310	1,890	2,512	2,279	2,287	9,278
An intellectual disability	184	2,154	5,008	5,867	5,331	18,544
Difficulty in learning, remembering or concentrating	160	2,450	9,467	13,391	11,725	37,193
Psychological or emotional condition	56	876	3,014	3,160	3,480	10,586
Other disability, including chronic illness	420	3,929	6,595	6,512	6,268	23,724
Difficulty in dressing, bathing or getting around inside the home	397	2,827	4,088	2,885	1,929	12,126
Difficulty in going outside home alone	362	2,652	4,758	4,140	3,439	15,351
Difficulty in working or attending school/college	306	2,036	4,657	5,151	6,002	18,152
Difficulty in participating in other activities	369	2,819	5,608	5,494	4,979	19,269
Total disabilities	2,710	22,765	48,290	51,463	48,025	173,253
Total persons with a disability	1,156	8,928	19,562	23,412	22,712	75,770
Average number of disabilities	2.34	2.55	2.47	2.20	2.11	2.29

Source: CSO (2012).

prevalent condition for children aged 19 years or less is a difficulty in learning, remembering or concentrating (37,193 in total), while 18,544 children had an intellectual disability, 10,586 had a psychological or emotional condition, 9,278 had a condition that substantially limits one or more basic physical activities, 4,910 were blind or had a serious vision impairment and 4,120 were deaf or had a serious hearing impairment. Table 5.2 also shows the numbers by age group with different types of limitations e.g. 12,126 had difficulty in dressing, bathing or getting around inside the home.

It is of particular note in relation to these disabilities that, on average, a child with a disability tends to have more than one condition or limitation. For example, for children with a disability aged less than one year, the average number of disabilities per child is 2.34 and this average remains broadly constant across the age distribution considered (see Table 5.2). Overall the 75,770 individuals in the State in 2011 aged between 0 and 19 years had a total of 173,253 disabilities, implying 2.29 disabilities per person on average. Indeed, in many instances individuals were reported to have five or more disabilities (data not presented here). For example, for those aged 5 years with a disability (3,201 children), 173 had 6 disabilities, 168 had 7 disabilities, 80 had 8 disabilities, 59 had 9 disabilities, 18 had 10 disabilities, while 7 children aged 5 years had 11 disabilities. This is important, since the presence of multiple disabilities is likely to impact significantly on the economic problems associated with childhood disability.

Literature review

International literature

This section examines the international literature in relation to the association between childhood disability and socioeconomic circumstances and outcomes. This literature is of particular interest in an Irish context, due to the very limited research undertaken to date on the topic in Ireland. At the outset it is worth stressing that understanding the nature of the relationship between disability and various socioeconomic indicators is complicated by the issue of 'reverse causality', whereby disability status impacts on socioeconomic outcomes and socioeconomic status impacts on the likelihood of disability. Since disentangling these two effects is complicated, much of the research to date has focused on the associations between these variables.

Socioeconomic status has long been a central issue in children's health inequalities research. The reason for this lies in the association between lower socioeconomic status and health, including issues that arise in relation to unequal access and utilisation of services. Another explanation is the process of 'health selection', in which lower socioeconomic status is a result of poor health (Haas, 2006). For example, from a childhood disability perspective the effects of caring for a child with a disability may have substantially adverse effects on parental educational attainment, labour force participation, income and economic well-being. Such caring is also likely to lead to substantial extra living costs associated with the disability (Burchardt and Zaidi, 2008). Consequently, when examining the interaction between child health and socioeconomic status, consideration must be given to the role of health selection in influencing families' transitions in social mobility and the likelihood of increased economic hardship.

Within this context, Emerson and Hatton (2007) provide evidence on the socioeconomic circumstances of children at risk of disability in Britain using data from the Families and Children Study. The criteria used to measure children at risk of disability was based on the primary carer's response to whether any of their children had a long-standing illness or disability which required extra care by the primary carer or affected their school/college attendance. The findings from the research show that families caring for a child at risk of disability were significantly disadvantaged in comparison to families with a non-disabled child across many socioeconomic indicators. In particular, they were 1.6 times more likely to be a lone-parent household, 2.5 times more likely to have neither parent in employment for more than 16 hours per week, while 37% of families with a child with a disability were living in poverty. Based on the use of a stepwise binary logistic regression model to control for household income and indebtedness, the findings show that both lone-parent and two-parent families caring for a child at risk of disability were 40–60% more likely to experience higher levels of hardship relative to other families. A limitation of the study, however, was that it did not control for other potentially relevant household characteristics, such as parental education.

Other international studies have examined the relationship between child disability and poverty controlling for household characteristics and found that the gap in social disadvantage fell when such characteristics were taken into account – see, for example, Shahtahmasebi et al. (2010). Nevertheless, the findings do indicate that these households experience greater social disadvantage and an increased likelihood of economic deprivation. This raises important questions about the health implications associated with this economic deprivation. For example, Duncan et al. (1994) focus on the impact of economic deprivation on early childhood development. Their findings showed that even when adjusting for other factors, family income and poverty status strongly influenced cognitive development and behaviour of children.

Also within this context, a number of studies have examined cumulative social disadvantage and child health in terms of both its immediate and long-term effects (Bauman et al., 2006; Case et al., 2002; Currie and Stabile, 2003; Smith, 2009). In particular, the literature notes a gradient in the relationship between socioeconomic status and health; that is, children from lower-income families tend to have poorer health than children from higher-income families (Case *et al.*, 2002). Parental education, family composition and income are all considered to be contributing factors (Bauman *et al.*, 2006). However, less consideration has been given to the contribution of the extra cost of childhood disability to this disparity. Case *et al.* (2005) contextualise the broader issue of economic status and health in childhood by examining the lasting impact of childhood health and circumstances. The results are based on data used from the National Child Development Study, which followed children born in Great Britain in the week of 3 March 1958 through to the age of 42. The findings showed that children who grew up in lower-income households experienced poorer health than children from higher-income households. When controlling for parental income, education and social class, the findings showed that children who experienced poorer health in childhood attained significantly lower educational qualifications, experienced poorer health and were more likely to be classified as having a lower socioeconomic status as adults. Interestingly, they found that prenatal and childhood health had a direct effect on the health and economic status of these adults at age 42, even when controlling for educational attainment, socioeconomic status and health in earlier adulthood. Case *et al.* (2005) make the point that the findings suggest greater focus should be given to health as a 'potential mechanism through which intergenerational transmission of economic status takes place'. This 'life course approach' is based on the fact that children who grow up in lower-income households are more susceptible to having poorer health status, which in turn impacts upon their health and economic well-being in adulthood, with the potential of affecting their own children.

One of the key issues to emerge from childhood disability research surrounds the issue of reverse causality and disentangling the dynamics between poverty and child disability (Porterfield and Tracey, 2003). Studies in the UK have shown that children with a disability experience greater socioeconomic disadvantage than other children (Blackburn *et al.*, 2010; Spencer *et al.*, 2009). Indeed, these findings are consistent with previous research identifying a social gradient in the prevalence of childhood disability (Emerson *et al.*, 2005; Gordon *et al.*, 2000). Moreover, in the UK, Blackburn *et al.* (2010) found evidence of clustering of child and adult disabilities. Data from the Family Resources Survey (2004/5) was used to show that children with a disability were over three times more likely to be living in a household with a parent who also had a disability than was a non-disabled child and 26% more likely to be living in a lone-parent household. Furthermore, Spencer *et al.* (2009) estimate that if all children and young people experienced the same prevalence rate of limiting long-term illness/disability (LLTI/D) as children in the most advantaged group, there would be a 41% reduction in the population prevalence of LLTI/D. Ongoing research in the UK is exploring the association between social disadvantage in early childhood and onset of LLTI/D in later childhood (Blackburn *et al.*, 2012). However, to date there are no available published studies which can provide evidence on the families' socioeconomic situation prior to the onset of childhood LLTI/D, due to a deficit of longitudinal data. Thus, the sequence of the causal pathway to childhood disability is not, as yet, fully understood.

Finally in relation to the association between socioeconomic indicators and childhood disability status, it is important to take account of the extra economic costs of disability as discussed by Cullinan and Lyons in Chapter 4. In this context, Burchardt and Zaidi (2008) utilised the same standard of living approach to estimate the extra costs associated with childhood disability in the UK, using data from the Family Resources Survey (2004/5). They found that families raising a child with a disability required between 10% and 18% higher incomes to achieve the same standard of living as families raising a child without a disability. This is important because existing evidence on the additional financial costs of childhood disability suggest that they leave families exposed to poverty and debt (Copps and Heady, 2007; Dobson and Middleton, 1998; Petrenchik, 2008). In this context, Stabile and Allin (2012) present a good overview of the direct, indirect and long-term costs incurred at a household level.

Irish literature
In an Irish context, only a small number of studies have been published to date in relation to the economics of childhood disability (Fitzgerald, 2004; Normand and Revill, 2010; O'Halloran, 2008). However, one advantage of these studies is that they provide important insights in relation to the specific costs associated with a particular condition or event, such as a hospital stay. For example, according to Fitzgerald's (2004) report on the financial cost of a child in hospital, the average daily cost incurred by parents for an in-patient visit was €80, whilst this cost rose to €96 for an out-patient visit. These cost findings, which are now slightly dated, were obtained from a postal survey of 110 parents who had a child hospitalised in one of four hospitals in Ireland. Nevertheless, the study points to the financial strain and potential for indebtedness associated with extra hospital visits incurred as a result of childhood illness and disability.

In a more recent study, Normand and Revill (2010) undertook a costs and outcomes analysis of alternative models of care for families caring for a child aged four years or less who suffers from severe intellectual and physical developmental delay, as a result of either being born with or having acquired a brain injury. The report was undertaken for the Jack and Jill Foundation (JJF), was based on a questionnaire completed by 28 families and considered direct and indirect costs borne by the families who received JJF home care. In terms of results, mean costs per year for family travel to health facilities were estimated to be €1,328, while the mean out of pocket direct costs for the family when the child was cared for at home and received JJF home care were €1,292. The mean indirect costs of reduced working hours, which are excluded in most studies in this field, were calculated to be €22,941 per year.

The Normand and Revill (2010) study also estimated the direct and indirect costs incurred by families when their child was hospitalised. The mean costs per year for family travel to hospitals were estimated to be €5,439, while the mean out of pocket costs incurred by the families when the child was hospitalised were €16,882. The indirect costs were estimated to be €27,728. Since many of these children experience complex needs, this is likely to have impacted on the findings. Nevertheless, one of the most important findings from the study is that it provided direct evidence on the efficiency and cost-effectiveness of the provision of home care as opposed to continuous care in a hospital setting. The study estimated that it costs almost nine times more for the State to deliver continuous care in an acute children's ward in a hospital at an average annual cost of €147,365, in comparison to the provision of JJF home care at an average annual cost of €16,422. Furthermore, given the three possible models of care outlined in the study, families chose JJF home care provision as the most preferred model of service delivery. The findings provided a convincing argument for government support to implement optimal policies based on the evidence that the JJF home care model provided the least costly model of care for both the State and the families.

Finally, in relation to previous Irish research in the area, in a study on the economic consequences of the non-provision of services for people with Asperger Syndrome in Ireland, O'Halloran (2008) found that over two-thirds of 25 parents of teenage and adult children interviewed had no option but to become a full-time carer. This meant they had to leave employment, despite 64% of the respondents wanting to return to participate in the workforce or attend college.

Notwithstanding the studies discussed above, significant gaps in the literature exist in relation to our understanding of the socioeconomic circumstances of families caring for a child with a disability in Ireland. In the remainder of this chapter, we attempt to address some of these gaps.

Data and methods

Data

The data used are from the first wave of the Growing Up in Ireland (GUI) survey conducted in 2007 and early 2008. This is a nationally representative survey of 8,568 children that examines issues concerning children, their caregivers, teachers and school principals. The main aim of the GUI survey is to allow an assessment of children in Ireland and to consider their development in the current social, economic and cultural environment, with a view to assisting in policy formation and service provision for children. The dataset includes approximately 14% of all nine-year-olds in the Republic of Ireland in 2008, with a two-stage clustered randomised sampling approach of 910 primary schools being used to generate the sample. In total, 50.8% of children within these schools were included and further details of the GUI survey, including the sampling procedures, can be found in Williams *et al.* (2009).

The GUI survey includes a wide range of variables of relevance for the analysis in this chapter, in terms both of identifying disability and of measuring a variety of socioeconomic and other indicators. The disability status of the child is based on the primary carer's response to the following questions:

> Does the Study Child have any on-going chronic physical or mental health problem, illness or disability? Yes/No;

and,

> Is the Study Child hampered in his/her daily activities by this problem, illness or disability? (1) Yes, severely; (2) Yes, to some extent; or (3) No.

Based on responses to the first question, a child's disability status can be ascertained and used to classify the disability status of his/her household, i.e. households with a child with a disability based on this question are classified as 'disabled', while households without a child with a disability are classified as 'not disabled'.[2] The second question is used to classify the severity of the disability, if any.

In terms of the various socioeconomic measures that are considered, these include variables relating to the labour market (primary carer's labour force participation status; whether a parent has had to turn down work activities as a result of family responsibilities), parental educational attainment, household social class, annual household income and the household's degree of ease or difficulty in making ends meet. More details on all of these variables as well as tables of descriptive statistics can be found in Roddy and Cullinan (2014).

Methods
Given these indicators, the goal is to investigate the association between each of them and the childhood disability status of households, when controlling for a range of other relevant household-level characteristics. This is represented by Equation [5.1]:

$$Y = f(D, \mathbf{X}, \varepsilon) \qquad\qquad [5.1]$$

where Y represents the particular socioeconomic variable under consideration (the 'dependent variable'). More specifically, separate versions of Equation [5.1] are estimated for the range of dependent variables, including: whether the primary carer participates in the labour force; whether work opportunities have been turned down by the household; whether the primary carer has a third-level education; whether the household is in the lowest social class; the log of household disposable income; and whether there are difficulties for the household in making ends meet. The goal in estimating these models is to investigate if there is an association between the outcome measure under consideration and the child disability status of the household. For example, is it the case that households with a child with a disability are more or less likely to have a primary carer in the labour force?

To do so, a range of 'explanatory variables' are included, such as D, which denotes the child disability status of the household (1 or 0, indicating Yes or No, respectively), and X, which represents a vector of control variables also thought to be related to Y. The error term in the model is represented by ε. Equation [5.1] is estimated using regression analysis. In all cases, except the model for annual household income, a binary logit model is estimated to explain a 'yes' or 'no' outcome. In addition, one ordinary least squares (OLS) regression model is estimated to examine the relationship between (log) annual household income and disability status. The choice of control variables X varies across models depending on data availability, previous research and tests for model robustness and goodness-of-fit. They include a range of maternal and paternal factors such as age, education, disability status, ethnicity and labour force status, as well as family, household and environmental factors such as household composition, housing tenure status, access to regular transport and location.

Results

Introduction

This section sets out an overview of the main results and findings from the econometric analyses discussed above. In presenting and discussing the results we divide the analysis into three separate groups of socioeconomic variables. These relate to: labour market outcomes; parental education and household social class; as well as household income and economic hardship. Detailed econometric results are presented in relation to labour force participation for illustrative purposes, while a summary overview of the key results and findings is presented for the other variables and models considered. More details are available for all of the estimated models in Roddy and Cullinan (2014).

Labour market outcomes

Table 5.3 sets out details of the association between the primary carer's labour force participation and the disability status of the child using four different models. The dependent variable in each case takes a value of 1 if the primary

Table 5.3 Logit models of primary carers' labour force participation, estimated marginal effects

	Model I No controls	Model II Controls	Model III No controls	Model IV Controls
Child with a disability (yes/no)	−0.062***	−0.042**		
Child with a disability and severe limitation in daily activities (yes/no)			−0.098	−0.101
Child with a disability and some limitation in daily activities (yes/no)			−0.075***	−0.051*
Child with a disability and no limitation in daily activities (yes/no)			−0.051**	−0.032
Age (years)		0.001		0.001
Single-parent household with 3 or more children (yes/no)		−0.216***		−0.216***
Couple household with 1 or 2 children (yes/no)		−0.124***		−0.124***
Couple household with 3 or more children (yes/no)		−0.291***		−0.291***
Non-Irish household (yes/no)		−0.070***		−0.070***
Primary carer has a disability (yes/no)		−0.138***		−0.139***
Primary carer has secondary education (yes/no)		0.200***		0.201***
Primary carer has third level education (yes/no)		0.412***		0.412***
Household located in a rural area (yes/no)		−0.015		−0.015
Household has access to regular public transport (yes/no)		−0.041***		−0.041***
AIC	11580.81	10684.74	11584.11	10687.89
Observations	8568	8530	8568	8530

Source: Analysis of GUI data.
Notes: The dependent variable (*Participation*) is an indicator variable taking a value of 0 if the primary carer does not participate in the labour force, a value of 1 if (s)he does.
The models are logit models with clustered standard errors and sample weights and the table reports the estimated marginal effects at the mean.
*** denotes significant at 1%, ** denotes significant at 5%, * denotes significant at 10%.
Full details of the control variables can be found in Roddy and Cullinan (2014).

carer participates in the labour force and a zero otherwise. All four models are binary logit models and the estimated marginal effects are presented. For example, Model I includes a single disability variable and no additional control variables and suggests that for households with a child with a disability there is a 6.2 percentage point reduction in the probability of labour force participation for a primary carer of a child with a disability. Since the estimated probability of participation for the base case where the household does not have a child with a disability is 59.1% (data not reported), this implies that the probability of participation for a primary carer of a child with a disability is significantly lower, i.e. on average (s)he is less likely to participate in the labour force than the primary carer of a child with no disability (52.9% versus 59.1%). This association is found to be statistically different from zero at a 1% level of significance. When a range of control variables are added in Model II, the estimated reduction is dampened to 4.2 percentage points, but still statistically significant.

Of course, it is not just the presence of a disability in a household that is likely to impact on participation rates, but also the severity of a child's disability. Thus, Models III and IV replace the single disability measure with a set of measures representing the extent to which a child is hampered by their disability. Model III, which does not include any additional control variables, suggests that the likelihood of labour force participation for a primary carer of a child with a disability who is severely limited in their daily activities is reduced by 9.8 percentage points, when compared to the likelihood of participation for a primary carer of a child without a disability. However, this estimate is not found to be statistically significant, though this could be due to the relatively small number of such children in the sample, which implies that the standard errors of the estimated coefficient will be inflated. For children with a disability who are somewhat limited by their disability, the likelihood of labour force participation for the primary carer is reduced by 7.5 percentage points (an estimate that is statistically significant), while for those not limited, the reduction is 5.1 percentage points. Thus, there is evidence of a strong gradient in the association between parental labour force participation and the severity of childhood disability. When the various control measures are added in Model IV, the corresponding probabilities of labour force participation are reduced by 10.1, 5.1 and 3.2 percentage points respectively, though only the estimated coefficient on disabled with some limitation is statistically significant, and only at a 10% level of significance. These results are summarised in the first row of Table 5.4.

The GUI also includes information in relation to whether or not the parents of children in the survey had to turn down work activities because of family responsibilities. A similar analysis to that conducted in relation to labour force participation shows that households with a child with a disability were 6.7 percentage points more likely (42.7% versus 36.0%) to turn down work activities due to family responsibilities than those with a child with no disability (see Table 5.4). When control variables were included this effect fell only slightly, to 6.0 percentage points, and in both cases these effects were

Table 5.4 Summary of main econometric results – comparisons relative to households with children without a disability

	No control variables				With control variables			
	All disabilities	Severely limiting disabilities only	Somewhat limiting disabilities only	Non-limiting disability only	All disabilities	Severely limiting disabilities only	Somewhat limiting disabilities only	Non-limiting disability only
Labour market outcomes								
Percentage point change in primary carer's probability of participation in the labour force	−6.2***	−9.8^{NS}	−7.5***	−5.1**	−4.2**	−10.1^{NS}	−5.1*	−3.2^{NS}
Percentage point change in probability of turning down work activities because of family responsibilities	6.7***	19.8**	14.1***	1.4^{NS}	6.0***	16.9*	13.6***	0.7^{NS}
Parental education and social class								
Percentage point change in primary carer's probability of having a third level education	−6.5***	−11.9*	−9.3***	−4.3*	−5.7***	−9.6^{NS}	−7.9**	−4.0^{NS}
Percentage point change in probability of household being in the lowest social class	1.0^{NS}	13.0***	0.7^{NS}	0.1^{NS}	−0.3^{NS}	8.2***	−1.1^{NS}	−0.1^{NS}
Household income and economic hardship								
Percentage difference in annual household income	−10%***	−20%**	−14%***	−6%***	−4%***	−7%^{NS}	−7%***	−2%^{NS}
Percentage point change in probability of household having difficulty in making ends meet	6.4***	12.4*	13.5***	1.6^{NS}	3.1**	5.8^{NS}	9.5***	−1.0^{NS}

Source: Analysis of GUI data.
Notes: *** denotes significant at 1%, ** denotes significant at 5%, * denotes significant at 10%, and NS denotes not significant. Full details of the econometric models upon which these estimates are based can be found in Roddy and Cullinan (2014).

found to be statistically significant. Furthermore, when severity of disability was included in the models in place of a single disability measure, the estimated effects suggest that families with a severely or somewhat limited child were considerably more likely to have to turn down work opportunities. These increases were estimated to be 19.8 and 14.1 percentage points without controls and 16.9 and 13.6 percentage points with controls, respectively.

Thus, overall, there appears to be evidence of a strong association between selected labour market variables and the disability status of children in the GUI survey. In particular, the primary caregiver of a child with a disability is less likely on average to participate in the labour force than a corresponding primary caregiver of a child without a disability and is also much more likely to have to turn down work opportunities as a result of family responsibilities, even after controlling for a range of other factors. Moreover, these associations are stronger for children with more severely limiting disabilities, suggesting a strong gradient in the effect of childhood disabilities on these labour market outcomes.

Parental education and social class
A similar analysis to that undertaken and presented in relation to labour force participation of the primary caregiver was also undertaken for variables relating to parental education and household social class, and the main results are presented in Table 5.4. In relation to parental education, the results suggest that the probability that the primary carer of a child with a disability has a third-level education is 6.5 percentage points lower (44.4% versus 50.9%) compared to the primary carer of a child without a disability when no additional control variables are included, and 5.7 percentage points lower when controls are added. Once again, these associations are even more pronounced when severity of disability is accounted for. For example, the reduction for the primary carer of a child with a severely limiting disability is 11.9 percentage points, compared to reductions of 9.3 and 4.3 percentage points in the cases of children who are somewhat or not limited by their disabilities, respectively. When control variables are included, these reductions fall to 9.6 percentage points for a severe disability (though this is not statistically significant), 7.9 percentage points for a somewhat limiting disability (statistically significant at the 1% level), and 4.0 percentage points for a disability that is not limiting (not statistically significant).

Table 5.4 also indicates differences in the social class of households with and without a child with a disability. Overall they suggest no statistically significant difference in the likelihood that a family with a child with or without a disability is in the lowest social class, even when controlling for a range of other factors. However, when the severity of the child's disability is accounted for, households with a severely limited child are found to be considerably more likely to be in the lowest social class, compared to families with a child without a disability. Similar associations are not found for children who are somewhat or not limited by their disability.

Overall, the results here suggest that there is a strong association between parental educational attainment and child disability status and that this association is more pronounced for more severe disabilities. Furthermore, while there is little difference on average between the social class of families of children with and without a disability, there is strong evidence suggesting a much higher likelihood of families with severely limited children being in a lower social class.

Household income and economic hardship

Table 5.4 also reports differences in the annual household income of families with and without a child with a disability. In the simplest model including a single measure of disability and no control variables, the estimates suggest that households with a child with a disability have annual incomes that are 10% lower than those of households with a child without a disability. When a range of other variables are controlled for, this differential falls to 4%. Once again, however, these average estimates mask considerable variation across the disability spectrum. For example, households with a severely disabled child have incomes that are 20% lower than in households with children without a disability, while the differential is 14% for somewhat limiting disabilities. However, these estimated differences fall to 7% in both cases when a range of other relevant variables are controlled for.

Overall these results suggest that while there are differences in income levels for disabled and non-disabled families, these can be explained by, for the most part, differences in household- and family-level characteristics. However, it is important to note that childhood disability may well be impacting on these other characteristics, for example through its effect on labour force participation and human capital accumulation for caregivers. Thus, while child disability status may not have a strong direct impact on or association with household income, it may have important indirect impacts on earnings. In this context, the estimated differences without the control variables are noteworthy.

In considering these results, it is also important to bear in mind that households with an individual with a disability tend to face greater costs than other comparable households. In such circumstances, similar levels of household income will not necessarily translate into similar levels of standard of living (see Cullinan and Lyons in Chapter 4). Indeed, it is likely that for families containing a disabled person, significant proportions of disposable income will be diverted from expenditures on 'everyday' goods and services to expenditures on 'disability-related' goods and services. Thus, as illustrated in Cullinan et al. (2013) in the case of older persons, this is likely to lead to a reduction in the standard of living of these households and to higher levels of deprivation and poverty.

Finally in this context, it is also informative to consider differences in the extent to which families with and without a child with a disability in the GUI survey find it difficult to make ends meet. The estimates presented in Table 5.4 suggest that, on average, childhood disability is associated with a considerable increase in the likelihood that a household will find it more difficult to make ends meet. Overall, the likelihood that a family with a disabled child has difficulty making ends meet is 6.4 percentage points higher than for a family without a disabled child (30.9% versus 24.5%), or 3.1 percentage points higher if differences across households are controlled for. Once again, however, there are also considerable differences depending on the severity of the child's disability (see Table 5.4).

Conclusions

This chapter has presented, for the first time, a detailed socioeconomic profile of childhood disability in Ireland. Using data from the GUI survey, it considers the association between a range of socioeconomic measures and the disability status of nine-year-old children. The findings are striking. They suggest that, overall, the primary carer of a child with a disability is considerably less likely to participate in the labour market and considerably more likely to turn down work opportunities, when compared to a primary carer of a child without a disability. Indeed, these differences are found to be more pronounced, the more limiting is the child's disability.

Similar patterns are also found in relation to parental education and social class. Parents of a child with a disability are less likely to be educated at third level and more likely to be in the lowest social class. Not surprisingly, these households also tend to have lower incomes and much greater difficulty in making ends meet. In fact, for all of the socioeconomic measures examined in this chapter, the presence of a child with a disability in a household is strongly correlated with worse outcomes. In considering these results, it is important to also acknowledge the intangible costs of childhood disability to the child, their family and society. Studies show that raising a child with a disability places complex demands upon various aspects of family functioning and may increase stress, as well as affecting family members' health and well-being (ISPCC, 2007; Reichman *et al.* 2008; Seltzer *et al.*, 2001; Sloper, 1999).

Finally, it is important to once again highlight the caveat that, in the absence of suitable 'instruments', analysis of cross-sectional data such as presented here provides evidence only of statistical associations between variables and does not identify or measure causal relationships. Thus, further work is required in order to better understand the pathways by which childhood disability impacts on these socioeconomic outcomes. Given the longitudinal nature of the GUI survey, the forthcoming second wave is likely to help in this regard.

Notes

1 It may also be related to changes in reporting behaviour between the two censuses, though this is unlikely to account for all of the change.
2 Unfortunately, while it was possible to identify (and control for) the disability status of the study child's parents in the GUI survey, this was not the case for his/her siblings (if any). To account for this, we considered a number of approaches. The first approach (and the one followed in this chapter) is to assume that children with or without a disability are equally likely to have a sibling with a disability. The second approach involved identifying the presence of another disability in the household by analysing disability-related payments to other family members in the GUI survey and controlling for this. Finally, the third approach involved undertaking the analysis using single-child households only. Using the latter two approaches, our results were not found to alter in any significant way, so that in this chapter we proceed on the basis of the assumption in the first approach. Further details can be found in Roddy and Cullinan (2014).

References

Bauman L., Silver E., Stein R. (2006) Cumulative social disadvantage and child health, *Pediatrics* 117, 1321–8.

Blackburn C., Spencer N., Read J. (2010) Prevalence of childhood disability and the characteristics and circumstances of disabled children in the UK: Secondary analysis of the Family Resources Survey, *BMC Pediatrics* 10, 1–12.

Blackburn C., Spencer N., Read J. (2012) Exploring the association between social disadvantage in early childhood with onset of limiting long term illness/disability (LLTI/D) in later childhood, paper presented at Childhood Disability and Social Disadvantage: Evidence and Implications for Policy and Practice conference, Scarman Training and Conference Centre, The University of Warwick, 28 September.

Burchardt T., Zaidi A. (2008) Disabled children, poverty and extra costs, in Sterlitz J., Lister R. (Eds) *Why Money Matters: Family Income, Poverty and Children's Lives*, UK: Save the Children.

Case A., Fertig A., Paxson C. (2005) The lasting impact of childhood health and circumstance, *Journal of Health Economics* 24, 365–89.

Case A., Lubotsky D., Paxson C. (2002) Economic status and health in childhood: The origins of the gradient, *American Economic Review* 92, 1308–38.

Copps J., Heady L. (2007) *What Price an Ordinary Life? The Financial Costs and Benefits of Supporting Disabled Children and their Families*, London: New Philanthropy Capital.

CSO (Central Statistics Office) (2012) *Profile 8: Our Bill of Health*, Dublin: Stationery Office.

Cullinan J., Gannon B., O'Shea E. (2013) The welfare implications of disability for older people in Ireland, *European Journal of Health Economics* 14, 171–83.

Currie J., Stabile M. (2003) Socioeconomic status and child health: Why is the relationship stronger for older children? *American Economic Review* 93, 1813–23.

Dobson B., Middleton S. (1998) *Paying to Care Findings – The Cost of Childhood Disability*, York: Joseph Rowntree Foundation.

Duncan G., Brooks-Gunn J., Klebanov P. (1994) Economic deprivation and early childhood development, *Child Development* 65, 296–318.

EDCM (Every Disabled Child Matters) (2007) *Disabled Children and Child Poverty*, London: EDCM.

Emerson E., Graham H., Hatton C. (2005) Household income and health status in children and adolescents in Britain, *European Journal of Public Health* 16, 354–60.

Emerson E., Hatton C. (2007) The socio-economic circumstances of children at risk of disability in Britain, *Disability and Society* 22, 563–80.

Fitzgerald E. (2004) *Sick Children, Money Worries – The Financial Cost of a Child in Hospital*, Ireland: Children in Hospital Ireland.

Gordon D., Parker R., Loughran F., Heslop P. (2000) *Disabled Children in Britain. A Re-Analysis of the OPCS Disability Surveys*, London: The Stationery Office.

Haas S. (2006) Health selection and the process of social stratification: The effect of childhood health on socioeconomic attainment, *Journal of Health and Social Behavior* 47, 339–54.

ISPCC (2007) *An Exploratory Study of the Impact of Childhood Disability on Individual Family Members, Relationships, Family Life and Dynamics*, Ireland: Irish Society for the Prevention of Cruelty to Children.

Normand C., Revill P. (2010) *There's No Place Like Home – A Cost and Outcomes Analysis of Alternative Models of Care for Young Children with Severe Disabilities in Ireland*, Dublin: The Centre for Health Policy and Management at the School of Medicine, Trinity College Dublin.

O'Halloran S. (2008) *A Study of the Economic Costs of the Non-Provision of Services for People with Asperger Syndrome in Ireland*, Ireland: Aspire – The Asperger Syndrome Association of Ireland.

Petrenchik T. (2008) Child disability in the context of poverty, A discussion paper prepared for the Ontario Ministry of Children and Youth Services.

Porterfield S., Tracey C. (2003) Disentangling the dynamics of family poverty and child disability: Does disability come first? Working Paper No. 03-01, Centre for Social Development, George Washington University, Washington, DC.

Reichman N., Corman H., Noonan K. (2008) Impact of child disability on the family, *Maternal and Child Health Journal* 12, 67–83.

Roddy A., Cullinan J. (2014) A socioeconomic profile of childhood disability in Ireland: Evidence from the Growing Up in Ireland survey, Discipline of Economics Working Paper Series, National University of Ireland, Galway.

Seltzer M., Greenberg J., Floyd F., *et al.* (2001) Life course impacts of parenting a child with a disability, *American Journal on Mental Retardation* 106, 265–86.

Shahtahmasebi S., Emerson E., Berridge D., Lancaster G. (2010) A longitudinal analysis of poverty among families supporting a child with a disability, *International Journal on Disability and Human Development* 9, 65–75.

Sloper P. (1999) Models of service support for parents of disabled children. What do we know? What do we need to know? *Child: Care, Health and Development* 25, 85–99.

Smith J. (2009) The impact of childhood health on adult labor market outcomes, *The Review of Economics and Statistics* 91, 478–89.

Spencer N., Blackburn C., Read J. (2009) Prevalence and social patterning of limiting long-term illness/disability in children and young people under the age of 20 years in 2001: UK census-based cross-sectional study, *Child: Care, Health and Development* 36, 566–73.

Stabile M., Allin S. (2012) The economic costs of childhood disability, *The Future of Children* 22, 65–96.

Williams J., Greene S., Doyle E., *et al.* (2009) *Growing Up in Ireland – National Longitudinal Study of Children: The Lives of 9-Year Olds*, Dublin: The Stationery Office.

6

Resource allocation for students with special educational needs and disabilities

Denise Frawley, Joanne Banks and Selina McCoy

Introduction

Inclusive education has increasingly become a focus of debate in the development of education policy and practice around the world (Farrell and Ainscow, 2002). Within these debates, there is an increasing focus on the nature of funding regulations and to what extent these facilitate an inclusive environment for students (Meijer, 2003; Parrish *et al.*, 1999). The funding of special education is extraordinarily complex. In order for inclusion to work effectively, schools need to be provided with the appropriate resources to meet the needs of their student body. Historically, funding arrangements for special education have been kept administratively separate from resources for general education (Ferrier *et al.*, 2007; Moore-Brown, 2001). In most jurisdictions, these and other factors have contributed to the creation of separate budgetary arrangements to ensure extra funding to support the educational needs of eligible students (Mitchell, 2010).

However, since the early 2000s funding models in special education have been under review in several countries. There is little consensus about the most effective funding model, with some countries promoting individual-based funding where resources are provided directly to individual students and others using general allocations provided to local authorities or schools for special educational need (SEN) and disability supports. Concern has also been raised over rising costs, efficiency and equity in the use of resources, and questions have been asked about the adverse incentives inherent in funding formulae, which may promote exclusion from mainstream education and over-referral into special education. Furthermore, the language of special education and use of categorical systems for resource allocation appears to run counter to the notion of inclusion, which undoubtedly has implications for the systems in place for securing extra provision (Winter and O'Raw, 2010). Funding is, therefore, a vital component of inclusion, with research suggesting that 'if a country advocates inclusion, then legislation and especially financial regulations have to be adapted to this goal' (Meijer, 1999; 2003, p. 19). Since funding mechanisms entail certain incentives, it can be the case that some of them promote and reward the segregation of students with SEN and disabilities. Fletcher-Campbell (2002) describes this as the 'implementation gap' which occurs when there are discrepancies between policy intentions and practical outcomes in terms of financing special education.

In Ireland, there has been intense debate about the most appropriate way to allocate resources for students with SEN and disabilities in school within the new policy environment of inclusive education. New legislation (under the Education for Persons with Special Educational Needs (EPSEN) Act, 2004) specified for the first time that, where possible, students with SEN in mainstream settings should be educated alongside their peers. Since the early 2000s there have been major reforms to the Irish funding model, from a system where all children were individually assessed and resourced according to the nature and type of disability to the existing model where there is a combination of individual allocation to students categorised as having 'low incidence' needs and a general model of funding allocated to schools (based on a number of set criteria) for children with 'high incidence' needs. Despite these dramatic changes there has been little discussion within the research and policy community about the most effective way in which to allocate resources in the light of the policy objectives outlined in the EPSEN Act. Given the trend towards 'throughput' or 'block funding' to schools in Ireland, there is a need to ensure that the existing criteria effectively target students with different types of SEN and disabilities across all school types.

The purpose of this chapter is to provide empirical evidence to inform how special educational needs can be best resourced in Ireland. The chapter provides, for the first time, evidence from a full census of primary and post-primary schools on the provision of resources to students with SEN and disabilities. By focusing on the nature and scale of the SEN population across primary and post-primary schools we examine the extent to which the criteria for special educational needs funding match the distribution of the SEN population across schools. We first examine the ways in which different countries approach SEN financing within the current climate of inclusive education policy. Findings from a National Census of Mainstream Schools (McCoy et al., 2014) are then outlined to examine the profile and characteristics of students with SEN across Irish primary and post-primary schools.

International special education funding models

Different funding models of special education are apparent internationally. There is, however, a movement away from individualised special education funding (centralised funding allocated to individual students) and towards decisions being made at a local/school level. According to Meijer (1999) there are three main funding models in place at an international level. These are: input- (demand), throughput- (supply) and output-based models. Each one has advantages and disadvantages, with the consequence that many countries employ a combination of funding models.

Input-based, demand-driven or categorical (Ferrier *et al.*, 2007) funding is based on allocating individual funding to identified students, the amount being based on the student's degree or severity of need. The model aims to ensure that special education funds are specifically targeted to meet the needs of students with identified disabilities or special needs. It is mostly used in countries with a relatively high proportion of students in segregated settings, especially where special schools are financed by central government on the basis of the number of students with SEN and the severity of the disability. Generally, this funding approach is based on the number of special needs students in a school and requires assessment procedures to establish the 'extra' support that is required (Pijl and Veneman, 2005). The funds are usually distributed according to a flat grant (equally weighted against all categories of identified need), are student weighted or are based on a census count (often adjustments are made based on the socioeconomic composition of a region). The first, flat-grant model, is commonly used in states of the USA, while parts of the UK implement the pupil-weighted approach which is further based on the severity of need (Peters, 2003). Since the early 2000s the Dutch government has taken major steps to develop a new form of input-funding known as the 'back-pack model' (Pijl and Veneman, 2005). The back-pack model is where a student is granted a financial pack that they can take to a school of their choice. The main rationale for this change was related to 'fairness' – the new system would be considered fair if it granted budgets to a largely identical student population (Pijl and Veneman, 2005). The proposal was to change from a supply-oriented form of financing to a demand-oriented model in order to guarantee that every student with SEN is financed in the same way. However, some are very critical of the 'back-pack' model, arguing that the Dutch system generally meets the criteria of objectivity and usefulness but fails in terms of 'fairness', in that the current model excludes groups of students formerly eligible for special needs funding (Emanuelsson *et al.*, 2005; Pijl and Veneman, 2005).

Despite these examples, there has been a gradual move away from the input-based approach internationally. Individual budgets have been criticised for reducing inclusive practice and for increasing costs, as input-driven models 'produce incentives to formulate needs' because of the extra funding attached to the diagnosis of disability (Graham and Sweller, 2011). Similar to the input or categorical funding model are voucher-based models which provide direct public payment to parents to cover their child's public or private school costs. The amount of the voucher varies depending on parental and student characteristics, such as the type and severity of the student's disability and parental income. The aim of these models is to increase parental choice and to promote competition between schools in order to increase the quality of educational services (Ferrier *et al.*, 2007). In the UK, a recent Green Paper on special educational needs funding has pointed to the introduction of a voucher-based model or 'personal budgets' to include funding for education and health support and social care (Poet, 2012).

Another model used in financing special education is the throughput or supply-driven funding model, where central government allocates funding to local authorities, regions or schools via a lump sum with possible adjustments for socioeconomic composition. This is the most common approach at an international level and involves the movement away from a needs-based and towards a service-based approach. It is therefore concerned with generating and maintaining special educational services for students in schools. In most cases, schools and local authorities receive additional funds for students whose needs are greater and for those who will need external assistance, such as local authority support services (Meijer, 1999). This model is often census based and allocates funding based on the number of students with certain weighted characteristics, such as socioeconomic status, gender or the type and degree of disability (Ferrier *et al.*, 2007). In the UK, the most common indicators are the number of students who are entitled to free school meals (Meijer, 1999) and gender (the funding is weighted in favour of male students (1.62:1) in recognition of the higher number of male students with 'statements' or diagnosed SEN (Banks and McCoy, 2011)).

The aims of these models are to simplify the overall funding mechanism and make the financing of special education independent of classification and placement decisions, thus removing the financial incentives to over-identify students as having a disability (Ferrier *et al.*, 2007). Some, however, are critical of these models and argue that it is almost impossible to track these funds to ensure that they are being used in relation to the children for whom additional resources were intended (Riddell *et al.*, 2006). Others have criticised where funding is allocated on the basis of the prevalence of SEN in a region or school, as it can create a perverse incentive to over-identify special educational needs. Between 2001 and 2004 the diagnosis of children with special educational needs in the province of Ontario, Canada became a major source of revenue for schools and resulted in a massive increase in public expenditure essentially because the system 'rewarded negative descriptors of pupils and there was no funding incentive to reward progress' (Ontario Ministry of Education, 2004; Winter *et al.*, 2006). As a result of this experience, the true purpose of assessment became distorted into a process described by some commentators as 'diagnosis for dollars' and 'bounty hunting' (Winter *et al.*, 2006). Other countries, and different states within the USA, have also found that linking resources to particular diagnostic categories is 'increasingly problematic because of fiscal incentives to place students in higher funded categories' (NCSE, 2006, p. 102).

Until recently, funding systems have tended to ignore or overlook the outputs and outcomes which the funding was designed to bring about. This is due, in part, to difficulties in creating consensus on agreed outcomes, but is also due to difficulties in seeing how inputs and outputs are part of the same funding equation (NCSE, 2006). Some countries have, however, begun to adopt the output model, which promotes the achievement of desired results. Output funding is where resources are allocated to 'outputs' such as achievement scores (the higher the achievement scores, the greater the funding) (Meijer, 2003). There is evidence, however, that more attention is beginning to be paid to outputs and outcomes in special education. This is due in part to studies which have found that the relationship between funding and outcomes – in mainstream as well as in special education – is either weak or non-existent. In the UK, for example, the Audit Commission found that although 15% of local authority expenditure on education went to special education, there was little evidence of how it was used, or what outcomes were achieved. Similarly, a study of school funding in Canada found that 'the link between marginal increases in spending and student outcomes appears to be rather weak' (Levin, 2004, p. 22; quoted in Winter et al., 2006). As a result of increased awareness about the importance of outcomes, the revised code of practice for special education in the UK has put greater emphasis on pupil outcomes as opposed to systems and procedures. Fletcher-Campbell (2002) argues, however, that there could be a problem of 'perverse disincentives' (e.g. a school may be so successful that it no longer qualifies for funding). On the other hand, some suggest that by focusing on quality outcomes, this model aligns special education with the mainstream accountability agenda (Shaddock et al., 2009). The output model is not used solely in any country but evidence can be seen in the USA in terms of the 'No Child Left Behind'[1] programme and in the United Kingdom through the publication of league tables (Peters, 2003).

A combination approach to funding is typical in many countries. In England and Wales there is evidence of a mixture of throughput- (task) based funding and input- (needs) based funding. Generally, the throughput model is most dominant in that the responsibility for the mainstream budget is in the hands of local authorities. The local authorities then decide on how to allocate resources to schools. The input model comes into play for students with more severe need (the statement procedure – where a child's needs are not deemed to be met at the school level and additional/individual-based funding is required). Likewise, Sweden uses a throughput-based model with elements of input-based support (for special schools) and New Zealand also incorporates a mixture of throughput and input funding, the latter of which is typical for severe need. Figure 6.1 gives a breakdown of the characteristics of each model,

Input model	Throughput model	Output model
Based on individual need	**Based on the services provided by a school or region**	**Usually based on achievement scores at the school level**
At the special school level, examples include: Austria, Belgium, France, Germany and the Netherlands. *At the pupil level*, examples include: the UK (for some SEN), the Czech Republic, Luxembourg, the Netherlands (so called 'back-pack' model).	*Via national governments to the local level*: Denmark, Finland, Greece, Norway, Sweden. *Via middle-government* Czech Republic, Denmark, France, the Netherlands (for 'milder' SEN), the UK.	It is not found anywhere in Europe in its purest form (Fletcher-Campbell, 2002).
Advantages SEN is identified and usually requires an assessment. Prevents certain pupils from 'slipping through the net'.	**Advantages** Costs are predictable and constant. It may result in decreasing numbers of pupils in segregated provision (Meijer, 1999).	**Advantages** Promotes achievement of desired results. Prevents 'perverse incentives', which is the notion that if schools enhance the levels of performance they find out that they do not qualify for additional resources (Fletcher-Campbell, 2003).
Disadvantages Costly. May reinforce low achievement, since there is no incentive to improve the quality of services (Meijer, 1999).	**Disadvantages** It could result in (temporary) lack of sufficient funding if many pupils have SEN in the area (Pijl and Veneman, 2005). May lead to inactivity or inertia, due to the fact that whether anything is done or not, funds will be available (Meijer, 2003).	**Disadvantages** May lead to a strong competitive climate between schools (Meijer, 1999). May reinforce the transfer of pupils with expected low gains in achievement scores to other parts of the system (Meijer, 1999).

Figure 6.1 Funding models

Primary	Post-primary
Introduced in 2005 with an explicit aim of promoting inclusive practices.	Introduced in 2012 with the aim of reducing administrative burden on schools.
Funds generally allocated to schools for students with the most common disabilities.	Movement from an individual-based model to a general model.

Based on
  • School enrolment (more pupils = funds)
  • Gender mix (boys and coed = funds)
  • Disadvantaged status (DEIS schools = funds)
	For 2012/13, funding based on numbers with most common disabilities in 2011/12. Unclear as to how funding will operate from 2013/14.

Figure 6.2 Overview of GAM at primary and post-primary

the advantages and disadvantages of each and some examples of countries that apply such a funding system.

Resource allocation in Irish schools

Like most countries, Ireland uses a combination of throughput- (general) and input- (individual) based funding. At primary and, more recently, post-primary level, a throughput model operates (known as the general allocation model or GAM at primary) (Figure 6.2). Alongside this model is an input or categorical model where students with 'low incidence' or less common disabilities are allocated funding based on the nature and type of disability. Under the throughput model, primary schools are allocated resources for students categorised as having 'high incidence'[2] disabilities, with resources dependent on a number of specific criteria including total enrolment and the gender and social mix of the student body (Special Education Circular SP ED 02/05 from the Department of Education and Skills). At post-primary level, a throughput model for students categorised as 'high incidence' has recently been introduced, with school allocations initially based on the 'high incidence' allocation received in the previous academic year (as yet it is unclear what criteria will be used from 2013/14 onwards). The model ensures that schools have a means of providing additional teaching support to students with special educational needs without having to make applications on behalf of individual students. The model is therefore not reliant on an individual diagnosis of a special educational need (NCSE, 2011). Each mainstream school is entitled to a general allocation of

Table 6.1 Criteria for additional teaching posts under the GAM (primary level)

Disadvantaged schools	○ 1st post at 80 students
	○ 2nd post at 160
	○ 3rd post at 240
	○ 4th post at 320 and so on
Non-disadvantaged	
Coeducational schools	○ 1st post at 145
	○ 2nd post at 315
	○ 3rd post at 495
	○ 4th post at 675 and so on.
*Small mixed schools (<145 students)	○ 1st post at 105
Boys' schools	○ 1st post at 135
	○ 2nd post at 295
	○ 3rd post at 475
	○ 4th post at 655, and so on
*Small boys' schools (<135 students)	○ 1st post at 100
Girls' schools	○ 1st post at 195
	○ 2nd post at 395
	○ 3rd post at 595
	○ 4th post at 795, and so on
*Small girls' schools (<195 students)	○ 1st post at 150

Source: DES, 02/05
Notes: * There is no additional general allocation made on the basis of enrolment between 100 and 135 (for small boys' schools); 105 and 145 (for small coeducational schools) and 150 and 195 (for small girls' schools) (DES, 02/05).

permanent teachers to assist it with students with learning difficulties and SEN arising from the more common disabilities.

Table 6.1 outlines the criteria for the allocation of additional teaching resources for schools, which include total enrolment and gender and social mix of the student body (under the Delivering Equality of Opportunity in Schools (DEIS) programme) in respect of students with high incidence SEN. The differentiation in funding level in respect of the gender mix of the student body has been the subject of some criticism. The decision to allocate more resources to single-sex boys' schools than to coeducational or single-sex girls' schools is based on the Special Education Review Committee (SERC) Report (Department of Education, 1993), which stated that the ratio of boys to girls in receipt of learning support was 3:2, and that the ratio of boys to girls with a specific learning disability was 7:3. Moreover, the 2003 school census by the Department of Education and Science showed that 65% of the children receiving support for high incidence SEN were boys, that is, roughly three boys for every two girls (INTO, 2005).

With the introduction of this model at primary level in 2005 and post-primary level in 2012, Irish schools have seen a move away from labelling and potentially stigmatising students, in that an assessment is not required for resource allocation. This also provides benefits at the school level with a reduction in administrative burden, given that funding is no longer dependent on the processing of individual assessments. However, the inability to track these funds and the potential mismanagement of resources at school level as a result is a concern, particularly where students with SEN are not receiving the appropriate funds/supports. Others argue that this model can lead to wide variation in provision. For example, the amount of time a student with a Mild General Learning Disability (MGLD)[3] receives, as well as the extent of differentiated teaching, depends on the experience, training and expertise of their teacher. Furthermore, with no reason to identify and assess students with disabilities there is 'no way of officially identifying how many MGLD students are being provided for in primary schools' (Stevens and O'Moore, 2009, p. 174).

Effective targeting of special educational needs funding

Given how the general model is currently devised for pupils with SEN and disabilities in Ireland, it is vitally important to look at the prevalence[4] of such need across different school contexts. One of the ways for throughput funding models to effectively target the SEN population is to consider the distribution of SEN students across schools. Using the National Census of Mainstream Schools[5] (McCoy et al., 2014), it appears, at first glance, that the general model at primary level is broadly 'targeting' the pupils most in need. Table 6.2 shows that DEIS Urban Band 1 (the most disadvantaged) and Urban Band 2 (the second most disadvantaged) schools are significantly more likely to have a higher prevalence of SEN[6] than rural DEIS schools and non-DEIS schools. However, all DEIS schools are treated the same under the general allocation model and are allocated enhanced funding. It can also be seen that increasing school size is associated with higher SEN levels. This is at odds with the funding model, which increases funding with size in a categorical manner. Moreover, the gender mix of schools is also a significant predictor of SEN prevalence. Coeducational primary schools (when compared to single-sex girls' primary schools) are more likely to have high SEN levels, while single-sex boys' primary schools have the highest SEN levels. Therefore, it does appear that overall the current model is partially targeting those schools most in need, such as students with SEN in single-sex boys' schools and coeducational settings.

These results have important policy implications, particularly in terms of the dominance of high SEN levels in Urban Band 1 DEIS, small and single-sex boys' schools. It would appear that overall the GAM model is effectively targeting those schools most in need in terms of gender mix and socioeconomic disadvantage. However, the results highlight the need for greater differentiation in the allocation of funding, with Urban Band 1 DEIS schools in need of

Table 6.2 Logistic regression model of the association between high SEN prevalence and school characteristics at primary level

	Coefficients
Constant	−1.974***
School characteristics	
DEIS (ref: non-DEIS)	
Urban band 1	0.674**
Urban band 2	0.590*
Rural	−0.046
School size (ref: <50)	
50–99 students	−0.225¬
100–149 students	−0.441**
150–230 students	−0.572***
231+ students	−1.165***
School type (ref: girls' primary)	
Boys' primary	1.798***
Coeducational primary	1.055**
N=2428 schools (unweighted data)	

Source: McCoy *et al.* (2014)
Notes: ***p<001; **p<.01; *p<.05; ¬p<.10.
Estimates compared to base categories: non-DEIS, less than 50 students and girls' primary.

enhanced funding over and above funds allocated to DEIS schools more generally. Further, the findings raise important questions around school size and SEN levels. It cannot be assumed that because a school is large in size, it has higher SEN prevalence rates. Moreover, given that there is no additional general allocation made on the basis of enrolment between 100 and 135 students (for small boys' schools) and between 105 and 145 students (for small coeducational schools), our finding that relatively small schools of between 100 and 149 students are predicting high SEN prevalence rates means that it might be necessary to revisit the GAM in the terms of its size criteria. There is a paucity of research around size and SEN prevalence, although one potential reason for this finding could be the greater identification of such pupils in smaller school contexts. Additionally, it might be the case that students with SEN and disabilities are adequately supported within the smaller school contexts, given the already reduced pupil–teacher ratio.

SEN prevalence in post-primary

In terms of post-primary, as already outlined, the system of resource allocation has recently changed to a system more akin to primary level. The 'general' model will move away from individual assessment, to the allocation of resources

Table 6.3 Logistic regression models of the association between high SEN prevalence and school characteristics at post-primary level

	Model 1 coefficients	Model 2 coefficients
Constant	−2.923***	−1.940**
School characteristics		
School type (ref: girls' secondary)		
Boys' secondary	1.116*	1.332***
Coeducational	1.180*	1.155*
Vocational	1.537**	0.682
Community/comprehensive	1.749***	1.857**
School size (ref: <200)		
200–399 students		−0.798*
400–599 students		−1.799***
600+ students		−2.135***
DEIS (ref: non-DEIS)		1.332*
N=498 schools (unweighted data)		

Source: McCoy et al. (2014).
Notes: ***p<001; **p<.01; *p<.05; ¬p<.10. Estimates compared to base categories: girls' secondary, less than 200 students and non-DEIS.

based on the previous year's incidence of the most common disabilities. In the same way as for primary, the prevalence of SEN students should be an important consideration in the development of such a model. The models in Table 6.3 predict the probability of post-primary schools having a high prevalence (>15%) of special educational needs. In the first model, school type[7] is a significant predictor, with a particularly strong likelihood of high SEN levels in community/comprehensive and vocational schools. Model 2 adds in two additional school measures, school size and DEIS status. Interestingly, when these factors are added, vocational schools lose their significant effect on SEN prevalence. This reflects the dominance of DEIS schools in the vocational sector, in that once account is taken of DEIS status, vocational schools no longer have a greater probability of high SEN levels. So while at first glance it appears that there is a big difference across school types in relation to SEN prevalence, when controls are put in place for size and DEIS status, the results change.

It would therefore appear that DEIS status is an important predictor of SEN prevalence at post-primary. In addition, single-sex boys' schools and community/comprehensive schools have higher SEN levels once we take account of DEIS status and school size. Like primary, school size is also significant in that smaller schools have a significantly higher prevalence of special educational needs, taking into account other school characteristics. These findings raise important implications for the introduction of the GAM at post-primary level and, while they support the literature that disadvantaged schools have a higher proportion of students with special educational needs (Lupton, 2004; Thrupp, 1999), this data source can serve as a valuable evidence base in the design of such a general allocation system and ensure the most effective allocation of resources.

Conclusions

The means of allocating resources to students with SEN and disabilities has, for a long time, perplexed policymakers around the world and continues to do so. As shown in this chapter, the issue of funding is central to national policy perspectives on inclusive education. There is therefore a reciprocal relationship between funding and paradigms of special educational needs (Mitchell, 2010). Given the fact that there appears to be no single consensus on the 'best' funding model and the fact that each one has its own advantages and disadvantages, combining a number of models seems to be the most desirable approach.

In Ireland this combination approach is being adopted, in that special education is currently financed using two distinct funding models – input and throughput funding. The model of input funding, which is based on a list of 14 disability categories, has received little attention both in this chapter and in research more generally. There is, however, a pressing need to re-examine the use of 'high' and 'low incidence' disability categories by the Department of Education and Skills in terms of how they fit within an inclusive framework as enshrined in the EPSEN Act, 2004.

In line with examples internationally, a second throughput model runs parallel to the input funding model at primary, and this has recently been introduced at post-primary level, based on a range of criteria including a school's disadvantaged status and gender mix. While overall the findings above show that the current throughput model at primary appears to be effectively 'targeting' students in terms of resource allocation, there is now evidence to show that greater differentiation is needed in the allocation of funding. Although schools with DEIS status are in receipt of favourable supports in terms of reduced pupil–teacher ratios and additional teaching hours, there is evidence to show that the current general allocation model, which treats all DEIS schools equally, is inefficient. In particular, the results highlight the need for greater differentiation in the allocation of resources across different DEIS bands, as well as according to gender mix, school size and the prevalence of SEN and disability. Most significantly, the substantial differential[8] in the prevalence of students with SEN between Urban Band 1 DEIS schools and both Rural DEIS and non-DEIS schools should be reflected in the allocation of resources. Moreover, given the finding that small schools are predicting higher SEN prevalence rates, the authors argue that the criteria might need to be revisited, particularly in terms of small boys' schools (of between 100 and 135 students) which receive no additional resource allocations.

At post-primary level, the DEIS status effect is strong and it appears to be partly underpinning the higher levels of SEN prevalence across different school types. In the same vein as primary level, school size is also significant in that smaller schools have a significantly higher prevalence of special educational needs, taking into account other school characteristics. Research has shown that, depending on the school context, the special educational needs of a child may or may not be recognised (Van der Veen *et al.*, 2010). It may therefore be the case that in small schools students with SEN may be picked up more easily. Another possibility is that smaller schools are more orientated towards providing for SEN pupils, thus attracting larger numbers of students with SEN. The exact criteria for the recently introduced throughput model are not yet known, however these findings, alongside further analysis of this data, would allow the development of an evidence-based funding model, thereby maximising effectiveness in the allocation of resources.

Overall, the findings of the research call into question the current practice of funding schools at a 'general' level based on outdated prevalence findings from the early 1990s, especially in the absence of any output measures. One notable aspect of international funding models missing from the Irish context is the focus on measuring student progress or outcomes, often used in output funding models. Research suggests that if a combination of funding models is to be adopted, perhaps the optimum system is a throughput model at the regional level with elements of the output model incorporated (Meijer, 1999). Much of the international literature points to the negative aspects of the throughput model being inactivity or inertia in schools, due to the fact that, whether anything is done or not, funds will be available (Meijer, 2003). By adopting elements of the output and throughput model, it is argued, schools can be accountable for their spending and the ongoing monitoring and evaluation of procedures can take place. Perhaps a focus on outcomes deserves greater attention as part of the funding mix in Ireland. It could be argued that, compared to criterion around evidence of need, student progress and outcomes can, at least, be defined (Farrell and Ainscow, 2002). The benefits of output funding where resources are linked to student progress certainly depend on the way in which the policy is implemented.

Inclusion as a concept is notoriously ambiguous both conceptually and practically (Hegarty, 2001). Underlying these discussions around SEN funding models are wider concerns about whether one funding model is more or less inclusive than another. Within the EPSEN Act, 2004, although there is a strong commitment to inclusive education, no mention is made of the ways in which to finance special education and the practical administrative ways in which inclusion can be achieved. Moreover, although inclusion is mentioned as a central aim of the introduction of GAM at primary level, there is no such underlying commitment at post-primary level. A significant budget is allocated to SEN[9] annually, so it is perhaps timely to evaluate the ways in which GAM funds are distributed at school level and examine the impact of these supports on the education of children with special educational needs. Using this new evidence base, there is now the opportunity to both refine the current GAM funding system at primary level and guide the development of a similar system at post-primary level.

Notes

1 The 'No Child Left Behind Act' of 2001 was signed into law in 2002 in the United States. At the core of this Act were a number of measures designed to drive broad gains in student achievement and to hold states and schools more accountable for student progress (US Department of Education, 2001).
2 The term 'high incidence' refers to these disabilities: borderline mild general learning disability; mild general learning disability; specific learning disability. The term 'low incidence' disability used by the Department for Education and Skills includes physical disability; hearing impairment; visual impairment; emotional disturbance; severe emotional disturbance; moderate general learning disability; severe/profound general learning disability; autism/autistic spectrum disorders; specific speech and language disorder; assessed syndrome along with one of the above low incidence disabilities; multiple disabilities in primary and post-primary schools (DES Circular Sp Ed 02/05).
3 MGLD is a high incidence disability. Usually these students have difficulty with most areas of the curriculum in school and therefore some may find it difficult to adapt to school life, showing signs of inappropriate or immature behaviour (NCSE, 2011).
4 The prevalence figure relates to the numbers of students with SEN in mainstream schools.
5 A full census of primary and post-primary schools was undertaken in 2011 (response rates of 80% and 74%, respectively), collecting valuable information on the nature and prevalence of SEN and the provision of resources to these students across all schools. All results are weighted so that they reflect the full population of primary and post-primary schools in Ireland. For more information see McCoy et al. (2014).
6 In this analysis, a high prevalence of SEN is defined as schools having more than 15% of pupils with SEN in their school. A low prevalence of SEN is defined as schools having fewer than 15% of pupils with SEN in their schools. Additional models (such as multinomial and ordinary least squares) were run using the SEN percentage categories and not the 15% cut-off, which further supported the results.
7 School type at post-primary refers to: single-sex boys' secondary; single-sex girls' secondary; coeducational secondary; vocational and community/comprehensive.
8 These differences were further supported by additional models, such as multinomial and OLS regression techniques.
9 In 2012 approximately 15% of public education budgets were allocated to support children with SEN (some €1.3 billion) (Dáil Éireann Debate, 2013).

References

Banks J., McCoy S. (2011) *A Study on the Prevalence of Special Educational Needs*, Trim: National Council for Special Education.

Dáil Éireann Debate (2013) *Volume 790, No 2, Written Answers No. 88, Special Educational Needs Expenditure*, accessed March 2013 at http://oireacht asdebates.oireachtas.ie/debates%20authoring/debateswebpack.nsf/takes/dail 2013013000066?opendocument.

Department of Education (1993) *Report of the Special Educational Review Committee (SERC)*, Dublin: Government Publications Sales Office.

Department of Education and Skills (2005) *Circular Sp Ed 07/02 Applications for Fulltime or Parttime Special Needs Assistant Support to Address the Special Care Needs of Children with Disabilities Sp Ed 07/02*, Dublin: DES. Accessed October 2012 at www.education.ie/servlet/blobservlet/spedc07_02.pdf.

Department of Education and Skills (2012) *Circular No. 0010/2012 Circular to the Management Authorities of Secondary, Community and Comprehensive Schools and the Chief Executive Officers of Vocational Education Committees on Revised Arrangements for the Provision of Resource Teaching Supports for the 2012/13 School Year*, Dublin: DES. Accessed November 2012 at www. education.ie/en/Circulars-and-Forms/Active-Circulars/cl0010_2012.pdf.

Education for Persons with Special Educational Needs (EPSEN) Act, 2004. Accessed January 2012 at www.oireachtas.ie/documents/bills28/acts/2004/A3004.pdf.

Emanuelsson I., Haug P., Persson B. (2005) Inclusive education in some Western European countries, in Mitchell D. (Ed.) *Contextualizing Inclusive Education: Evaluating Old and New International Perspectives*, Abingdon, Oxfordshire: Routledge.

Farrell P., Ainscow M. (2002) *Making Special Education Inclusive: From Research to Practice*, London: David Fulton Publishers.

Ferrier F., Long M., Moore D., Sharpley C., Sigafoos J. (2007) *Investigating the Feasibility of Portable Funding for Students with Disabilities*, Report for the Department of Education, Science and Training, Monash University.

Fletcher-Campbell F. (2002) The financing of special education: Lessons from Europe, *Support for Learning* 17, 19–22.

Graham L., Sweller N. (2011) The Inclusion Lottery: Who's in and who's out? Tracking inclusion and exclusion in New South Wales government schools, *International Journal of Inclusive Education* 15, 941–53.

Hegarty S. (2001) Inclusive education: A case to answer, *Journal of Moral Education* 30, 243–9.

INTO (Irish National Teacher Organisation) (2005) *EOLAS*, Issue 02/05.

Lupton R. (2004) Schools in disadvantaged areas: Recognising context and raising quality, CASE Paper 76, ESRC Centre for Analysis of Social Exclusion, London: London School of Economics.

McCoy S., Banks J., Frawley D., Watson D., Shevlin M., Smyth F. (2014, forthcoming) *Responding to Need? Understanding Special Class Provision in Ireland*, Dublin/Trim: Economic and Social Research Institute /National Council for Special Education.

Meijer C.J.W. (Ed.) (1999) *Financing of Special Needs Education: A Seventeen-country Study of the Relationship between Financing of Special Needs Education and Inclusion*, Middelfart: European Agency for Development in Special Needs Education.

Meijer C.J.W. (Ed.) (2003) *Special Education across Europe in 2003*, Middelfart: European Agency for Development in Special Needs Education.

Mitchell D. (2010) *Education that Fits: Review of International Trends in the Education of Students with Special Educational Needs*, Christchurch, New Zealand: Ministry of Education.

Moore-Brown B. (2001) Case in point: The administrative predicament of special education funding, *Journal of Special Education Leadership* 14, 42–3.

NCSE (National Council for Special Education) (2006) *Implementation Report, Plan for the Phased Implementation of the EPSEN Act 2004*, Trim: NCSE.

NCSE (2011) *Children with Special Educational Needs, Information Booklet for Parents*, Trim: NCSE. Accessed December 2012 at www.ncse.ie/uploads/1/ChildrenWithSpecialEdNeeds1.pdf.

Ontario Ministry of Education (2004) *Review of Growth in Claims for Students with Severe Special Needs*, Ontario, Canada: Ministry of Education.

Parrish T.B., Chambers J.G., Guarino C.M. (Eds) (1999) *Funding Special Education*, Thousand Oaks, CA: Corwin Press.

Peters S.J. (2003) *Inclusive Education: Achieving Education for All by Including Those with Disabilities and Special Education Needs*, The Disability Group, Washington, DC: The World Bank. Accessed December 2012 at www.hiproweb.org/fileadmin/cdroms/Education/EducationIntegreeEN.pdf.

Pijl S.J., Veneman H. (2005) Evaluating new criteria and procedures for funding special needs education in the Netherlands, *Educational Management, Administration & Leadership* 33, 93–107.

Poet H. (2012) *Changes to the funding of Special Educational Needs and Disability (SEND) Provision: Views of Lead Members*, Local Government Association Research Report, Slough: National Foundation for Educational Research.

Riddell S., Tisdall K., Kane J., Mulderrig J. (2006) *Literature Review of Pupils with Additional Support Needs*, Edinburgh: Scottish Executive Social Research.

Shaddock A., MacDonald N., Hook J., Giorcelli L., Arthur-Kelly M. (2009) *Disability, Diversity and Tides that Lift all Boats: Review of Special Education in the ACT*, Chiswick, NSW: Services Initiatives.

Stevens P., O'Moore M. (2009) *Inclusion or Illusion? Educational Provision for Primary School Children with Mild General Learning Disabilities*, Dublin: Blackhall Publishing.

Thrupp M. (1999) *Schools Making a Difference: Let's be Realistic!* Buckingham: Open University Press.

US Department of Education (2001) No Child Left Behind Act, accessed January 2013 at www2.ed.gov/policy/elsec/leg/esea02/index.html.

Van der Veen I., Smeets E., Derriks M. (2010) Children with special educational needs in the Netherlands: Number, characteristics and school career, *Educational Research* 52, 15–43.

Winter E., Fletcher-Campbell F., Connolly P., Lynch P. (2006) Resource requirements for the diagnosis and assessment of special educational needs in Ireland, Research report, unpublished, Trim: National Council for Special Education.

Winter E., O'Raw P. (2010) *Literature Review of the Principles and Practices Relating to Inclusive Education for Children with Special Educational Needs*, Trim: National Council for Special Education.

7

Ageing, disability and policy

Eamon O'Shea

Introduction

One in ten Europeans has a disability and that percentage is likely to increase along with the ageing of the population in the coming decades. For example, there will be more than twice as many people aged 80 years or older in 2050 across OECD countries than there are currently, and their share of the population will rise from 4% in 2010 to 10% in 2050 (OECD, 2013). Between one quarter and one half of these people will need help in their daily lives, due to reduced functional and cognitive capabilities. In Ireland, there are currently 595,335 people with disabilities, accounting for 13% of the population (Central Statistics Office (CSO), 2012). The numbers of people with a disability increase with age, and of the total number of people with a reported disability in the 2011 Census, 43% were aged 60 years or over. The link between age and disability becomes even clearer when looking at the numbers with a disability as a percentage of their relevant age group. For example, the percentage of all 10- to 14-year-olds with a disability is 8%, while the corresponding proportion for the 85 and over age group is 72%. Given population ageing, particularly in the older age categories, the relationship between age and disability is likely to be a key policy issue for all governments in Europe, but especially in Ireland, in the coming decades.

Older people with disabilities in Ireland include people with a disability acquired at a younger age and those who acquire a disability later in life. Disability may be physical or cognitive or both, and can be exacerbated by social forces and social structures. People who enter the ageing process with a disability may have their primary identification as a disabled person already firmly established. They may have had different life experiences from non-disabled people: lack of an employment history, fewer assets for retirement and (in some cases) pre-existing high dependency. Conversely, people who acquire a disability in older age may choose the ageing community as a primary identification, rather than the disability community. Since impairment is seen as a normal part of ageing by many, some older people do not tend to see themselves as disabled and prefer to separate disability from ageing. They see themselves as older with a disability, rather than having a disability at an older age.

This chapter is largely concerned with the relationship between ageing and disability and whether there exists the possibility of a common approach to thinking about policy questions in relation to ageing and disability and their various interfaces. At the moment, older people and people with disabilities tend to be treated as two very distinct groups in Ireland in relation to policy formulation, policy implementation, practice and service delivery, in spite of the considerable overlap between the two groups in relation to needs and core aspirations, particularly in relation to autonomy and connectivity. A life course perspective would likely reveal many influences and experiences that serve to unite people with a disability and those who acquire a disability in later life. Yet, in contemporary debates about social care for older people, ageing and disability tend to be treated separately. In social services, disability programmes and ageing programmes have been distinct for many decades. This is not unique to Ireland and is a feature of many other countries. In the USA, for example, older and younger adults with disabilities advocate from different positions related to chronological age. Disability rights groups tend to prioritise advocacy by people with disabilities themselves, while older adults tend to be represented by much younger, and often professional, advocates (Putnam, 2007).

The gain made by the disability movement in the development of a social model of disability contains many lessons for groups and organisations representing older people in the political process. Currently, the service models of care used in disability and ageing programmes are different across many European countries (OECD, 2013). Attitudes to choice, autonomy and empowerment vary and there is no evidence of convergence in respect of an ageing disability interface in regard to public policymaking. Disability programmes typically incorporate concepts of independence, autonomy, self-direction and empowerment. In contrast, ageing programmes tend to follow the medical model more closely, with health and social care professionals having a much more direct input into the decision-making process. As more people age with disability, the medical model of ageing will come under increasing scrutiny from people demanding a social model of care provision. The trend in the future will likely be towards the integration of the medical and the social models through the adoption of a bio-psychosocial approach to ageing and disability. In this context, this chapter explores the implications of a more integrationist approach for older people and their families.

The arguments in favour of a closer alliance between the disability and ageing sectors are obvious, particularly in relation to the adoption of the social model of disability. Currently, older people are placed in situations of dependency through inappropriate institutional arrangements and narrowly conceived social policies, including inappropriate placement in long-stay facilities. Choice is denied to older people in respect of social care services, which are determined mainly through an administrative and financial model designed to meet the needs of providers and budget holders rather than clients. This would not be tolerated in the disability sector or by the highly organised and politicised disability movement. Whilst the rights-based model has been led by disability groups, it is equally applicable to older people. Citizenship and entitlement are equally relevant to people with disability and to older people, if only because so many people with disabilities are older. The search for common ground between the disability and ageing sectors through the formation of coalitions of interests and alliances can yield significant benefits in terms of quality of life and well-being for people with disabilities, whatever their age. It also recognises the diversity in the ageing experience and that each person will age in unique ways at different times. So, rather than developing policy solutions for specific age groups, many countries are now beginning to fund services and environments that allow people to age in place and can respond to individuals' unique and changing needs.

Living with a disability

The National Disability Authority Act, 1999 defines 'disability' to mean 'a substantial restriction in the capacity of a person to participate in economic, social or cultural life on account of an enduring physical, sensory, learning, mental health or emotional impairment'. This is broader than the traditional definitions, which tend to equate disability with dependency linked to physical, sensory and/or intellectual impairment, but without the emphasis on participation in economic, social and civic life. The classic 'medical model' locates disability as an individual problem, directly caused by disease, trauma or other health condition. Treatment is conceived of in terms of medical care (WHO, 2002). The 'social model' of disability originated in the disability movement in the United Kingdom and United States and distinguishes impairment, which is a condition of the body, from disability, which is a situation of social exclusion caused by the organisation of society. The model puts the emphasis on social institutions and the environment, rather than on the individual. It also stresses the role of empowerment, participation and leadership of disabled people in effecting change. The Independent Living Movement has emphasised the importance of breaking the association between dependence and being able to do things for oneself. It has challenged the idea that having to rely on others should inevitably lead to reduced autonomy and control. Though differences in interpretation of the social model exist, the influence of social factors on the experience of disablement has now been widely accepted, as evidenced in the World Health Organization's (WHO) International Classification of Functioning, Disability and Health (WHO, 2002).

Notwithstanding the important distinction between the social model and the medical model, disability at any age is likely to be lived and experienced in a very personal way. Disability, while strongly influenced by social conditions, social processes and social structures, is, more often than not, experienced alone. People with arthritis feel pain; people with stroke suffer loss; people with depression are not able to cope. People report difficulties with walking, with getting up stairs, with seeing, with hearing, with communicating and with coping. The intensity with which these disabilities are experienced will influence the ability of older people to remain independent in older age. Loss and decline accompanies disability and impacts on the individual's sense of self and on their identity. People may be unable to recognise themselves or their former self when confronted with debilitating levels of pain and discomfort. They find it hard to continue, particularly when confronted with multiple disabilities.

And yet there is good evidence that the majority of people with disabilities continue and manage to live fulfilling lives, in spite of the odds that are stacked against them (Murphy *et al.*, 2007). They maintain self-identity and preserve meaning in their lives. They find new levels of resolve and new spirit within themselves, which allows them to adapt to their impairment and adjust their expectations to the fact of disability. Of course, all of our lives and actions are influenced by our mental outlook, attitudes and personality characteristics (Gabriel and Bowling, 2004). Therefore, a person's psychological resources have a big impact on how disability is perceived and accommodated. Some people consider themselves independent, even when the nature of their disability might suggest otherwise to an impartial observer. This ability to find compensatory strategies has been labelled 'selective optimisation with compensation' (Baltes and Baltes, 1990). There is some evidence that the ability to operationalise coping strategies in response to disability is associated with higher levels of life satisfaction and improved quality of life (Freund and Baltes, 1998). Older people often draw on lifetime experience, some of which was fashioned in less abundant economic circumstances, to make the best of what they have now, rather than focus on negative aspects of their lives. The attitude is one of adjusting, of accepting one's lot, of making the best of things in the face of adversity.

People also tend to compare themselves with others and make downward social comparisons with those who are (in their view) worse off than themselves. The rationalisation of disability through comparison with others in worse circumstances is an attempt to come to terms with the disability and reach some reconciliation with the constraints imposed through reference to others less fortunate than themselves. People's subjective valuation of quality of life can be significantly enhanced if they compare themselves to people worse off than themselves, rather than to healthy individuals. For example, Heidrich and Ryff (1993) found that subjective valuations of quality of life in older women were high, regardless of health state, because the reference point for these women was those with health problems, rather than healthy individuals. Social comparison may also be informed by a pervasive view among older people that, since impairment is a normal part of ageing, they are not disabled in the same way as younger people with similar impairments are, and consequently are better off. The ability to rationalise disability in this way may be particular to older people and may explain, to some degree, why disability is less politicised in older age.

It is not difficult therefore to see how people's subjective assessment of their quality of life is sometimes more positive than objective measures. The existence of this so-called 'satisfaction paradox' is well established in the gerontological literature (Walker, 2006). What for many younger, disability-free people would be an intolerable life is portrayed in a more positive light by older people experiencing the disability. People look for positives and search for new meanings, anything to make sense of their current predicament. It may also be easier to come to terms with disability if people are given time to adapt to their disability, and that sudden-onset disability can have devastating consequences for people. There may well be age cohort effects behind the satisfaction paradox, reflecting reduced expectations of this and previous older generations. If that is the case, it is unlikely to last indefinitely as expectations and demands expand rather than contract among future age cohorts in Ireland. Future generations may find it more difficult to come to terms with disability, even though they may spend less time in disability than do the current older generation.

Social model of disability

Social health for older people comprises a definition of individual well-being that is distinct from both physical and mental health. Social health is concerned with older people's ability to function as members of the community and includes measures of people's connectedness to others in terms of interpersonal interactions and social participation. The social model distinguishes impairment from dependency. It refers to the possibility that dependency is created through social forces and social structures impacting on the ability of older people to take control of their own lives (Townsend, 1981). Economic deprivation can also prevent people from being able to participate meaningfully in economic and social life, both absolutely and relative to prevailing social standards. The disability movement has been much more successful than the ageing sector in identifying and overcoming social obstacles to independence and in promoting social policies that respect the rights of younger people with disabilities. Within the ageing sector, older people are often excluded from decision making. They are consulted less often when it comes to service provision or placement decision making. Their problems tend to be personalised and, very often, medicalised.

In a study on ageing and disability conducted for the now dissolved National Council on Ageing and Older People, Murphy *et al.* (2007) found that older people with disabilities were conscious of the limitations imposed on their autonomy and independence by social forces and social structures. Some of them spoke about ageing, about being treated as second-class citizens in their daily life. They did not have entitlements to services but were dependent on the vagaries and vicissitudes of the health and social care system and the budgetary system that underpinned resource allocation in this area. For example, many older people were dependent on voluntary organisations for critical equipment such as sensory aids. Others paid for services such as chiropody, rather than continue to wait indefinitely for public provision. People also complained about physical barriers to their independence, such as poorly designed houses and public buildings. The absence of public transport also created an artificial dependency for some older people. People reported having to pay for taxis to enable them to access some health and social care services. People could not visit family and friends because of poor public transport, particularly in rural areas. Many participants also spoke about the absence of information as a barrier to accessing services and to participation generally. Too many people simply did not know what their entitlements were.

There are strong arguments, therefore, for the adoption of a broader definition of dependency that incorporates physical, mental, social and economic functioning. There is much that the ageing sector can learn from the disability movement in the development of a social model. Yet, disabled people's organisations are not working with older people to any great extent in Ireland, especially given the number of older people with a disability in the population. While there are difficulties in orchestrating this relationship, not least the potential resistance among older people to being labelled disabled, and the focus within the disability movement on younger people, increased integration is necessary. Much has already been achieved in the context of recent equality legislation and through the 2005 Disability Act. But much more remains to be done to find some common ground between older people and disabled people. There is a real need for disability awareness and equality work with advocacy groups representing older people and with agencies providing services to older people (Priestly and Rabiee, 2002).

Ageing and disability

An important question is whether there are particular age-related aspects to disability and whether it is possible to capture disability relationships through a single version or theory of ageing. The lesson from the social model of disability is that ageing cannot fully be represented in terms of a deficit model which sees old age simply as a medical problem. But neither can ageing be captured by a heroic model which implies the denial of ageing and the continuation of a life of unlimited opportunities in economic and social life. Older people with disabilities want to be independent, but most are conscious of the range of personal and social limitations and constraints imposed by their condition. Theirs is a post-medical, post-social world where biological, psychological and social conditions combine in a complex way to determine well-being and quality of life. Ageing with a disability cannot, therefore, be understood without a forensic and ethnographic examination of the person and the community within which they live.

One of the advantages of a person-centred approach is that it allows consideration of all of the factors that make life different for an older person with a disability than for a younger person with a disability. It has already been suggested above that life course experience may help older people to rationalise their disability in more positive terms than younger people with disability. Conversely, age may also confer disadvantages. Ageism is a pervasive fact for older people in Ireland (The Equality Authority, 2002). It leads to prejudice and discrimination and ultimately may contribute to a different experience between younger and older people with disability. Ageism may exacerbate the potential for exclusion that disability presents. In an environment of sustained retrenchment in health and social care spending, older people with a disability may be placed at the end of the queue for health and social care services. Rationing is most problematic for older people when it is least overt (Dey and Fraser, 2000). In Ireland, there is some evidence of rationing by age through delay rather than through overt denial of services (Murphy *et al.*, 2007). One of the key features of being old with a disability in Ireland seems to be that of perpetual waiting; people wait for services and appointments that sometimes never come.

Older people are also very conscious of the various losses that accompany age. They lose family and friends. Their life is characterised by diminishing social networks, sometimes leading to isolation and loneliness. In some cases, people are dealing with the onset of disability at the same time as mourning the loss of a loved one through bereavement. They can be fearful of a future without the support of family and friends. They are acutely aware of the various thresholds associated with their disability and are conscious of the marginal impact that changes in their own condition or their social networks can have on their ability to cope and continue to live independently. They may be fearful of their own mortality. Changes to the local neighbourhood can exacerbate the isolation sometimes felt by older people with a disability. New people may move in, leading to new relationships having to be formed, which may be difficult for older people if disability reduces the opportunities for social contact. Communication may diminish and potential solidarity relationships may never develop. Social connectedness declines and so does quality of life.

Policy issues

There have been many developments in the disability sector in terms of policy and legislation in recent years (NESC, 2012). The trend of policy has been towards a rights-based approach, with enhanced support for independent living and greater emphasis on personal assistance. The National Disability Strategy introduced in 2004 was the key policy document driving change in the disability sector. The focus in this Strategy was empowerment, participation and the integration of people with disabilities into mainstream society. Underpinning the Strategy was the Disability Act 2005, which proclaimed the right of people with disability to an assessment of need. However, while individual need assessment for children under 5 years has commenced, similar provision for older children and adults has been deferred indefinitely. Moreover, there was always ambiguity as to where older people fitted into the Strategy anyway, given the separation between disability and ageing in the policy process. A major reason why many of the provisions of the Strategy have been put on hold has been budgetary constraints arising from the current economic crisis. This has created dissatisfaction and frustration with progress, particularly given the widespread initial support for the provisions of the Act and the Strategy. Complicating matters has been the absence of an implementation framework linked to the development of a comprehensive information system on older people with disabilities. Without proper information systems that link needs to resources it has proved difficult to monitor the implementation of the Act, particularly in relation to older people. One of the difficulties at the moment is that information about what outcomes have been achieved is relatively poor.

Most people agree that the role and importance of the person with a disability needs to be emphasised at all times in the provision of health and social care. Care should be person centred and specific to the diverse needs of older people. This points to the need to develop comprehensive and localised systems of information on the needs of older people with disabilities, including the provision of local centralised information centres where older people with disability can get information on entitlements and allowances.

The development of the first National Disability Survey by the CSO has been a really important development in regard to developing the information base in Ireland, but it is not enough. We need integrated information on older people with disability that covers all aspects of their lives, including data on family relationships and social networks. We need to understand more about attitudes to disability among older people and their perceptions of the social conditions that cause social dependency. Data on the economic circumstances of older people is also critical to understanding care patterns and care trajectories into the future. Information is necessary to both understand and create the conditions whereby younger and older people can live independent but connected lives. Data on what people can and cannot do in a physical sense is only part of the story. The elimination of economic and social constraints to independence requires the development of much more complex datasets. This is the essence of the social model of disability and only by having this information can it be implemented and fully supported. For example, ending nursing home care is an overt goal of the disability movement. Older people, in contrast, seem reconciled to nursing homes as an inevitable consequence of dependency, perhaps because they remain unaware of other possibilities (Kane and Kane, 2001).

The older person should also be centrally involved in all decision making with respect to what care is provided and how care is arranged. This approach will allow the social, emotional and psychological needs of people to be given equal weighting to the physical and health needs in the provision of services. This should be done through careful monitoring of the effects of different types of care and stimuli on older people with disabilities in different types of settings. A core element of policy should be that every disability story is different, even if key quality of life domains are the same for most people. For people with dementia, especially, the care process must always seek to protect and nurture the sense of self that remains with the older person. The narrative of the lives of people with dementia must be highlighted through careful dialogue, interventions and therapies that seek to connect with the wholeness of the person's life and not just the dementia component.

Connecting with other people is also an important part of healthy living. So many people with disabilities can feel cut off from other people. Their disability may make it difficult to keep in contact with others, or people reduce contact with them because of their disability. The latter can occur more frequently for people with dementia and depression than for other disability groups. Connecting with other people is important, irrespective of type of disability. People with disabilities at all ages value the opportunity to reciprocate care and support from family and friends. They want to give something back. The social model of disability has been very successful in empowering younger people with disability to take control of their own lives and maintain equal relationships with family and friends. The disability movement has succeeded in removing disabling barriers and providing enabling supports so that people can continue to be part of their community. This approach facilitates higher levels of social contact for younger people with disability and has resulted in improved quality of life for that group. The absence of a similar model for older people means that their potential for participation in social, civic and cultural life is weaker. Their dependency is exacerbated; their potential for reciprocity is reduced. This can be changed only through the development of new connectedness measures that could be used to track the impact of policy on maintaining and developing the social world of people with disabilities.

Preventing dependency should be a key goal of public policy. The objective of dependency prevention is to give every ageing individual the greatest possible opportunity of remaining free of disability in old age or, if they do acquire a disability, of being as independent as possible. Healthy ageing and the prevention of dependency requires an investment at an early age in healthy living. Disability for many people is not inevitable and investment now in health promotion and primary care could significantly reduce the numbers of people suffering from depression, stroke and dementia in future years. Any reduction in disability in the future will have important implications for social spending on health and social care, thereby potentially justifying an increase now in expenditure on health promotion and dependency prevention.

The prevention of physical dependency and mental incapacity can be encouraged at three levels: primary, secondary and tertiary. Primary prevention lies first and foremost in the diagnosis and treatment of causal illnesses through behavioural change, vaccination, screening programmes and the identification of potential risk factors in relation to heart disease and some cancers. An investment in suitable housing for dependent older people and the adoption of appropriate assistive technologies and smart homes can also enable community-based living for as long as possible for older people with disabilities. The concept of age-friendly cities and environments is also a way of integrating the needs of older people and of people with disabilities in the development of a society for all ages. Making local places and spaces age friendly is very important for the support of older people with disabilities living at home; all the more so given the absence of comprehensive community-based care in the community. Even where services exist for older people they are poorly coordinated and weakly integrated. There is almost no cross-over between disability services and age-related services. The weakness of community care for older people is generally not challenged in policy circles, but it still does not lessen the impact of the absence of such community-based services on the quality of life of people with disabilities. For all the recent focus and support for home care packages, it is hard to escape the conclusion that the community care system has failed older people with disabilities.

Overcoming ageist attitudes within society is the first step in preventing social dependency in old age. Public policy must continue to challenge ageism and ageist behaviour through effective legislation, regulation and public information campaigns on ageing with a disability. Groups advocating on behalf of older people for equality and human rights have much to offer here, but they need to connect more with their counterparts in the disability sector who have been more successful in challenging discriminatory practices and policies. Ironically, those with the most severe ageist attitudes can sometimes be older people themselves who have low expectations in regard to what society should do for them. Training and education programmes need to target older people as much as younger people if such attitudes are to change. An absence from mainstream society should not be accepted as a normal part of ageing; thankfully, it is not tolerated for younger people with disabilities, so why should it be tolerated for older people with disabilities? The key mind-set to be changed here is that of older people themselves.

Conclusions

This chapter has examined the issue of ageing and disability, with specific focus on the social model and the need for an integrated approach to disability at all ages. The numbers of older people with disability will increase in the future in line with the ageing of the population. So too will the number of people entering old age with a disability. It is important that all older people with a disability, whatever its source, receive adequate care and support services, as they are a particularly vulnerable group and at risk of discrimination. Disability tends to have a negative influence on quality of life. In almost all circumstances, however, the effect of disability on quality of life may be mediated by forces outside of the disability. The psychological aspect of the disabled person may enable them to cope well with their disability. Environmental and social support will further reduce the impact of any disability on quality of life. So, whilst disability carries the potential to reduce quality of life, mitigating factors may serve to reduce the negative effects of a disability.

Public policy has a vital role to play in improving the quality of life of older people. Health and social services need to work together to ensure that older people with disabilities get the services they need. Practical interventions such as hearing aids, reading glasses, rehabilitation, barrier-free housing and transport can yield huge benefits for older people with disabilities. These services are, for the most part, not expensive, which makes their absence all the more incomprehensible. These services are also much more available for younger people with disabilities, suggesting considerable age discrimination. Advocacy services are much weaker for older people with disabilities than for younger people with disabilities, which may explain some of the inequalities in provision. A more person-centred focus would help to integrate ageing and disability services. So too would a declaration of universal human rights which would place older people firmly at the centre of decision making throughout the ageing process, with or without a disability.

References

Baltes P.B., Baltes M.M. (1990) Psychological perspectives on successful aging: The model of selective optimization with compensation, in Baltes P.B., Baltes M.M. (Eds) *Successful Aging: Perspectives from the Behavioral Sciences*, New York: Cambridge University Press.

CSO (Central Statistics Office) (2012) *Profile 8: Our Bill of Health*, Dublin: Stationery Office.

Dey I., Fraser N. (2000) Age-based rationing in the allocation of health care, *Journal of Aging and Health* 12, 511–37.

Freund A.M., Baltes P.B. (1998) Selection, optimization, and compensation management: Correlations with subjective indicators of successful aging, *Psychology and Aging* 13, 531–43.

Gabriel Z., Bowling A. (2004) Quality of life from the perspectives of older people, *Ageing & Society* 24, 675–91.

Heidrich S.M., Ryff C.D. (1993) The role of social comparison processes in the psychological adaptation of elderly adults, *Journal of Gerontology* 48, 127–36.

Kane R., Kane R. (2001) What older people want from long-term care and how they can get it, *Health Affairs* 20, 114–27.

Murphy K., O'Shea E., Cooney A., Casey D. (2007) *The Quality of Life of Older People with a Disability in Ireland*, Dublin: National Council on Ageing and Older People.

NESC (National Economic and Social Council) (2012) *Quality and Standards in Human Services in Ireland: Disability Services*, Dublin: NESC.

OECD (Organisation for Economic Co-operation and Development) (2013) *A Good Life in Old Age: Monitoring and Improving Quality in long-Term Care*, Paris: OECD.

Priestly M., Rabiee P. (2002) Same difference? Older people's organisations and disability issues, *Disability & Society* 17, 597–611.

Putnam M. (2007) *Ageing and Disability: Crossing Network Lines*, New York: Springer Publishing Company.

The Equality Authority (2002) *Implementing Equality for Older People*, Dublin: The Equality Authority.

Townsend P. (1981) The structured dependency of the elderly: A creation of social policy in the twentieth century, *Ageing & Society* 1, 5–28.

Walker A. (2006) Towards an international political economy of ageing, *Ageing & Society* 25, 815–39.

WHO (2002) *Active Ageing: A Policy Framework*, Madrid: WHO.

8

The economics of dementia

Paddy Gillespie and Sheelah Connolly

Introduction

Dementia describes the group of symptoms caused by the gradual death of brain cells, leading to the progressive decline of functions such as memory, orientation, understanding, judgement, calculation, learning, language and thinking (Luengo-Fernandez *et al.*, 2010). There is no single cause of dementia, with a combination of risk factors, both known and unknown, believed to influence its onset and progression. Within this risk factor profile, increasing age is by far the strongest contributor, with the prevalence nearly doubling every five years from the age of 65 years onwards (Lobo *et al.*, 2000). The most common forms of dementia include Alzheimer's disease, which accounts for approximately 60% of all cases, vascular dementia, Lewy bodies and fronto-temporal dementia (Luengo-Fernandez *et al.*, 2010). Dementia is one of the leading causes of disability among older people. It is a terminal disease, with those affected expected to live three to nine years following diagnosis (Ganguli *et al.*, 2005; Helzner *et al.*, 2008; Larson *et al.*, 2004; Xie *et al.*, 2008). It is a particularly debilitating condition, as it affects those capabilities on which everyday life depends. Given the diverse nature of the illness, people with dementia require a wide range of formal health and social care and informal care services. Such services are delivered in a variety of settings, including hospitals, residential care settings or the person's home, and by a variety of providers, such as health and social care professionals, family members and friends.

The burden of dementia is enormous, affecting both the individual and their caregivers on personal, emotional, financial and social levels. The cost of caring for people with dementia worldwide was estimated to be US$604 billion in 2010 (Wimo and Prince, 2010), which included the costs of informal care provided by unpaid family and others, social care provided by community care professionals and in residential home settings, and health care provided in primary and secondary medical facilities. Indeed, this burden is projected to spiral in the near future as, given the ageing profile of the global population, the number of people with dementia worldwide is expected to grow from an estimated 35.6 million in 2010 to 65.7 million by 2030 and to 115.4 million by 2050 (Wimo and Prince, 2010). Given such projections, concerns are growing over the ability of an already resource-constrained formal and informal care infrastructure to cope with the expected increase in need. To address these concerns, policymakers in many countries have developed, or are in the process of developing, national action plans for dementia. In Ireland, the government plans to introduce a National Strategy for Dementia in 2014 which will go on to shape the nature of health and social policy for dementia. This process will be informed by an evidence-based policy approach, building on existing best practice nationally and internationally, to determine what type of care is to be provided, where it is to be delivered, and the personnel best suited to deliver it. Within the field of evidence-based policy, economic analysis is playing an increasingly prominent role, given the budget constraints facing health systems worldwide and the growing importance of issues of cost and cost-effectiveness. Indeed, in light of the growing pressures facing policymakers in relation to dementia, economic methods are likely to play a central role in informing decisions regarding service provision for people with dementia in the future.

This chapter explores the research on the economics of dementia in Ireland, which, while still in its infancy, is a growing field of analysis. The chapter begins with a brief overview of the methods applied by economists to address issues in relation to dementia and dementia care, before going on to describe three examples of these methods in an Irish context. The first presents the results of a cost-of-illness study which explores the economic burden of dementia in Ireland, while the second presents the results from a microeconometric study which explores the drivers of formal and informal dementia care costs in Ireland. The third explores the continuing evolution of dementia care in Ireland and presents an argument that health technology assessment will play a central role in informing this process in the future.

Health economic analysis of dementia in Ireland

Applying economic analysis to the study of dementia is a relatively new field of research, with the first comprehensive collection of literature presented in the book *Health Economics of Dementia* in 1998 (Wimo *et al.*, 1998). Since then, the discipline has expanded, with more and more studies being produced every year. Within this literature, applied empirical work can be grouped into three categories: (1) cost of illness; (2) applied health econometrics; and (3) health technology assessment. In brief, cost-of-illness techniques are used to express, in monetary terms, an estimate of the total cost of a particular disease to society.

Applied health econometric techniques are typically used to explore the determinants of health status, health care utilisation or cost. Health technology assessment techniques are used to evaluate interventions or technologies, examining issues such as their clinical and cost effectiveness. In the following three sections, recent examples from the Irish literature are presented for the first two methods and the potential future role of the third is explored.

Estimating the cost of dementia in Ireland: a cost-of-illness study

A recent study by Connolly *et al.* (2012) used a cost-of-illness approach to estimate the economic and social costs of dementia in Ireland. Cost-of-illness studies require the identification, measurement and valuation of all resources related to a particular disease, and the output, expressed in monetary terms, is an estimate of the total burden of a particular illness to society. While not without their critics in terms of methodology (Drummond, 1992) and usefulness (Byford *et al.*, 2000), cost-of-illness studies are useful in determining not only resource use associated with a particular illness, but also the distribution of costs among different resource categories. In the case of the latter, this goes to highlight those particular care pathways within the overall health system which shoulder the majority of the care burden. Such evidence is of particular interest to decision makers charged with the design of policy to meet future care needs. The methodological approach adopted and the results produced by Connolly *et al.* (2012) are presented in the current section.

In that study, a societal perspective was adopted, with all costs included regardless of where they fell. An annual time frame was assumed, with all costs due to dementia estimated for the most recent year for which data were available. The methodological process involved identifying, measuring and valuing all resources used by those with dementia. The starting point for the analysis was to estimate the total number of people with dementia in Ireland and the settings in which they receive care. The next step was to identify and estimate resource use in each care setting. Data on resource use and unit costs were obtained from a variety of national and, where necessary, international sources. Resource use was then valued using unit cost data and combined to calculate total costs per care setting and the overall total cost to society. All costs are presented in euro (€) currency in 2010 prices. Where necessary, unit cost estimates extrapolated from an earlier period were adjusted using an appropriate inflation index (Central Statistics Office, 2010).

An estimate of the prevalence of dementia was obtained from a study by Cahill *et al.* (2012), which estimated that 41,470 people were living with dementia in Ireland in 2010. This estimate was generated by applying the EuroCoDe (Alzheimer Europe, 2009) age- and gender-specific dementia prevalence rate formulae to demographic data from the 2006 Census of

Population of Ireland (Central Statistics Office, 2007). Unfortunately, there is no reliable data on where people with dementia in Ireland reside, therefore national and international evidence was used to allocate the estimated 41,470 people with dementia across various settings including the community, acute, psychiatric and long-stay care sectors. Connolly *et al.* (2012) estimate that 63% or 26,104 of those with dementia reside in the community, 2% or 644 in acute care, 1% or 456 in psychiatric care, and 34% or 14,266 in various long-stay facilities. For those living in the community, costs relating to informal care as well as primary, community, out-patient and medication-related costs were considered, while for those in the other three sectors, the costs included those relating to that particular sector. In addition, in keeping with cost-of-dementia studies in other countries, the cost associated with productivity losses related to premature mortality were also considered. The costing process is described below and in Table 8.1 for the four resource categories included in the analysis: (1) formal health and social care; (2) residential care; (3) informal care; and (4) productivity losses from premature mortality.

Formal health and social care includes all services provided in primary, community, acute and psychiatric settings. For those living in the community, data on utilisation rates of general practice, registered nurse, physiotherapist, psychologist, chiropodist, occupational therapist and social worker consultations, respite care, meals on wheels and home help services, out-patient consultations, accident and emergency admissions and medications were obtained from a published Irish study (Gillespie *et al.*, 2012). Data on the number of people with dementia in the hospital sector were derived from the Hospital In-Patient Enquiry Scheme, while information on the number of people with dementia in long-stay psychiatric hospitals and units was obtained from the National Psychiatric In-Patient Reporting System. Unit costs for formal health and social care services (see Table 8.1) were derived from a variety of published and unpublished national sources. The results from the analysis indicate that the combined cost of formal health and social care services for dementia in 2010 amounted to €147,947,223.

With respect to residential care, Connolly *et al.* (2012) estimated that there were approximately 14,266 people with dementia living in long-stay care in Ireland. Unit costs for residential care were based on the maximum weekly financial support available under the Health Service Executive's Nursing Home Support Scheme, which provides financial support for people assessed as needing long-term nursing home care in public and private long-stay facilities. The results indicate that the total cost of residential care amounted to €731 million, at an average cost per resident of €51,251 per annum. While the average weekly cost of private nursing home care was less than that in public homes, more people resided in private nursing homes, meaning that private provision accounted for a higher proportion of residential care costs.

Table 8.1 Estimating the costs of dementia in Ireland for 2010

Resource category	Measure	Unit cost (€)	Average use	Total use	Resource cost (€)	Total cost (€)	%
Health and social care						147,947,223	9%
General hospital admission	Per night	809	42.20	605	20,996,099		
Psychiatric hospital admission	Per night	339	187.00	456	38,684,162		
Accident and emergency hospital admission	Per admission	265	0.38	9,920	2,632,432		
Day-case hospital admission	Per admission	711	1.00	132	93,798		
Geriatrician visit (outpatient clinic)	Per visit	156	0.50	13,052	2,030,023		
Neurologist visit (outpatient clinic)	Per visit	156	0.12	3,132	487,206		
Psychiatrist visit (outpatient clinic)	Per visit	156	0.52	13,574	2,111,224		
General practice (GP) visit	Per visit	50	4.40	114,858	5,742,880		
Physiotherapist visit	Per visit	28	0.38	9,920	279,636		
Occupational therapist visit	Per visit	28	0.16	4,177	117,741		
Other specialist visit	Per visit	28	0.68	17,751	500,401		
Respite day care service	Per visit	97	15.20	396,781	38,570,437		
Home help service	Per visit	18	32.80	856,211	15,813,879		
Meals on wheels service	Per meal	7	12.40	323,690	2,202,575		
Registered nurse visit	Per visit	32	2.00	52,208	1,674,769		
Social worker visit	Per visit	28	0.16	4,177	117,741		
Anti-dementia drugs	Per day	1.88	75%	19,678	13,469,664		
Anti-depressant drugs	Per day	0.59	9%	2,349	502,763		
Anti-anxiety drugs	Per day	0.04	4%	1,044	15,245		

Table 8.1 (Continued)

Resource category	Measure	Unit cost (€)	Average use	Total use	Resource cost (€)	Total cost (€)	%
Anti-psychotic drugs	Per day	3.33	6%	1,566	1,904,548		
Residential care						731,148,816	43%
Public nursing home	Per week	1245	1.00	5,543	333,848,712		
Private nursing home	Per week	876	1.00	8,723	397,300,104		
Informal care						807,499,128	48%
Caregiving by person in employment	Per hour	22	8.33	26,104	573,324,381		
Caregiving by person not in employment	Per hour	5	8.33	26,104	234,174,747		
Productivity losses							
Working years lost (human capital approach)	Per year	29,113*		27	4,339,591	4,339,591	<1%
Total economic burden						1,690,934,758	

Source: Connelly *et al.* (2012).
Notes: Unit costs presented in € in 2010 prices.
* future earnings discounted at an annual rate of 4%.

People with dementia living in the community are generally cared for by family members and friends. For the purpose of the analysis by Connolly *et al.* (2012), it was assumed that people with dementia receive an average of 8.33 hours of informal care per day. This was based on the results from two small-scale Irish studies which present estimates of the amount of care provided by informal caregivers to people with dementia living in the community. The first study, by O'Shea (2003), was based on data for 98 caregivers and found that, on average, they were providing 11.6 hours of care per day. A second study, by Gallagher *et al.* (2010), of 100 patients and their carers found that individuals received, on average, 5.06 hours of informal care per day. The difference between the two studies is most likely explained by the severity of dementia, with those in the former study being at a more advanced stage than those in the later study. The figure for informal care hours adopted in the analysis by Connolly *et al.* (2012) was based on the average of these two estimates.

One of the most contentious issues in health economic analysis relates to how informal care should be valued. In this case, an opportunity cost approach, which assigns a value commensurate to that of what the individual could have earned were they not engaged in caregiving, was used to value informal care time. Data from a published Irish study (Gillespie *et al.*, 2012) on the labour force participation status of caregivers were used to categorise caregivers as either employed (29%) or not employed (71%). For the employed group, the opportunity cost of caring was valued at the average industrial wage (€21.81 per hour), mainly because the average weekly number of paid hours worked was only 29, suggesting that if people were not caring they could potentially be engaged in further paid work. Of those not in employment and caring, almost all were not actively seeking employment, having reached retirement age, taken early retirement, never engaged in paid work or had health-related problems. For this group, the opportunity cost of time was valued as a percentage (25%) of the average industrial wage, on the assumption that only leisure time is sacrificed in order to care. Multiplying these estimates of the value of informal care by the number of hours of care provided by informal caregivers provided an estimate of €807 million as the cost per annum of informal care for people with dementia. Notably, this is viewed as a conservative estimate, as alternative approaches, such as the replacement cost method, would generate much higher cost estimates (McDaid, 2001).

The fourth category of cost included in the analysis was the lost productivity, valued in terms of foregone earnings, associated with premature mortality from dementia. It was assumed for the analysis that the proportion of people with dementia aged 65 years and over who were still working was negligible. Data on the number of deaths of people with dementia aged less than 65 years in 2010 were obtained from the Central Statistics Office. The total number of working years lost due to premature death was calculated relative to the normal retirement age. The cost of working years lost was valued using average annual earnings. As these earnings would have arisen in future years, they were discounted to their present value at a rate of 4% (HIQA, 2010). Average annual earnings data were applied to the total working years lost, to generate the total loss associated with dementia. The results indicate that lost productivity due to premature mortality from dementia amounted to €4.3 million.

Combining costs across the four individual resource categories, the total cost of dementia in Ireland in 2010 was estimated at €1.69 billion. Of the total cost, just under half, or 48%, was accounted for by informal care provided by family and friends, while 43% was due to residential long-stay care. Formal health and social care provision, linked mainly to primary and community care, comprised only 9% of the total cost of dementia. Based on the estimated 41,740 people with dementia in Ireland, the average annual cost per person was €40,511. Although relatively few cost-of-illness studies have been carried out in Ireland, making it difficult to compare the economic cost of dementia with other conditions or diseases, the limited evidence that is available suggests that dementia is associated with a relatively high economic burden. This has been confirmed in a UK analysis which, using a similar methodology to cost a number of conditions, reported that the economic and social costs of dementia were almost twice those for cancer and three-times those of heart disease (Luengo-Fernandez et al., 2010).

The work by Connolly et al. (2012) is the second study on the economic costs of dementia in Ireland. A previous study estimated the total annual cost of dementia to be IR£248 million, with an average cost of IR£8,261 per person in 1998 (O'Shea and O'Reilly, 2000). The large rise between the 1998 and 2010 estimates likely reflects the significant increase in costs over the intervening decade, more realistic assumptions with respect to prevalence and more comprehensive data on resource use and unit costs (Connolly et al., 2012). The updated estimates are broadly in line with those from other international studies. The average cost per person with dementia was estimated at over £25,000 for the UK in 2005/6 (Knapp et al., 2007) and at over €36,000 for Northern Europe in 2008 (Wimo et al., 2011). In addition, the distribution of costs is comparable, with informal care accounting for 55% of total costs in the UK (Luengo-Fernandez et al., 2010) and 56% in Northern Europe (Wimo et al., 2011).

The analysis by Connolly et al. (2012) can be extended, albeit on the basis of strong underlying assumptions, to explore the likely future costs of dementia in Ireland. Cahill et al. (2012) provided both low and high estimates of the expected number of people with dementia in Ireland up to 2041. For example, the low estimates suggested that the number of people with dementia in Ireland would increase to 67,493 by 2021, 100,047 by 2031 and 140,580 by 2041. Table 8.2 shows the expected annual costs of dementia in those years based on

Table 8.2 Estimating the costs of dementia in Ireland for 2021, 2031 and 2041

Numbers with dementia	2021		2031		2041	
	67,493	69,066	100,047	103,279	140,580	147,015
	Cost (€)		Cost (€)		Cost (€)	
Health and social care	240,786,157	246,397,948	356,924,905	368,455,299	501,529,313	524,486,641
Residential care	1,189,954,836	1,217,688,067	1,763,907,538	1,820,890,248	2,478,536,305	2,591,990,431
Informal care	1,314,216,027	1,344,845,304	1,948,103,816	2,011,036,953	2,737,357,787	2,862,659,376
Productivity losses	7,062,745	7,227,350	10,469,329	10,807,538	14,710,868	15,384,253
Total cost	2,752,019,764	2,816,158,669	4,079,405,588	4,211,190,038	5,732,134,272	5,994,520,700

Source: Cahill et al. (2012) and Connolly et al. (2012).
Note: Unit costs presented in € in 2010 prices.

low and high prevalence rate assumptions. Based on the low prevalence rates, the total annual cost of dementia, in real terms, would be expected to increase to €2.75 billion by 2021, €4.08 billion by 2031 and €5.73 billion by 2041, while the high prevalence rates would see the annual total cost of dementia increase to €2.82 billion by 2021, €4.21 billion by 2031 and €5.99 billion by 2041.

These estimates, however, are based on a range of assumptions. For example, the prevalence predictions are based on current population projections, which are further based on a range of assumptions regarding fertility and migration. In addition, the dementia projections are based on the assumption that age- and gender-specific prevalence rates will remain constant over time. Furthermore, the cost estimates are based on the assumption that resource use and unit costs also will remain unchanged. These limitations notwithstanding, the results provide useful indicators of the general trends in expected prevalence and costs if the Irish population ages as predicted by the Central Statistics Office. Moreover, they highlight, in stark and meaningful terms, the increasing demands that will placed on the formal and informal dementia care infrastructure in Ireland in the near future.

Modelling the cost of dementia in Ireland: a microeconometric study

There is a growing international empirical microeconometric literature which explores the relationship between disease severity, resource use and cost of care for people with dementia. A recent study by Gillespie et al. (2012), based on data from the Enhancing Care in Alzheimer's Disease (ECAD) study, used econometric techniques to model costs of care for a sample of patients with Alzheimer's disease and amnestic mild cognitive impairment in Ireland. In particular, the analysis sought to explore the effects of patients' dependence on others and functional capacity on costs of care, while controlling for a range of demographic, socioeconomic and clinical characteristics. The underlying premise is that as the disease progresses the patient's functional capacity worsens and they become increasingly dependent on others. Therefore, interventions that improve patient independence may have economic as well as clinical benefits. In the current section, the methodological approach and results of the study by Gillespie et al. (2012) are described.

The analysis included data collected as part of the ECAD study (Gallagher et al., 2010). In brief, 100 participants were identified from referrals to a memory clinic associated with a university teaching hospital in Dublin and recruited for the study. Notably, only community-dwelling patients were included, i.e. individuals living in residential care settings were not eligible to participate in the study. Diagnoses of dementia were made through clinical team consensus by a neuropsychologist and consultant geriatrician or psychiatrist in the memory clinic following neuropsychological assessment, together with relevant haematological and neuroimaging investigations. A range of data were collected for each participant via medical assessments and structured interviews with their caregivers.

Two cost outcomes were included as dependent variables in the econometric analysis. These included: (i) formal health and social care costs, and (ii) informal care costs. Formal care costs included general practitioner practice visits, hospitalisations, out-patient clinic consultations, accident and emergency visits, respite care, meals on wheels services and additional health and social care professional consultations. The average cost of formal and social care was estimated to be €1,845 (standard deviation (SD): 3,363) per patient over a six-month period. The cost of informal care involved assigning a value to each hour of care received by a person with dementia from a family or friend caregiver. Following a similar approach to that presented in the previous sub-section, an opportunity cost method was adopted to value informal care, as data were available on the labour force participation status for each carer. The mean cost per patient of informal care was estimated to be €33 (SD: 51) per day and €4,959 (SD: 6,470) over a six-month period.

The impact on cost of a number of independent variables, including patient dependence and function, as well as demographic and socioeconomic characteristics, was considered in the analysis. Patients' dependence on others was measured using the Dependence Scale (DS) (Stern et al., 1994). The DS is a 13-item measure which is administered to a knowledgeable caregiver and asks questions regarding levels of dependence. A total dependence score may be derived by summing scores on all 13 items, providing a continuous index ranging from 0–15, with higher scores indicating greater dependence. Patient function was assessed with the Disability Assessment for Dementia (DAD) scale (Gelinas et al., 1999). The DAD is a validated, multi-item instrument that assesses 10 activities of daily living, including 6 instrumental activities of daily living (telephoning, performing housework/leisure activities, preparing meals, taking medications, going on an outing and managing finance/correspondence) and 4 basic activities of daily living (dressing, eating, hygiene and continence). The DAD is completed via an interview with a caregiver in which they are asked to rate the patient's actual performance on observed activities of daily living over the preceding two weeks. The maximum score on the scale is 40, with higher scores indicating greater functional capacity.

Other clinical measures included cognitive function, neuropsychiatric symptoms, anxiety, depression and comorbidity status. Cognitive function was measured using the Mini Mental State Examination scale (Folstein et al., 1975). Neuropsychiatric symptoms were assessed with the Neuropsychiatric Inventory (Cummings et al., 1994). Anxiety and depression status were recorded in a binary, yes or no, format. Comorbidity status was defined as having one or more coexisting chronic conditions from a list including ischemic heart disease, diabetes, congestive heart failure, chronic lung disease, musculoskeletal disease, hypertension, psychosis and cerebrovascular disease. The demographic and socioeconomic data included in the analysis were age, sex, educational attainment, medical card and private health insurance status.

A multivariate generalised linear model was used to explore the effects of the patients' clinical, socioeconomic and demographic characteristics on costs of care. Each dependent cost variable was modelled in its raw untransformed scale so that the estimated regression coefficients for each independent variable are interpreted in terms of their incremental effect on the mean cost of care. For continuous variables, the coefficient estimates the unit change in cost for a unit change in that variable. For dichotomous variables, the coefficient estimates the unit change in cost relative to the reference group for that variable.

Table 8.3 shows the associations between the various clinical and demographic variables and formal health and social care costs and informal care costs. Probably due to the small sample, few explanatory variables were statistically significant. Turning first to the formal health and social care costs, only one variable reached statistical significance: patient function, as measured by the DAD scale score. The results indicate that a one unit improvement in patient function was associated with a €189 (p-value = 0.002) reduction in formal health and social care costs over a six-month period. In the analysis of informal care costs, two variables were significant: patients' dependence on others (DS score) and patient function. The results for the DS score indicate that a one unit increase in patient dependence on others is associated with a €667 (p-value = 0.030) increase in informal care costs over a six-month period, while a one unit improvement in patient function was associated with a €224 (p-value = 0.019) reduction in informal care costs over a six-month period.

In summary, the results indicate that poorer function was associated with both higher formal and informal care costs, while more severe levels of dependence were associated with higher informal care costs. Notably, these results suggest that measures of patient function and dependence play independent roles in explaining variations in costs of care. The results for Ireland broadly reflect those of the growing international literature which explores the relationship between disease severity and costs of care for dementia. The majority of studies have examined the effect of functional capacity on costs and have consistently reported a positive relationship between increasing functional deficits and higher costs (Taylor et al., 2001; Small et al., 2002; Hill et al., 2006; Jonsson et al., 2006; Zhu et al., 2006a; Zhu et al., 2006b). While the effect of dependence on costs is less well known, the current literature also suggests a positive relationship between increasing dependence on others and higher costs of care (Murman et al., 2007; Zhu et al.,

Table 8.3 Econometric modelling of the costs of dementia in Ireland

Variable/model	Model 1 Formal health and social care cost Beta (SE)	Model 2 Informal care cost Beta (SE)
Dependence scale	191 (167)	667 (308)**
DAD scale	−189 (61)***	−224 (95)**
Age	−17 (54)	37 (78)
Gender		
Female (base-category)	–	–
Male	−901 (740)	975 (1134)
Education level		
Primary (base-category)	–	–
Secondary	871 (905)	−1329 (1272)
Third	343 (902)	−1633 (1241)
GMS status		
Ineligible (base-category)	–	–
Eligible	228 (834)	−670 (1376)
Private health insurance status		
Uninsured (base-category)	–	–
Insured	−808 (913)	−2359 (1449)
Comorbidity (other chronic disease)		
None (base-category)	–	–
1 or more other chronic disease(s)	1284 (770)	−486 (927)
Anxiety	−1661 (1269)	478 (1424)
Depression	−474 (1029)	−543 (1201)
Neuropsychiatric inventory (NPI) score	−18 (18)	−1 (21)
Mini mental state examination (MMSE) score	109 (81)	−109 (135)
Constant	5476 (3195)	9904 (5599)
AIC	18.92	19.64
Log likelihood	−808.925	−909.084

Source: Gillespie et al. (2013).
Notes: ** = $p < 0.05$; *** = $p < 0.01$.
SE – bootstrapped standard errors based on 1,000 replications.

2008a; Zhu et al., 2008b). As in the study by Gillespie et al. (2012), Zhu et al. (2008a, 2008b) suggest that increased dependence and functional deficits are independently associated with a higher total cost of care.

Limitations of the analysis included the sample, which was not representative of the general dementia population and particularly those living in residential care. It is also important to note the cross-sectional nature of the study, concerns of collinearity between the independent variables, and the small sample size. To address the latter, bootstrapped standard errors were estimated (see Gillespie *et al.*, 2012). Furthermore, some of the data were reported by carers and might be subject to bias.

From a policy perspective, these studies highlight the potential cost savings which may be expected to arise from improving patients' function and lessening their dependence on others. Indeed, assuming the findings of Gillespie *et al.* (2012) are transferable to the general cohort of people living in the community with dementia in Ireland, it follows that improvements in patient independence could lead to significant reductions in costs of care. This would suggest that the design and implementation of modes of care which delay movements to higher levels of functional impairment and dependence should be prioritised, as they have the potential to yield substantial economic, as well as clinical, benefits. Nonetheless, the clinical and cost effectiveness of such interventions would need to be examined before they could be adopted in practice.

Health technology assessment and dementia in Ireland

The techniques of health technology assessment are used to evaluate health and social care interventions or technologies in terms of their clinical and cost effectiveness. These techniques, which include cost effectiveness, cost utility, and cost-benefit analysis, compare alternative interventions in terms of health outcomes generated and resource costs incurred. Evidence from such studies is used to identify the most efficient means of allocating available health and social care resources to achieve health outcomes of interest. As yet, such techniques are not applied widely in the field of dementia in Ireland. In part, this is due to the complexity of undertaking such evaluations in this clinical area and, in particular, to the difficulties associated with measuring health outcomes for people with dementia. These difficulties notwithstanding, ongoing examples of Irish studies include the Technology Research for Independent Living project, which is an evaluation of technology solutions for older people, including those with dementia, and the Dementia Reminiscence-based Education Programme for Staff study, which is an evaluation of reminiscence therapy for people with dementia living in residential care (O'Shea *et al.*, 2011). It is argued here that these examples mark the start of a process whereby health technology assessment will become a central cog in informing policy for dementia care in Ireland and elsewhere. This argument is presented in terms of three related issues which reflect the contextual environment within which dementia policy and resource allocation will be decided upon in the future.

First, the evolving nature of the decision-making process with respect to health and social care resource allocation in Ireland will increase the need for such techniques. The fiscal constraints facing health systems worldwide have highlighted the need for an explicit consideration of value for money in decisions regarding public expenditure. Indeed, and as outlined above, in the case of dementia such fiscal constraints will become more pronounced, given the predicted increases in prevalence. As a result, the methods of health technology assessment are likely to become a formal part of the decision-making process for policymakers charged with allocating health and social care resources for people with of dementia.

Second, the changing policy environment with respect to dementia care in Ireland will increase the need for such techniques. The government has stated its aim to develop a national dementia strategy which will shape the nature of dementia care services in the country. Indeed, Cahill *et al.* (2012), in an exploratory document prepared to inform the drafting of the national strategy, call for a broad, eclectic and holistic perspective for the planning and provision of care services for people with dementia. Such a perspective, they suggest, should support the individual from the time of diagnosis until the time of death, regardless of whether the person resides in their own home, in hospital or in some form of residential care. A guiding principle will be a person-centred approach which values and respects the uniqueness of the individual and views them as someone with rights and responsibilities and who still has something to contribute to society. In addition, efforts should be made to balance the interests of the individual with those of their family, friends and health and social care professionals. To address these multiple policy goals requires a wide range of health and social care and informal care interventions. At one end of the disease pathway, preventive interventions will be required to advise on life-style risk factors which, if continued, may accelerate or aggravate the dementia. At the other end, interventions will be required to meet the needs of people with dementia and their caregivers. Furthermore, choices will have to be made as to which interventions will be provided at any given time. To inform such resource allocation decisions, the techniques of health technology assessment will have a role to play.

A third and related issue in terms of the changing nature of dementia care will be the increasing role of technology and innovation in supporting the provision of such care. This is closely aligned with the idea of 'ageing-in-place' and the now well established desire of older people to stay in their own home as they age. The recognition of this preference will be central to ageing and dementia policy in Ireland. To this end, an important factor will be how technological advancements and innovation will enable and enhance the provision of home-based care. While there will be a need to ensure that the burden of care is not simply transferred from the formal system to the informal system, as highlighted above, if new models of home-based care can enhance patient independence this may lead to reductions in both the formal and informal care burden. Within this context, Connected Health, which is a term used to describe all aspects of information and communication technologies in the field of health and social care (Bogan *et al.*, 2010), will have an important role to play. This encompasses the fields of eHealth, digital health, health informatics, telemedicine, mHealth, ambient assisted living and the use of supportive technologies in ageing. In general, these approaches make use of software, hardware, medical devices, telecommunications and other technologies to connect the patient in their home to their health and social care system. In doing so, they seek to improve patient outcomes, reduce risks and achieve efficiencies (Bogan *et al.* 2010). In this environment of technological innovation, the issue of who will pay for expensive new technologies, as well as questions over their clinical and cost effectiveness, will become increasingly relevant. The methods of health technology assessment are likely to play an important role in informing the decision-making process in this regard.

Conclusions

Dementia is one of the leading causes of disability in older people. With the number of people with dementia worldwide expected to increase dramatically, enormous pressures will be placed on existing formal and informal care services. To address this concern, governments in many countries are in the process of developing action plans and strategies for dementia care. In Ireland, the government intends to introduce a National Strategy for Dementia which will shape the future of dementia care provision in the State. Economic analysis is playing an increasingly prominent role in policy formulation, given the budget constraints that health systems face worldwide and the growing importance of issues of cost and cost effectiveness. This chapter presents an overview of heath economic research on dementia in Ireland which, while still in its infancy, is a growing field of analysis. Estimates of the overall costs of dementia in Ireland, based on a cost-of-illness methodology, reveal that the burden of the condition is considerable and is likely to increase significantly. These findings are broadly in line with international evidence on costs of dementia at the national level. The results from a microeconometric analysis suggest that improving patient independence may result in significant cost savings to both the formal and informal care systems. Again, these findings form part of the growing international evidence base which examines the impacts of dependence on others and functional capacity on costs of care for people with dementia. Finally, it is argued that the context within which dementia care is provided in Ireland and internationally, the continuing fiscal constraints facing health systems, the proposed policy framework and the role of technological innovation will all necessitate a central role for health technology assessment in informing how future policy is formed and resources are allocated in the area of dementia.

References

Alzheimer Europe (2009) *Number of People with Dementia in Europe Higher than Previously Thought*, Luxembourg: Alzheimer Europe Press Release, 13 July 2009.

Bogan D., Spence J., Donnelly P. (2010) *Connected Health in Ireland – An All Island Review*, Belfast: BioBusiness Ltd. Available at www.cardi.ie/userfiles/Connected_Health_in_Ireland_An_All_Island_Review.pdf.

Byford S., Torgerson D., Raftery J. (2000) Cost of illness studies, *British Medical Journal* 320, 1335.

Cahill S., O'Shea E., Pierce M. (2012) *Creating Excellence in Dementia Care: A Research Review for Ireland's National Dementia Strategy*, Living with Dementia Research Programme, School of Social Work and Social Policy, Trinity College Dublin.

Central Statistics Office (2007) *Census of Population – Volume 3: Household Composition, Family Units and Fertility*, Dublin: Stationery Office.

Central Statistics Office (2010) *Inflation Indices 2010*, Dublin: Stationery Office.

Connolly S., Gillespie P., O'Shea E., *et al.* (2012) Estimating the economic and social costs of dementia in Ireland, *Dementia*, DOI: 10.1177/1471301212442453.

Cummings J.L., Mega M., Gray K., Rosenberg-Thompson S., Carusi D.A., Gornbein J. (1994) The neuropsychiatric inventory: Comprehensive assessment of psychopathology in dementia, *Neurology* 44, 2308–14.

Drummond M. (1992) Cost of illness studies: a major headache? *PharmacoEconomics* 2, 1–4.

Folstein M.F., Folstein S.E., McHugh P.R. (1975) Mini-mental state: A practical method for grading the cognitive state of patients for the clinician, *Journal of Psychiatric Research* 12, 189–98.

Gallagher D., Ni Mhaolain A., Coen R., Walsh C., Kilroy D., Belinski K., Bruce I., Coakley D., Walsh J.B.., Cunningham C, Lawlor B.A. (2010) Detecting prodromal Alzheimer's disease in mild cognitive impairment: Utility of the CAMCOG and other neuropsychological predictors, *International Journal of Geriatric Psychiatry* 25, 1280–7.

Ganguli M., Dodge H.H., Shen C., Pandav R.S., DeKosky S.T. (2005) Alzheimer disease and mortality: A 15-year epidemiological study, *Archives of Neurology* 62, 779–84.

Gelinas I., Gauthier L., McIntyre M., Gauthier S. (1999) Development of a functional measure for persons with Alzheimer's disease: The disability assessment for dementia, *American Journal of Occupational Therapy* 53, 471–81.

Gillespie P., O'Shea E., Cullinan J., Lacey L., Gallagher D., Ni Mhaolain A., Lawlor B. (2012) The effects of dependence and function on costs of care for Alzheimer's disease and amnestic mild cognitive impairment in Ireland, *International Journal of Geriatric Psychiatry*, DOI: 10.1002/gps.3819.

Helzner E.P., Scarmeas N., Cosentino S., Tang M.X., Schupf N., Stern Y. (2008) Survival in Alzheimer disease: A multiethnic, population-based study of incident cases, *Neurology* 71, 1489–95.

Hill J., Fillit H., Thomas S.K., Chang S. (2006) Functional impairment, healthcare costs and the prevalence of institutionalisation in patients with Alzheimer's disease and other dementias, *PharmacoEconomics* 24, 265–80.

HIQA (Health Information and Quality Authority) (2010) *Guidelines for the Economic Evaluation of Health Technologies in Ireland*, Dublin: HIQA.

Jonsson L., Eriksdotter Jonhagen M., Kilander L., Soininen H., Hallikainen M., Waldemar G., Nygaard H., Andreasen N., Winblad B., Wimo A. (2006) Determinants of costs of care for patients with Alzheimer's disease, *International Journal of Geriatric Psychiatry* 21, 449–59.

Knapp M., Prince M., Albanese E., Banerjee S., Dhanasiri S., Fernandez J., Ferri C., McCrone P., Stewart R. (2007) *Dementia UK*, London: Alzheimer's Society.

Larson E.B., Shadlen M.F., Wang L., McCormick W.C., Bowen J.D., Teri L.. (2004) Survival after initial diagnosis of Alzheimer disease, *Annals of Internal Medicine* 140, 501–9.

Lobo A., Launer L.J., Fratiglioni L., Andersen K., Di Carlo A., Breteler M.M., Copeland J.R., Dartigues J.F., Jagger C., Martinez-Lage J., Soininen H., Hofman A. (2000) Prevalence of dementia and major subtypes in Europe: A collaborative study of population-based cohorts, Neurologic Diseases in the Elderly Research Group, *Neurology* 54, S4–9.

Luengo-Fernandez R., Leal J., Gray A. (2010) *Dementia 2010: The Economic Burden of Dementia and Associated Research Funding in the United Kingdom*, England: Alzheimer's Research Trust.

McDaid D. (2001) Estimating the costs of informal care for people with Alzheimer's disease: Methodological and practical challenges, *International Journal of Geriatric Psychiatry* 16, 400–5.

Murman D.L., Von Eye A., Sherwood P.R., Liang J., Colenda C.C. (2007) Evaluated need, costs of care, and payer perspective in degenerative dementia patients cared for in the United States, *Alzheimer Disease and Associated Disorders* 21, 39–48.

O'Shea E. (2003) Costs and consequences for carers of people with dementia in Ireland, *Dementia* 2, 201–9.

O'Shea E., Devane D., Murphy K., Cooney A., Casey D., Jordan F., Hunter A., Murphy E. (2011) Effectiveness of a structured education reminiscence-based programme for staff on the quality of life of residents with dementia in long-stay units: A study protocol for a cluster randomised trial, *Trials* 12, 41.

O'Shea E., O'Reilly S. (2000) The economic and social costs of dementia in Ireland, *International Journal of Geriatric Psychiatry* 15, 208–18.

Small G.W., McDonnell D.D., Brooks R.L., Papadopoulos G. (2002) The impact of symptom severity on the cost of Alzheimer's disease, *Journal of the American Geriatric Society* 50, 321–7.

Stern Y., Albert S.M., Sano M., Richards M., Miller L., Folstein M., Albert M., Bylsma F.W., Lafleche G. (1994) Assessing patient dependence in Alzheimer's disease, *The Journals of Gerontology* 49, M216–22.

Taylor D.H., Schenkman M., Zhou J., Sloan F.A. (2001) The relative effect of Alzheimer's disease and related dementias, disability, and comorbidities on cost of care for elderly persons, *Journals of Gerontology Series B: Psychological Sciences and Social Sciences* 56, S285–93.

Wimo A., Jönsson L., Gustavsson A., McDaid D., Ersek K., Georges J., Gulácsi L., Karpati K., Kenigsberg P., Valtonen H. (2011) The economic impact of dementia in Europe in 2008 – Cost estimates from the Eurocode project, *International Journal of Geriatric Psychiatry* 26, 825–32.

Wimo A., Jönsson B., Karlsson G., Winblad B. (1998) *Health Economics of Dementia*, Chichester, UK: John Wiley & Sons.

Wimo A., Prince M. (2010) *World Alzheimer Report 2010: The Global Economic Impact of Dementia*, London: Alzheimer's Disease International.

Xie J., Brayne C., Matthews F.E. (2008) Survival times in people with dementia: Analysis from population based cohort study with 14 year follow-up, *British Medical Journal* 336, 258.

Zhu C.W., Leibman C., McLaughlin T., Zbrozek A.S., Scarmeas N., Albert M., Brandt J., Blacker D., Sano M., Stern Y. (2008a) Patient dependence and longitudinal changes in costs of care in Alzheimer's disease, *Dementia and Geriatric Cognitive Disorders* 26, 416–23.

Zhu C.W., Leibman C., McLaughlin T., Scarmeas N., Albert M., Brandt J., Blacker D., Sano M., Stern Y. (2008b) The effects of patient function and dependence on costs of care in Alzheimer's disease, *Journal of American Geriatric Society* 56, 1497–503.

Zhu C.W., Scarmeas N., Torgan R., Albert M., Brandt J., Blacker D., Sano M., Stern Y. (2006a) Clinical characteristics and longitudinal changes of informal cost of Alzheimer's disease in the community, *Journal of American Geriatric Society* 54, 1596–602.

Zhu C.W., Scarmeas N., Torgan R., Albert M., Brandt J., Blacker D., Sano M., Stern Y. (2006b) Longitudinal study of effects of patient characteristics on direct costs in Alzheimer disease, *Neurology* 67, 998–1005.

9

The costs of community living for people with intellectual disabilities

Aoife Callan

Introduction

International trends favouring greater presence in the community on the part of adults with intellectual disability have strengthened in recent years (Mansell *et al.*, 2007; NDA, 2008). Thus far, this process of 'deinstitutionalisation' is at varying degrees of progress across developed countries. In the United States, for example, the population of people with intellectual disabilities living in public institutions peaked at 194,650 in 1967; by 2004, this number had declined to 41,653 (Prouty *et al.*, 2005). In the United Kingdom (UK) too, a marked reduction in institutional provision and increase in community-based residential supports has taken place in recent decades (Emerson and Hatton, 1998). In other countries, however, such as many Central and Eastern European countries, the dominant provision of care remains institutional care, with policy discourse concentrated on upgrading and renovating current institutions, rather than on the development of community living provisions (Mansell *et al.*, 2007). Nonetheless, decades of change in providing supports for people with intellectual disability have culminated in an overall enhancement of the quality of living environments for adults and widespread international consensus that long-stay institutions are neither desired nor needed (Tossebro *et al.*, 1996).

Ireland, with a population of 4.6 million, has endorsed a policy of community living for people with intellectual disability. From the Report of the Commission of Inquiry on Mental Handicap in 1965 to the landmark National Disability Strategy (NDS) in 2004 enshrining the enhancement of service provision for people with disabilities, the last 49 years have witnessed the transition of people with intellectual disability from institutional to community living (Fahey *et al.*, 2010; NDA, 2008; Review Group on Mental Handicap Services, 1990). This is reflected in the numbers of people living in community group homes (4,127) exceeding those in institutional settings (2,743) in 2011. By way of comparison, in 1997 there were 2,825 people registered as living in community homes, with 3,539 living in residential centres[1] (Kelly and Kelly, 2011; Mulvaney, 2004). Nevertheless, there is still a marked need for more residential places to support people with intellectual disability to live in the community, most notably given the greying population of adults with intellectual disability (Fahey et al., 2010). Of critical note for policymakers is that since 1975 the increase in numbers registered with the National Intellectual Disability Database (NIDD) is principally among two age cohorts: those aged between 35 and 54 years and those aged 55 years and over (Kelly, 2012). For the latter group in particular, the majority currently reside in community group homes or residential centres (Kelly, 2012). Consequently, demands on community-based services are likely to increase as a result of both greater absolute numbers of older people with intellectual disability and increasing average ages within this group. Policymakers in Ireland, therefore, must strive for coherence in planning appropriate supports and specific services for older people, particularly in a new financial environment (Department of Health and Children, 1997).

The move from institutional living to community inclusion and individual supports sparked a range of post-institutional research focusing on outcomes, quality of supports and costs across a range of diverse community residential settings. Typically, research measuring user outcomes identifies community living as being associated with a number of positive user outcomes in comparison to institutional living (Emerson and Hatton, 1994; Kozma et al., 2009). In addition, a range of studies investigated the quality of supports and outcomes for residents across a range of community-based residential settings (Fahey et al., 2010). In the UK, for example, Emerson et al. (2000) identified comparative advantages for residents in dispersed as opposed to congregate campus-based housing. These advantages included a more homely setting, more recreational opportunities, less institutional care and a greater likelihood that residents would name a person who was not a paid staff member, family member or another person with intellectual disability as a member of their social network. In campus-based housing, residents were found to be more likely to receive regular health checks, to have more contact with health professionals, to engage in more daily activities and to experience less risk of exploitation in the local community (Emerson et al., 2000). Thus, the authors suggest that variability in quality exists within any particular approach to providing residential supports.

Cost analysis of institutional and community care, on the other hand, has yielded varied results (Emerson et al., 2000; Mansell et al., 2007). According to Mansell and Beadle-Brown (2009a), there is little evidence to suggest any difference in costs between community living and institutional settings, once estimations are based on comparable needs of residents and comparable estimates of the quality of care. Knapp et al. (1997), however, suggested that while community care is more cost-effective for residents with less severe mental health difficulties, there is a threshold where hospital-based care becomes more cost-effective as the severity of mental health difficulties increases. Continuing the cost analysis to differing community-based residential settings, in the UK-based companion study to this chapter Emerson *et al.* (2000) investigated the quality and costs of residential supports for 500 people with intellectual disabilities living in dispersed housing, village campus settings or NHS hostels. Results highlighted village communities as the least expensive option when compared to dispersed housing, but village communities were rated slightly lower in the quality of their outcomes.[2] Nevertheless, the study concluded that both settings demonstrated benefits for their residents. For full details and results of the UK study, see Emerson *et al.* (2000) and Emerson *et al.* (2004). Furthermore, Mansell and Beadle-Brown (2009b) in their systematic review of 10 studies found clustered housing less expensive than dispersed housing, but noted that the studies which controlled for user characteristics found no statistical difference in costs. Currently there is no overall mechanism in Ireland to link service models and costs either with indicators of the quality of residential supports or with user outcomes. To bridge this gap, the National Disability Authority commissioned research on costs and outcomes of differing supported accommodation (NDA, 2008). Nevertheless, outside of systematic reviews, there is relatively little empirical evidence relating costs to user outcomes of different residential supports in Ireland (NDA, 2008).

Data from a study that examined the costs, characteristics and outcomes of community residential facilities in Ireland form the basis of this chapter. The study, conducted by Walsh *et al.* (2000a; 2000b) and funded by the (then) Department of Health and Children, aimed to generate essential information on the outcomes and costs of the two main types of residential support provided to Irish adults with intellectual disabilities, namely dispersed housing and group homes. The specific research aims of the original study were: (a) to compare the characteristics of the people living in residential campuses and group homes and the supports received; (b) to identify comprehensive costs associated with each type of provision; and (c) to explore the relationships between costs and user outcomes associated with each type of residential provision. Interview and observational data for the study were gathered during 1998–2000, and analysis of cost data was completed in spring of 2001 (Walsh *et al.*, 2000a; 2000b; 2000c; 2000d; 2001a; 2001b). The purpose of this chapter is twofold. First, it draws together and summarises key findings from the Walsh *et al.* (2000a; 2000b) study. Second, it contributes to the findings of Walsh *et al.* (2000a; 2000b) by presenting a detailed exploration of the costs associated with each type of Irish residential support setting and the relationship between costs and respondent characteristics.

Data collection

Participants

In the Walsh *et al.* (2000a; 2000b) study, a cross-sectional design was undertaken and the sample was drawn from 11 Irish organisations providing residential services to people with intellectual disability. These organisations were considered to be exemplars of good and/or typical practice in providing one of two types of residential provision for people with intellectual disability: village campus settings (typically characterised as on-site residential accommodation) or group home residences (typically characterised as being located within the community and referred to as dispersed housing). A total of 125 adults with intellectual disability were randomly selected from these residences to participate in the study. Written informed consent was obtained from each participant, and where this was not directly possible, agreement was obtained from the person's independent advocate, the closest family member or the chief executive of the provider organisation (see Emerson *et al.*, 2000). If agreement could not be obtained, another resident was randomly selected from the sampling frame.[3]

Measures

Information pertaining to each participant's residential setting was obtained using a range of measures and followed the protocol developed by Emerson *et al.* (2000) for the companion UK study. The Architectural Features Scale (AFS; Thompson *et al.*, 1990) was used to collect information on aspects of the physical environment of each residential setting. Internal consistency of the AFS was high (Cronbach's alpha = 0.86; n=125). A modified version of the Residential Services Setting Questionnaire (Emerson *et al.*, 1995) examined the size and location of the setting, the demographics of co-residents and the number and qualifications of staff. No information was available on the psychometric properties of this questionnaire. The Residential Services Working Practices Scale (Felce *et al.*, 1995) was used to determine the extent to which organisations implemented an 'active support' approach to the care provided for residents (Emerson and Hatton, 1994; Felce *et al.*, 2000; Jones *et al.*, 1999; McGill and Toogood, 1994). Active support involves the implementation of procedures within the setting that relate to individual planning, assessment and teaching, the planning of daily and weekly activity, arranging staff support for resident activity and the training and supervision of staff. Finally, the Group Home Management Interview (Pratt *et al.*, 1980) was used to rate the extent to which the four cardinal features of 'total institutions' (block treatment; depersonalisation; rigidity of routines; and social distance) were present within each setting. Internal consistency in the study (n=125) ranged from 0.32 (rigidity of routine) to 0.72 (depersonalisation) and was deemed acceptable. Characteristics of each of the care settings are reported in detail in Fahey *et al.* (2010).

Information about the participating residents and the specific support they received was collected by survey methods and by interviews with key informants. Part 1 of the *Adaptive Behavior Scale – Residential and Community*, 2nd Edition (ABS) (Nihira *et al.*, 1993) was used to collect information on the abilities and skills of the person and the presence of co-morbid disabilities. Reliability in the study was high, Cronbach's alpha reaching 0.98 (n=125). Challenging behaviour was assessed using the Aberrant Behavior Checklist (Aman *et al.*, 1995) and Cronbach's alpha for this scale was 0.94 (n=125). The PAS-ADD Checklist (Moss *et al.*, 1996; Moss *et al.*, 1998) was administered to screen for the presence of psychiatric disorder (reliability 0.66, n=125), while the Autism Screening Questionnaire (Howlin, 1996) was used to screen autism spectrum disorder. Internal consistency of the Autism Screening Questionnaire in the study was considered good, with Cronbach's alpha = 0.85 for the full scale (n=125). Finally, a Choice Scale developed specifically for the study (Emerson *et al.*, 1999) was used to identify opportunities for self-determination. The study recorded a high Cronbach's alpha = 0.95 (n=125).[4]

Information from families was obtained using a Family Questionnaire (Hatton *et al.*, 1995). The families' perception of the quality of care provided for their relatives has been previously reported and is not discussed here (see Walsh *et al.*, 2001c). While the views of individual residents regarding the quality of their residential settings were obtained for UK residents in the companion study, it did not prove feasible to do so across the 11 participating agencies in Ireland by the time all other data had been gathered.

Gathering cost data

Financial data were gathered by the (then) Centre for Health Economics, University College Dublin, using the protocol developed for the UK study (Emerson *et al.*, 2000). Income, expenditure and use of services over the previous three months were recorded on behalf of each participant on a revised version of the Client Service Receipt Inventory (Beecham, 1995). Additional costing information pertaining to residents was gathered on the Residential Services Setting Questionnaire (Emerson *et al.*, 1995). Collating this information, an individualised cost per participant was calculated for a final sample of 109 participants. These costs were then grouped under the headings of pay costs, non-pay current costs and the annualised value of capital costs for further analysis (Table 9.1).

Table 9.1 Cost typology

Cost grouping	Description
Pay costs	Direct salary, Pay Related Social Insurance, payments by employer and superannuating costs, holidays and replacement costs
Non-pay current costs	Overhead costs including local administration costs and sponsoring organisation administration costs
Capital costs – annualised value	Annualised insurance valuations
Total costs	Sum of pay, non-pay and capital costs

As presented in Table 9.1, analysis of costs began with pay costs at the level of direct staffing costs within each residential centre or group home, as pay costs are typically the single most important element of costs in the residential sector. Non-pay current costs are essentially overhead costs and include local administration costs and the administration costs of the sponsoring organisation itself.[5] In addition to local administration costs, an attempt was made to estimate the administration costs of the organisation per resident and include this in the total.

Estimating capital costs often proves problematic, as balance sheet values reflect accounting practices and generally embody depreciated valuations. Accordingly, insurance valuations, which were based on replacement cost or current market values, were taken as the capital valuation. These capital costs were then annualised over a 60-year time frame and discounted at 8%. Furniture and fittings were valued at depreciated cost or, in some cases where replacement furniture was necessary because of damage or breakage, at annual costs over the effective lifetime of the asset. Total costs were then calculated by summing the three cost groups together. Since the estimate is based on individual residents, rather than a simple average cost, and includes the annualised value of the capital cost, it must necessarily differ from the average cost estimated by service providers.[6]

Statistical analysis

Statistical and econometric analysis was conducted using Stata 11.0 (Stata Corporation, College Station, Texas, USA). Descriptive statistics of respondents in each residential community setting were calculated. Univariate analysis was undertaken and consisted of independent t tests for continuous variables, Kruskal-Wallis (Mann-Whitney) tests were used for ordinal or non-normal continuous variables and χ^2 tests for categorical variables. A multivariate

Generalised Linear Model (GLM) was also undertaken to explore the effects of a range of variables on total cost per patient.

Results

We first compare the characteristics of the participants living in village campuses with those in dispersed homes to develop an understanding of the levels of dependency of individuals residing in each facility type. We then present a brief discussion of the nature of support provided to participants, followed by a comparison of six key outcomes for residents by each facility type. Next, we present both raw costs and costs adjusted for the levels of ability of residents in each type of residential facility. This is followed by results of the GLM.

Characteristics

There were a number of significant differences between group characteristics, specifically in relation to age, gender, residential history, aberrant behaviour, ability and autism. Table 9.2 details the characteristics of participants in both village campuses and dispersed homes. Across both settings, there was a greater proportion of men compared to women, although the difference was more pronounced in village campuses than in dispersed homes. At a national level, the proportion of men with intellectual disability is greater than women, with an overall ratio of 1.35:1 (Kelly, 2012).

Typically, those in village settings were, on average, younger but had also spent a longer period of time living in their current village campus. This is also reflected in the significantly higher proportion of those in village campuses who had moved there directly from their family home and in the lower frequency of changing residential setting in the last seven years. While there was little difference in the number of health conditions between residents, it is clear that those in village campuses were significantly less able (as measured by their Adaptive Behaviour Scale (ABS) score) than those in dispersed housing. Residents in village campuses also displayed significantly higher levels of challenging behaviour (as measured by their Aberrant Behavior Checklist (ABC) score) than those in dispersed housing. There was also a significantly higher proportion of residents in village campuses with autism compared to those in dispersed housing. It is evident, therefore, that levels of dependency were generally higher among residents in village campuses than among those in dispersed housing. As noted by Emerson et al. (2004), such differences are not uncommon in analyses of residential facilities and their residents. However, such differences should be taken into account when analysing costs between care facility type, in order to avoid confounding of highly correlated variables such as ability and aberrant behaviour (Emerson et al., 2004).

Table 9.2 Characteristics of individuals by type of care setting

		Village campus, N=60	Dispersed housing, N=65	Significance
Age	Average in years	35.6	40.4	p < 0.05
	Range	19–75	19–66	
	Standard deviation	14.8	10.5	
Gender	% men	73.3 (n=44)	50.8 (n=33)	p < 0.05
	% women	26.7 (n=16)	49.2 (n=32)	
Residential history	Average age when left home (s.d.)	19.2 (14.9)	21 (13.1)	NS
	Average years in current setting	8.5	5.7	p < 0.01
	Family home as previous home (%)	78.9	25.8	p < 0.01
	Mean number of moves in previous 7 years	0.56	1.13	p < 0.01
Number of health conditions	Mean number of health conditions (range)	1.75(0–6)	1.8(0–7)	NS
Adaptive behaviour	Total ABS score (s.d.)	114.2 (65.6)	212.3 (64.2)	p < 0.01
	Range	7–248	71–313	
Challenging behaviour	Total ABC score (s.d.)	25.4 (22.6)	13.8 (12.9)	p < 0.01
	Range	0–89	0–51	
Autism criteria reached	Percentage	40%	23.8%	p < 0.01
Sensory impairments	Visual impairment	5%	1.6%	NS
	Hearing impairment	0%	3.2%	NS
Personal plan	% has personal plan	55%	79%	p < 0.01
Number of occupants				
Fewer than five	Less than five occupants	6.6%	41.7%	p < 0.01
Between six and eight	Between six and eight occupants	51.6%	46.7	NS
Nine or more	Nine or more occupants	41.7%	11.7%	p < 0.01

Notes: NS = not significant.
(s.d.) = standard deviation in parentheses.

Nature of support provided to participants

There were differences between models in regard to the supports received by residents (see Fahey *et al.*, 2010 for details of supports provided by model type). In summary, dispersed housing obtained a higher homeliness score, a higher score on the Architectural Features Scale compared to the village campuses and, on average, had a smaller number of residents per facility. Residents were also more likely to have had health checks in the last year. Generally, village campuses had more residents per facility but staffing ratios were higher, which may be indicative of the higher levels of care needs as characterised by their residents (see Table 9.2). Residents in village campuses were more likely to have had contact with health professionals, such as a psychiatrist or a physiotherapist, in the previous three months than those in dispersed housing.

Outcomes

The focus of this section is on six key outcomes including individual choice, social networks, health, diet, activity and victimisation (Table 9.3). Differences were observed between residents in village campuses and dispersed housing across choice scores, social networks, activity and victimisation. In terms of choice, as measured by the Choice Scale (Hatton *et al.*, 2004), residents in group homes reported greater opportunities for self-determination than those in village campuses. Those in dispersed homes also reported a greater social network, averaging a network of about 22 people, as compared to 17 people for those residing in village campuses. Social networks across both groups were largely comprised of other individuals with intellectual disabilities, as well as staff members. In the case of residents in village campuses, staff comprised a significant proportion of their social networks (approximately 61% of the social network).

Assessments of residents' weight among those in group homes, as compared to the norms, indicated that female residents tended to be over-represented as 'obese' and under-represented as 'normal' across both models of care provision. Engagement by all residents in physical activity across both settings was low, particularly among those in village campuses. Across both facility types, diet was generally considered sufficient and cigarette smoking was uncommon. Finally, an examination of safety issues suggested that those in village campuses were less likely to suffer victimisation, as compared to those in dispersed housing.

Costs

The second research aim was to identify comprehensive costs associated with each type of residential provision. Details of the univariate analysis conducted on the raw pay costs, non-pay costs, annualised capital costs and total costs are summarised in Table 9.4. Original costs were gathered and computed in

Table 9.3 Outcomes across residential type

		Village campus N=60	Dispersed housing N=65	Significance
Choice	Mean choice score	46.8	69.5	$p < 0.01$
Social networks	Mean no. in social network	17	22	$p < 0.05$
	Family as % of social network	17.9%	13.36%	$p < 0.05$
	Staff as % of social network	61.3%	42.5%	$p < 0.01$
	People with learning disabilities as % of social network	17.6%	36.4%	$p < 0.01$
Health	% who are of normal weight	25%	24.5%	NS
	% of men who are obese	22.7%	29.6%	NS
	% of women who are obese	46.7%	43.3%	NS
Diet	% whose diet is considered OK	76.7%	78.5%	NS
	% with three or more bad diet behaviours	11.7%	15.4%	NS
	% who smoke	10%	15.4%	NS
Activity	Mean no. of times a participant undertook light activity in last 4 weeks	26.6	35.7	$p < 0.02$
	Mean no. of times a participant undertook vigorous activity in last 4 weeks	2.47	2.10	NS
	Physically incapable of some activity	46.7%	26%	$p < 0.01$
Victimisation	% who have been a victim of crime	5%	15.5%	$p < 0.01$
	% who have been a victim of teasing or verbal abuse	10%	20%	NS

Note: NS = not significant.

Irish pounds and have been converted to euros. In contrast to the findings from the UK (see Emerson *et al.*, 2000; Emerson *et al.*, 2004), costs were higher for individuals residing in village (larger residential) centres when compared with those in dispersed housing. Results of independent *t* tests indicated that cost differences – pay, non-pay, capital and total – between the two residential models were statistically significant (total costs: $t = 6.3$, $df = 107$, $p < 0.001$). It is unsurprising that pay costs are the significant driver of costs of both care models, constituting almost 60% of the total costs for an average village facility and 73% of the total costs for an average dispersed home model of residential care.

Table 9.4 Raw average weekly cost of residential support

	Village campus, N=60	Dispersed housing, N=65	Significance
	2000 (Euro)[a]	2000 (Euro)[a]	
Pay costs	614.04	466.66	$p < 0.05$
(SD)	(249.64)	(342.62)	
[95% CI]	[549.55–678.53]	[368.25–565.07]	
Non-pay costs	264.95	102.02	$p < 0.01$
(SD)	(73.89)	(42.76)	
[95% CI]	[245.86–284.03]	[89.74–114.30]	
Capital costs annualised value	146.49	69.18	$p < 0.01$
(SD)	(16.50)	(44.26)	
[95% CI]	[142.28–150.75]	[56.47–81.90]	
Total average costs	1025.48	637.87	$p < 0.01$
(SD)	(281.98)	(358.12)	
[95% CI]	[952.64–1098.32]	[535.01–740.74]	

Notes: SD denotes standard deviation, CI denotes confidence interval.
[a] Converted from Irish pounds to € using conversion rate of Irl£0.7875 = €1.
Tests for differences in means conducted using both parametric and non-parametric comparisons of means. Non-parametric results reported.

Differences between ability and aberrant behaviour of residents in both models may affect analysis of between-residence differences in raw costs and such correlations should be taken into account. Therefore, using a GLM controlling for age, aberrant behaviour and ability, we also predicted costs for each model type (results not presented). The analysis indicated a narrowing of the difference in costs but significant differences prevailed ($p < 0.01$), with total costs equating to €921.78 for village campuses and to €742.34 for dispersed housing. Full results are available on request from the author.

Modelling costs of community residential care facilities
Annual costs, based on the individual resident costs as calculated and presented in Table 9.4, range from approximately €33,000 for those in dispersed housing to over €53,000 for those in village campuses. Therefore, it is important to understand drivers of individual costs within each type of care facility. To explore the relationship between respondent characteristics, inputs such as facility size (in terms of the average number of residents per housing type) and costs, we employed a GLM with a gamma distribution and a log link, the results of which are detailed in Table 9.5. All standard errors are bootstrapped with 1,000 iterations to account for the relatively small sample size.

Table 9.5 Results of GLMs, estimated coefficients

	Village campus	Dispersed housing
Female	0.917	1.029
Age 19 to 30	1.354***	0.845
Age 30 to 50	1.197	0.93
ABS score	0.998**	0.996***
ABC score	0.999	1.015***
No personal plan	0.934	1.168
Five or fewer	0.881	0.874
Nine or more	0.861**	0.537***
AIC	15.646	14.596
N observations	60	37

Notes: Base categories: male, age 50 plus, physically inactive, has personal plan, between six to eight residents. * p<0.01; **p<0.05; ***p<0.10.

Despite the differences in the proportions of men and women within each facility type, gender does not significantly influence costs in either residential model. However, age is significantly related to costs in village campuses, with the youngest cohort demonstrating significantly higher costs relative to the oldest cohort. Age is not, however, a significant driver of costs in dispersed housing facilities. In both models of residential facilities, lower levels of ability (as demonstrated by the ABS score) are associated with increasing individual costs. Furthermore, scores of aberrant behaviour (as demonstrated by the ABC score) are positively related to costs in dispersed housing.

For both dispersed housing and village campuses the number of occupants per residential setting demonstrated a significant relationship to costs.[7] Within both settings, facilities with nine or more occupants have lower costs relative to occupants of between six and eight occupants, which may reflect economies of scale.

Conclusions

Community living for people with intellectual disability has been encouraged and supported for a number of decades in Ireland. Systematic reviews have demonstrated the merits of community living and social inclusion and have highlighted the relative cost-effectiveness of delivering care in the community to individuals with intellectual disability (Mansell *et al.*, 2007). Yet, there is a notable gap in the Irish literature linking costs and outcomes of current community residential provision. This chapter aims to bridge this gap by bringing together relevant information from a study on resident characteristics, costs and outcomes of two types of community residential facilities for people with intellectual disability in Ireland: village campuses and dispersed housing.

The findings highlight the higher average cost per resident for village campuses relative to dispersed housing, driven by differences in staff costs. This is in contrast to the findings of the UK companion study, which found lower average costs associated with village campuses. Assessments of residents indicated higher dependency (in terms of both ability and challenging behaviour) across residents in village campuses, as compared to those in dispersed housing. Similarly, a distinct pattern is evident in the outcome measures across the two residential settings. Those in village campuses rated slightly lower across a range of outcome measures including self-determination, engagement in activities, ability to be physically active and having a smaller social network.[8] However, residents in village campuses fared better in terms of lower levels of reported victimisation than did those in dispersed housing. Thus, heterogeneity both within and across residents in each type of community care facility is highly evident. In addition, supports provided in each community setting attributed dispersed housing with higher homeliness scores and architectural scores relative to village campuses. The higher dependency levels of residents in village campuses may also be reflected in the higher number of staff supports compared to dispersed housing. Nevertheless, when we controlled for confounding factors such as ability, challenging behaviour and age on costs, the relatively higher costs remained for village campuses. We were also interested in exploring the relationship between costs and a range of variables. Costs, unsurprisingly, proved to be significantly associated with ability, challenging behaviour, the number of occupants in each type of care setting and, in the case of village campuses, the age of residents.

In conclusion, the recent debate in Irish community care policy for people with intellectual disability calls for further and complete integration into dispersed housing facilities within the community. Given the evidence from this study, this method of community residential provision demonstrated lower costs, as compared to village campuses. However, village campuses accommodated a higher proportion of people with more severe or profound intellectual disability. It is also clear that there are different patterns of benefits and supports for each facility type. Thus, in order to maximise inclusion and community living for people with intellectual disability, the conclusion from this work is that the provision of choice in terms of community living facilities may provide the optimal outcome for people of different levels of intellectual disability. Furthermore, with an ageing population of people with intellectual disability, policymakers should strive to utilise both cost and outcome data to develop the optimal and flexible community living policy for people with intellectual disability.

Finally, some limitations should be acknowledged. Participants for this study were selected randomly from the population of adults receiving residential supports within each participating service organisation. It may be assumed with confidence that the features of these organisations are represented in the findings. However, the organisations themselves were not randomly selected and, therefore, the results are limited in their representativeness of community and group homes nationally. Furthermore, while 125 individuals made up a sample of 2% of all Irish adults with intellectual disabilities living in similar residential settings at the time of the study (Mulvaney, 2004), caution should nevertheless be exercised in generalising these findings to all other group homes or campus settings in Ireland.

Acknowledgements

The author would like to thank Patricia Noonan Walsh, Joseph Durkan, Christine Linehan, John Hillery, Eric Emerson and Chris Hatton for providing the data that form the basis of this chapter, which is from a study funded by the (then) Department of Health and Children. The author would also like to thank Seán Lyons for his work on the dataset, and all for their helpful advice on this chapter. Any conclusions drawn, or errors which may inadvertently appear, are entirely the author's own.

Notes

1 Data taken from the National Intellectual Disability Database, established in 1996.
2 For an in-depth discussion of the costs of community living for residents with intellectual disability, see Mansell et al. (2007).
3 All individuals in each organisation were anonymised and then randomly selected, stratified by each organisation. The selected anonymised participants were returned to each organisation using a unique identifier and each organisation was requested to commence the process of obtaining consent from each selected resident for participation.
4 Fahey et al. (2010) also reported descriptive statistics of the characteristics of residents, their supports and quality of life per residential community type.
5 When it came to the house-specific direct running costs, a distinction was drawn between those items which residents themselves paid for out of their own entitlements and those borne by the organisation. In general, residents made a weekly contribution to cover the costs of food, heat and light and these were excluded from overall costs.
6 The main difference arises in relation to staff costs, which here are resident specific, rather than averaged.
7 The relationship between outcome variables such as number of health conditions, homeliness score, BMI, time spent in current setting, autistic, number in social network and family visits were highly insignificant and, as such, are not presented in detail here.
8 It is important to note that we did not control for confounding factors on outcomes.

References

Aman M.G., Burrow W.H., Wolford P.L. (1995) The aberrant behavior checklist – Community: factor validity and effect of subject variables for adults in group homes, *American Journal on Mental Retardation* 100, 283–92.

Beecham J. (1995) Collecting and estimating costs, in Knapp M.R.J. (Ed.) *The Economic Evaluation of Mental Health Care*, Aldershot: Arena.

Department of Health and Children (1997) *Enhancing the Partnership: Report of the Working Group on the Implementation of the Health Strategy in Relation to Persons with a Mental Handicap*, Dublin: Department of Health & Children.

Emerson E., Alborz A., Felce D., Lowe K. (1995) *Residential Services Setting Questionnaire*, Manchester: Hester Adrian Research Centre, University of Manchester.

Emerson E., Hatton C. (1994) *Moving Out: The Impact of Relocation from Hospital to Community on the Quality of Life of People with Learning Disabilities*, London: Her Majesty's Stationery Office.

Emerson E., Hatton C. (1998) Residential provision for people with intellectual disabilities in England, Wales and Scotland, *Journal of Applied Research in Intellectual Disabilities* 11, 1–14.

Emerson E., Robertson J., Gregory N., Hatton C., Kessissoglou S., Hallam A., Knapp M., Jarbrink K., Netten A., Walsh P.N. (1999) *Quality and Costs of Residential Supports for People with Learning Disabilities: A Comparative Analysis of Quality and Costs in Village Communities, Residential Campuses and Dispersed Housing Schemes*, Manchester: Hester Adrian Research Centre, University of Manchester.

Emerson E., Robertson J., Gregory N., Hatton C., Kessissoglou S., Hallam A., Knapp M., Jaerbrink K., Netten A., Walsh P.N. (2000) Quality and costs of community-based residential supports, village communities and residential campuses in the United Kingdom, *American Journal on Mental Retardation* 105, 81–102.

Emerson E., Robertson J., Hatton C., Knapp M., Walsh P.N. (2004) A comparison of costs and outcomes of supported accommodation in England, in Stancliffe R.J., Lakin K.C. (Eds) *Costs and Outcomes: Community Services for People with Intellectual Disabilities*, Baltimore, MD: Paul H. Brookes Publishing.

Fahey A., Noonan Walsh P., Emerson E., Guerin S. (2010) Characteristics, supports, and quality of life of Irish adults with intellectual disability in life-sharing residential communities, *Journal of Intellectual and Developmental Disability* 35, 66–76.

Felce D., Lowe K., Emerson E. (1995) *Residential Services Working Practices Scale*, Cardiff: Welsh Centre on Learning Disabilities Applied Research Unit.

Felce D., Lowe K., Beecham J., Hallam A. (2000) Exploring the relationships between costs and quality of services for adults with severe intellectual disabilities and the most severe challenging behaviours in Wales: A multivariate regression analysis, *Journal of Intellectual and Developmental Disability* 25, 307–26.

Hatton C., Emerson E., Robertson J., Henderson D., Cooper J. (1995) The quality and costs of services for adults with multiple disabilities: A comparative evaluation, *Research in Developmental Disabilities* 16, 439–60.

Hatton C., Emerson E., Robertson J., Gregory N., Kessissoglou S., Walsh P.N. (2004) The Resident Choice Scale: A measure to assess opportunities for self-determination in residential settings, *Journal of Intellectual Disability Research* 48, 103–13.

Howlin P. (1996) *Autism Screening Questionnaire*, London: St George's Medical School.

Jones E., Perry J., Lowe K., Felce D., Toogood S., Dunstan F., Allen D., Pagler J. (1999) Opportunity and the promotion of activity among adults with severe mental retardation living in community residences: The impact of training staff in Active Support, *Journal of Intellectual Disability Research* 43, 164–78.

Kelly C. (2012) *Annual Report of the National Intellectual Disability Database Committee 2010*, Dublin: Health Research Board.

Kelly F., Kelly C. (2011) *Annual Report of the National Intellectual Disability Database Committee 2010*, Dublin: Health Research Board.

Knapp M., Chisholm D., Astin J., Lelliott P., Audini B. (1997) The cost consequences of changing the hospital–community balance: The mental health residential care study, *Psychological Medicine* 27, 681–92.

Kozma A., Mansell J., Beadle-Brown J. (2009) Outcomes in different residential settings for people with intellectual disability: A systematic review, *American Journal on Intellectual and Developmental Disabilities* 114, 193–222.

Mansell J., Beadle-Brown J. (2009a) Cost-effectiveness of community living for people with intellectual disability: An international perspective, paper presented at the National Disability Authority Annual Conference, Dublin, 6 October.

Mansell J., Beadle-Brown J. (2009b) Dispersed or clustered housing for adults with intellectual disability: A systematic review, *Journal of Intellectual and Developmental Disability* 34, 313–23.

Mansell J., Knapp M., Beadle-Brown J., Beecham J. (2007) *Deinstitutionalisation and Community Living – Outcomes and Costs: Report of a European Study, Volume 2: Main Report*, Canterbury: Tizard Centre, University of Kent.

McGill P., Toogood S. (1994) Organising community placements, in Emerson E., McGill P., Mansell J. (Eds) *Severe Learning Disabilities and Challenging Behaviours: Designing High Quality Services*, London: Chapman & Hall.

Moss S., Prosser H., Costello H., Simpson N., Patel P. (1996) *PAS-ADD Checklist*, Manchester: Hester Adrian Research Centre: University of Manchester.

Moss S., Prosser H., Costello H., Simpson N., Patel P., Rowe S., Turner S., Hatton C. (1998) Reliability and validity of the PAS-ADD Checklist for detecting psychiatric disorders in adults with intellectual disabilities, *Journal of Intellectual Disability Research* 42, 173–83.

Mulvaney F. (2004) *Annual Report of the National Intellectual Disability Database Committee 1998/1999*, Dublin: Health Research Board.

NDA (National Disability Authority) (2008) *A Contemporary Developments in Disabilities Services Paper*, Dublin: National Disability Authority.

Nihira K., Leland H., Lambert N. (1993) *Adaptive Behavior Scale – Residential and Community*, Austin, TX: Pro-Ed.

Pratt M.W., Luszcz M.A., Brown M.E. (1980) Measuring the dimensions of the quality of care in small community residences, *American Journal of Mental Deficiency* 85, 188–94.

Prouty R.W., Smith G., Lakin K.C. (Eds) (2005) *Residential Services for Persons with Developmental Disabilities: Status and Trends Through 2004*, Minneapolis, MN: University of Minnesota, Institute on Community Integration, Research and Training Center on Community Living.

Review Group on Mental Handicap Services (1990) *Needs and Abilities, A Policy for the Intellectually Disabled*, Dublin: The Stationery Office.

Thompson T., Robinson J., Graff M., Ingenmey R. (1990) Home-like architectural features of residential environments, *American Journal on Mental Retardation* 95, 328–41.

Tossebro J., Aalto M., Brusen P. (1996) Changing ideologies and patterns of services: The Nordic countries, in Tossebro J., Gustavsson A., Dyrendahl G. (Eds) *Intellectual Disabilities in the Nordic Welfare States*, Kristiansand: Norwegian Academic Press.

Walsh P.N., Linehan C., Hillery J., Durkan J., Emerson E., Robertson J., Gregory N., Hatton C., Kessissoglou S., Hallam A., Knapp M., Jaerbrink K., Netten A. (2000a) *Quality and Outcomes of Residential Settings Provided for Irish Adults with Intellectual Disability: An Analysis of Quality in Irish Village Campus Settings*, Dublin: Centre for the Study of Developmental Disabilities, National University of Ireland, Dublin.

Walsh P.N., Linehan C., Hillery J., Durkan J., Emerson E., Robertson J., Gregory N., Hatton C., Kessissoglou S., Hallam A., Knapp M., Jaerbrink K., Netten A. (2000b) *Quality and Costs of Residential Supports for Irish Adults with Intellectual Disability – Brief Summary Report*, Dublin: UCD Centre for the Study of Developmental Disabilities, National University of Ireland, Dublin.

Walsh P.N., Linehan C., Hillery J., Durkan J., Emerson E., Robertson J., Gregory N., Hatton C., Kessissoglou S., Hallam A., Knapp M., Jaerbrink K.,

Netten A. (2000c) *Quality and Outcomes of Residential Settings Provided for Irish Adults with Intellectual Disability: A Comparative Analysis of Quality in Irish Village Campus Settings and Group Home Settings*, Dublin: Centre for the Study of Developmental Disabilities, National University of Ireland, Dublin.

Walsh M., Linehan C., Walsh P.N., *et al.* (2000d) *Quality and Outcomes of Residential Settings Provided for Irish Adults with Intellectual Disability: Observational Study*, Dublin: Centre for the Study of Developmental Disabilities, National University of Ireland, Dublin.

Walsh M., Linehan C., Walsh P.N., *et al.* (2001a) *Quality and Outcomes of Residential Settings Provided for Irish Adults with Intellectual Disability: Predicting Variation in Quality and Costs*, Dublin: Centre for the Study of Developmental Disabilities, National University of Ireland, Dublin.

Walsh P.N., Linehan C., Hillery J., *et al.* (2001b) *Quality and Outcomes of Residential Settings Provided for Irish Adults with Intellectual Disability: Summary*, Dublin: Centre for the Study of Developmental Disabilities, National University of Ireland, Dublin.

Walsh P.N., Linehan C., Hillery J., *et al.* (2001c) Family views of the quality of residential supports, *Journal of Applied Research in Intellectual Disabilities* 14, 292–309.

10

The economics of mental health services

Brendan Kennelly

Introduction

Mental health services include a broad range of services, from home and community-based facilities such as day hospitals and out-patient facilities, to acute care units and residential care services. This chapter presents a broad overview of key economic issues facing the provision of such services in Ireland. The key issues that are addressed include: (a) the nature and extent of mental illnesses in Ireland; (b) the resources spent on care provided to people with mental illnesses; and (c) the economic cost of mental illness in Ireland. I also review some examples of economic evaluation of mental health interventions in Ireland and a contingent valuation study that estimated the willingness to pay for a mental health programme.

Mental illnesses of all kinds account for one of the largest categories of the burden of disease with which health systems must cope. The World Health Organization (WHO) has estimated that mental disorders are responsible for more than 10% of the lost years of healthy life in the world and for over 30% of all years lived with disability. The size of this burden is due to the relatively high prevalence of mental disorders and both the duration and intensity of many episodes of mental disorders. Not surprisingly, these high disease burdens are reflected in large economic costs. The cost of mental illnesses has been estimated at between 3% and 4% of GDP in many European countries, including Ireland (O'Shea and Kennelly, 2008). The majority of these costs are lost output costs due either to an inability to work due to a mental illness or due to premature death caused by a mental illness. Cost-of-illness estimates typically do not include any estimate of the human burden of an illness and this is likely to be a particularly important issue in the case of mental illness.

Since 2006, most discussions of mental health issues in Ireland have been conducted in the light of a major report on mental health policy in Ireland, *A Vision for Change* (Department of Health and Children, 2006). The report set out a comprehensive policy framework for mental health services in Ireland. It proposed a holistic view of mental health problems incorporating biological, psychological and social aspects. A person-centred inclusive approach to mental health care was an important part of this view, and the report argued that much more attention should be given to the process and locus of care. *A Vision for Change* was an important landmark for the development of services for people with mental health problems in Ireland. A formal implementation plan, covering the period from 2009 to 2013, was issued by the Health Service Executive (HSE) in 2009. A series of valuable annual reports up to and including 2012 assessing the progress, or lack thereof, in implementing *A Vision for Change* have also been published. The reports follow a consultation process that is open to service providers, advocacy groups and other interested parties. Unfortunately, recent news reports indicate that these annual progress reports will no longer be published.

The incidence of mental ill health in Ireland

The first step with any analysis of the system of care for people with mental illness in any country is to estimate the needs of the population. Ideally, the starting point should be a psychiatric morbidity survey that includes a representative sample of the population and administers a standardised test that will allow a deduction to be made as to whether a respondent meets some established criteria for mental illness. The respondents in the survey who satisfy such criteria are then resurveyed with additional questions about their health and social conditions. The second-phase interview should be conducted by clinically trained research interviewers who have the skills to diagnose less common disorders such as psychosis and personality disorders. Unfortunately, this kind of survey has never been carried out in Ireland. This is a severe limitation for health planners trying to decide what services to supply, and also for researchers trying to analyse the overall effectiveness of the system of mental health care in Ireland. As we will see throughout this chapter, data limitations continue to plague researchers on mental health policy in Ireland.

In the absence of a comprehensive psychiatric morbidity study, researchers in Ireland have to rely on smaller surveys to estimate the likely prevalence of mental health problems. The Health Research Board (HRB) conducted two population-level surveys of psychological well-being and distress in Ireland (Tedstone Doherty *et al.*, 2007; Tedstone Doherty and Moran, 2009). In both cases about 1,000 people aged 18 or over were surveyed. Questions regarding use of mental health services in the previous year as well as self-reported mental health were included. In addition, the General Health Questionnaire (GHQ) was completed by respondents. A score of 4 or more on this index indicates a moderate or severe level of mental distress.

The most recent survey was conducted in November and December of 2007. Overall, 12% of respondents received a score of 4 or higher on the GHQ, while 12% of the respondents reported that they had experienced a mental health problem in the previous year. Of the sample, 1.2% stated that their mental health problem had severely affected their physical health and 1.4% said it had severely affected their social activities. Six per cent of people said they were taking psychotropic medication at the time of the survey. Almost 10% of the respondents had visited their GP about a mental health problem in the previous year. However, an interesting finding is that fewer than half of those who reported a mental health problem in the previous year had attended a GP about this problem. This suggests that about 3% of the sample had visited their GP about a mental health problem but also responded that they did not have a mental health problem in the previous year. Whether this is due to stigma or whether the people in question felt that their mental health problem had been cured is not clear. Over 5% of the respondents had been in contact with at least one of a range of secondary mental health services and 2.2% said they had been in contact with in-patient psychiatric services. This is much higher than the number of adults who were admitted to in-patient services for that year.

A second useful source of information on mental health is the Slán survey, the most recent of which was also carried out in 2007 (Barry et al., 2009). This included face-to-face interviews with 10,364 adults. Respondents were asked a series of questions about their mental health as part of a longer survey about health and well-being. One question referred to non-specific psychological distress, which was measured using the five-item Mental Health Index. Of the sample, 7% (6.3% of men and 7.5% of women) were identified as having probable mental health problems. This figure is considerably lower than other population-level surveys on mental health in Ireland in the past 10 years, such as the HRB survey referred to earlier. Barry et al. (2009) suggest that respondents may be less inclined to disclose their true level of psychological distress in face-to-face interviews.

The Slán survey also provided information that would lead to a probable diagnosis of (a) a major depressive disorder and (b) a generalised anxiety disorder (GAD). A diagnosis of a major depressive disorder means that the respondent fulfils the criteria for an episode of depression for at least two weeks of the previous 12 months. Respondents were also asked whether they had had depression in the previous 12 months and, if so, whether it had been diagnosed by a doctor. A diagnosis of a GAD means that the respondent fulfils the criteria for GAD for at least 6 of the previous 12 months.

Overall, 6% of the respondents were assessed as having a probable major depressive disorder in the past year (8% of women, 5% of men). About 6% of the sample reported that they had had depression in the previous 12 months, with over three-quarters of this group reporting that the depression had been diagnosed by a doctor. Interestingly, fewer than half of the group that reported they had been depressed were diagnosed as having a probable major depressive disorder as measured by the CIDI-SF instrument. This might be the result of their having received appropriate treatment or because they were depressed for a relatively short period. Overall, over 3% of the respondents were diagnosed as having had a GAD in the previous year. The rates for depressive disorder and GAD were similar to what had been found in other surveys.

Eurobarometer has occasionally asked questions about mental health and the most recent survey of mental health in the European Union (EU) is based on fieldwork carried out in February and March 2010 (European Commission, 2010). Twelve per cent of respondents in Ireland and 15% of respondents across the EU reported that they had sought professional help with a psychological or emotional problem in the previous 12 months. Six per cent of people in Ireland reported that they had taken anti-depressants in the previous 12 months, which is the same as the EU average in the survey. Respondents were also asked whether they had accomplished less than they would have liked in the previous four weeks because of an emotional problem such as depression or anxiety. Almost two-thirds of the Irish respondents said this had never been the case, while just over half of the EU respondents said so. Thus, Irish people seem less inclined to think that whatever emotional problems they might be experiencing have an impact on their ability to achieve their potential in day-to-day activities.

Expenditure on psychiatric services

Reliable data on admissions to all psychiatric hospitals are available since 1965. The data shows that the admission rate increased from 535 per 100,000 of total population in 1965 to 928.8 per 100,000 in 1981. Since then it has fallen steadily and was equal to 413.9 per 100,000 in 2011. The actual number of admissions was 15,440 in 1965, 29,392 in 1986 and 18,992 in 2011. The decline in admissions since 2005 is in line with the long-standing policy objective of treating more people in primary and community care, rather than in hospitals. Cross-country comparisons in this area are challenging, due to different definitions and reporting requirements. Nevertheless, data supplied to the World Health Organization suggests that Ireland has one of the lowest admission rates in the EU. For example, the admission rate per 100,000 was 968.6 in Belgium, 836.4 in Denmark and 778.4 in Austria.

As well as the data on admissions and length of stay, an annual census of the people in psychiatric units and hospitals on a particular day is collected by the HRB and the Mental Health Commission. The move away from hospitalisation is very clear from this data. There were over 19,000 people in psychiatric hospitals in 1963, over 10,000 in 1987 but fewer than 3,000 in the most recent census of mental hospitals, in 2010. From an economic perspective the number of in-patient days is of particular interest, as it is generally the most expensive type of care. Since 2005 the total number of in-patient days has declined from 603,599 to 484,879. The percentage of these days accounted for by public psychiatric hospitals has fallen from 36% to 23% in the same period. This decline is scheduled to continue in the next few years as more of the public psychiatric hospitals are scheduled to close. The decline in the number of psychiatric beds per 100,000 population in Ireland between 1991 and 2011 was the largest in the OECD and Ireland is now just below the OECD average on this indicator (OECD, 2013b).

There is considerable confusion about the level of expenditure on mental health in Ireland and there are still significant gaps in what is known about how much is spent on mental health services by the government in Ireland. Even less is known about how spending is allocated to different services within the overall budget and about how much is spent by private individuals on mental health services. Nevertheless, some progress has been made in collecting consistent financial data in recent years. The 2012 budget included a special allocation to improve the collection of mental health expenditure data and, hopefully, that allocation will bear fruit in the not too distant future. The 2012 edition of the *Revised Estimates* for the Health Services Executive contains information on the out-turn for 2011, as set out in Table 10.1.

The figure of €712 million reported in Table 10.1 is significantly lower than had been published the previous year, when the estimated expenditure for 2011 was €920 million. The explanation for the discrepancy is that the 2012 figures were restated in line with the HSE's National Service Plan. Central costs such as pension costs that had been formerly apportioned to care programmes were instead apportioned to a corporate heading. A similar problem arose in 2005 and 2006. The *Health in Ireland: Key Trends 2007* document reported that mental health expenditure in 2006 was €825 million,

Table 10.1 Mental health expenditure, 2011

	Provisional out-turn for 2011 (€m)
Long-stay residential care	413
Community services	195
Psychiatry of later life	7
Counselling services	14
Other mental health services	83
Total mental health	712

Source: Department of Public Expenditure and Reform (2012).

while the *Health in Ireland: Key Trends 2009* document reported it to be €984 million (Department of Health and Children, 2007; 2009). Thus, it is impossible to create a long time series of the most basic number of interest to researchers and policy analysts – the amount spent by the government on mental health.

Consistent figures for public spending on mental health are available in the HSE National Service Plans for the past few years. The data show that expenditure has declined from €787 million in 2009 to €711 million in 2012, although the latter figure may be revised later. The more accurate figures for recent years represent progress and are a welcome development. They seem to be generally accepted as being an accurate estimate of the amount of money spent on certain mental health services.

There are a number of difficulties with focusing too much attention on the proportion of the health budget spent by the government on mental health care. First of all, as the data in Table 10.1 indicate, the amount spent on the mental health programme is itself subject to arbitrary change. In 2009, for example, it makes a significant difference if one uses €1,007 million (the figure available from *Health in Ireland: Key Trends 2010*) or €787 million (the figure available in the HSE National Service Plan) in the numerator of the ratio. If the difference in the two numbers for 2009 and subsequent years is due to issues such as pension costs, it is important to note that no adjustment seems to have been made to the denominator (total public health spending) to account for such matters. The question of where occupational public sector pensions should be included in government expenditure is a broader one. There is a case for taking all such expenditures across the public sector and including them as a separate item.

Second, the amount spent in the mental health programme does not include a few large items of expenditure on mental health – such as prescription charges for medication for mental illnesses and medical services provided to people with mental health problems by GPs that are paid by the government – although expenditure on these items by the State is included in the denominator of the ratio. A third difficulty concerns the correct number for the denominator when calculating these ratios. In recent years there has been a very large increase in appropriations-in-aid which are included in the HSE Gross Public Health spending total, but are excluded from the net total (in 2010, for example, the difference was over €3.5 billion). Finally, the significant role played by the private sector in mental health care in Ireland makes it particularly important that international comparisons are treated very carefully.

To get a more accurate estimate of the total spent by the government on mental health we need to adjust for various items that are excluded. To this end, I have calculated that expenditure by the government on medication for mental health problems was approximately €204 million in 2010.[1] Expenditure by the State on medication for mental health problems increased almost five-fold between 1998 and 2008 and has declined by about 8% since then.

Another significant item not included is the amount spent on services provided by GPs for people with mental illnesses. Little is known about the proportion of GP consultations that are related to mental health issues. The HRB survey of mental health in the Republic of Ireland found that 10% of respondents in the Republic of Ireland had attended a GP for mental health problems. This was a survey of the general population and about 40% of the general population have access to the General Medical Scheme. Based on this, I estimated that 15% of the cost of GP visits under the General Medical Scheme could be attributed to mental illnesses. In 2010, the total amount paid to doctors in the GMS was €493.83 million, and 15% of this is €74.07 million. Combining this figure with the estimate of the amount spent on medications would add €278 million to the amount spent by the government on mental health in 2010, an increase of over 38%.

The spatial distribution of resources for mental care is another topic that has been analysed in recent years. *A Vision for Change* recommended that extra funding be provided for areas that exhibit social and economic disadvantage with associated high prevalence of mental health problems. A systematic attempt to examine how the allocation of health care resources across geographic areas would be affected in a new resource allocation model was carried out by Staines and colleagues in a report commissioned by the HRB and the HSE. Staines *et al.* (2010a) noted that it was difficult to ascertain exactly how resources are allocated between care groups at LHO (local health office) level and that budgets did not reflect service provision to the population at LHO level. They proposed a resource allocation model in which resource allocation in Primary Continuing and Community Care (which includes mental health) would be driven by LHO population and weighted by age and gender-specific estimated need. These allocations should be further refined using LHO data on deprivation and health care utilisation (Staines *et al.*, 2010b). The difference between the current allocations and the proposed allocations are very large for some LHOs, as illustrated in Table 10.2.

It is clear from these examples that current levels of funding are not necessarily related to need or demand and that some areas with high funding maintain high levels of institutional care with less than fully developed community-based alternatives. Previous research by O'Keane *et al.* (2005) also found that there was no clear relationship between financial allocation and the provision of clinical services. They concluded that money allocated to mental health was probably being side-tracked to other areas in the health service, an issue that has continued to occur in recent years.

A Vision for Change also argued that catchment boundaries should be realigned in order to reflect the current social and demographic composition

Table 10.2 Mental health care per capita allocation, 2007 (€m)

Local health office	Actual expenditure	Expenditure under proposed model	Variation
Dublin North Central	420.1	188.2	−231.9
Galway	271.1	70.1	−100
Longford/Westmeath	285	182	−103
Meath	31.7	148	116
North Cork	285.4	183.9	−101.5
North Tipperary/East Limerick	28.7	166	137.3
Sligo/Leitrim/West Cavan	304.3	192.7	−111.6
West Cork	54.8	193.4	138.6

Source: Brick et al. (2010) based on Staines et al. (2010b).

Table 10.3 HSE mental health budget by super catchment area, 2010 (€)

Super catchment area	Per capita budget
Limerick, Clare, North Tipperary	166
Donegal, Sligo, Leitrim, West Cavan	218.2
Galway, Mayo, Roscommon	299.7
North Lee, North Cork	221.4
South Lee, West Cork, Kerry	132.7
Wexford, Waterford	145
Carlow, Kilkenny, South Tipperary	267.6
North Dublin	139.6
Louth, Meath, Cavan, Monaghan	127
North West Dublin, Dublin North Central	225
Dun Laoighre, Dublin South East, Wicklow	147.4
Dublin West, Dublin South West, Dublin South City	129.5
Laois, Offaly, Longford, Westmeath, Kildare, West Wicklow	132.5

Source: HSE.

of the population. There is some evidence that this is underway, as shown in a recent report that obtained information from the HSE on how the mental health budget was allocated to what are called super catchment areas in 2010 (Table 10.3). Even though these areas are much larger in terms of population than the LHO areas used in the Staines et al. (2010a, 2010b) analysis, there is still a large difference of over 100% between the lowest and highest per capita allocation. Caution should be exercised in interpreting these figures, as the HSE has 11 separate accounting systems that encompass approximately 12,000 individual cost centres and the accounting systems are not always consistent with each other.

The Irish mental health system in a comparative context

Since the early 2000s, a number of attempts have been made to compare mental health systems from economics and health services perspectives (Knapp *et al.*, 2007; Lauriks *et al.*, 2012; WHO, 2011). These research efforts have been greatly hampered by substantial gaps in basic data on mental health outcomes and expenditure. Indeed, many of the research projects in this area have themselves focused on the collection of comparable cross-country data (Knapp *et al.*, 2009).

Much attention in the media and policy debates is given to the issue of what proportion of the public health budget is spent on mental health programmes. This proportion is often used to make cross-country comparisons. The WHO has published a series of country briefs that include data on the proportion of the health budget spent on mental health for 2011. Ireland is one of several countries for which the proportion is listed as 'not available'. For countries that do report this data the proportion varies from between 10% and 13% in the Netherlands, Germany and France to less than 6% in Portugal, Spain and Finland (where it is only 3.9%). Assuming that the 2011 figures for mental health expenditure in the *Revised Estimates* publication are correct, the corresponding ratio for Ireland is around 5%.

The situation is even more difficult as regards outcome indicators. Lauriks *et al.* (2012) provide a systematic review identifying 1,480 unique performance indicators that are used internationally to measure the performance of public mental health care. They find that fewer than 3% of performance indicators actually assess the efficiency, cost or expenditure of mental health care systems. Most countries which collect data on mental health quality and performance tend to focus on hospital care and measures of utilisation. There is also a wide variation between countries as regards the indicators which are collected. This makes international comparative work more difficult. Other factors that make efficiency and performance measurement very challenging in mental health care include the difficulties in measuring outputs and outcomes, the complex nature of mental health care, interactions with non-health sectors and the seriously marginalising social consequences of mental ill health, which may impact on measurement (Moran and Jacobs, 2013).

Since 2010 international organisations such as the EU, the WHO and the OECD have supported a number of initiatives to develop a better evidence base for comparative analysis in mental health care. The 2013 *Health at a Glance* survey from the OECD (2013a) included more indicators of mental health than previous editions had. The OECD Mental Health Expert Group will publish a major comparative report on mental health care performance and expenditure in 2014 and we can expect further progress in comparative mental health care analysis in the near future.

The cost of mental illness

The amount spent on mental health care by the government represents just one part of the total economic cost associated with mental illness. The primary aim of cost-of-illness studies is to draw attention to the economic burden of a particular illness or condition, where economic burden refers to the value of all resources used in the prevention, diagnosis and treatment of that condition, as well as the productivity and welfare losses incurred as a result of the condition. While insufficient as a basis for resource allocation (for which information about the effectiveness, and possibly the value, of an intervention are also needed), appropriate estimates of the cost of illness is an important part of health economics and policy analysis (Chisholm *et al.*, 2010). Poor mental health imposes a variety of consequences on individuals, families and caregivers, and society. The most important consequence is the pain (physical, emotional, mental and existential) experienced by individuals whose mental health is poor. Other consequences include the effects on physical health, personal relationships, access to employment and housing, ability to participate in society and a higher risk of being imprisoned. In addition, the vast majority of families and caregivers devote considerable amounts of time and resources to helping loved ones cope with the effects of mental health problems. Finally, the wider society provides health and other services to people with mental health problems.

O'Shea and Kennelly (2008) calculated the total economic cost of mental illness in Ireland to be over €3 billion in 2006. Most of the costs were associated with lost productivity, as can be seen in Table 10.4. These figures do not include any estimate of the human cost of mental illness. The figures were based on a series of assumptions regarding the prevalence of mental illness, the effect of mental illness on one's ability to work, the effect of mental illness on carers, the effect of mental illness on one's ability to do unpaid work, and, finally, and crucially, unit costs of various mental health care services. The authors noted the need for more reliable data in all of these areas. In particular, a comprehensive psychiatry morbidity study could give us a much better idea

Table 10.4 Overall distribution of the cost of mental health problems in Ireland, 2006

Category	Cost (€ million)	%
Health and social care	716.8	23.8
Other direct care	286.8	9.5
Lost output	2,002.9	66.7
Total	3,006.5	100

Source: O'Shea and Kennelly (2008).

of the impact that mental health problems have on employment, hours worked (paid and unpaid) and wages earned.

A complementary approach is to conduct illness-specific cost-of-illness studies. For example, Behan *et al.* (2008) calculated the economic cost associated with schizophrenia in Ireland. They estimated that the overall cost was over €460 million in 2006. About a quarter of these costs were direct health care costs, with most of the remainder being due to lost output due to illness or premature mortality. While the data on the prevalence of schizophrenia underlying the study are likely to be more reliable than the prevalence data in the O'Shea and Kennelly (2008) study (which covered all mental illnesses), data problems were still a major problem for Behan *et al.* (2008), who noted the lack of comprehensive data on community-based services, as well as reliable unit cost data.

Economic evaluation of mental health services in Ireland

The high costs associated with mental illnesses, allied to the fact that choices have to be made on how scarce resources are allocated, have led many people to argue in favour of the use of cost-effectiveness and cost-benefit analysis to guide policy decisions regarding the allocation of resources for the treatment and support of people with mental health problems. This section reviews the available evidence on economic evaluations of specific mental health services in Ireland. Unfortunately, the evidence is very limited, as very few studies exist that combine accurate economic data and reliable data on mental health outcomes. While there are particular difficulties in conducting good economic evaluations in the mental health area, the main reasons for the lack of available studies are the absence of reliable information such as data on unit costs in mental health and the failure to incorporate adequate information systems when new interventions in the mental health area are introduced.

There is growing concern about the increase in the cost of some treatments for mental health problems. Some of the newer treatments for severe forms of depression and schizophrenia are very expensive. Not surprisingly, many people feel that there is a pressing need to determine whether the newer treatments are cost-effective. The potential use of cost-effectiveness analysis is not confined to new treatments. It is relevant for all aspects of resource allocation in mental health care, particularly in relation to the balance of care decision making along the continuum of care. The economic impacts of mental health problems are wide ranging and in many cases long lasting, given the chronic nature of many mental health problems. These impacts will be felt not only by service users, but also by their families and wider society.

Two examples of economic evaluation of mental health interventions in Ireland were published in 2012. Gibbons *et al.* (2012) examined whether changing to a community-based model of service delivery in the Kildare/West Wicklow catchment area would be more or less cost-effective than the traditional model, which was oriented towards in-patient care. The catchment area is divided into five sub-areas, each with its own mental health team. Two of the areas that were thought to rely on different models of care were selected for comparison. The North East sector follows a comprehensive community model with access to a day centre, a day hospital and a home care team, as well as access to a full range of relevant professional disciplines. The Mid East sector at the time of the study (2008) relied far more on a traditional service model that placed a strong reliance on in-patient care. Data on clinical activity levels and costs were collected for both areas, as well as some evidence on the satisfaction of service users and family members with the services in the respective areas.

Gibbons *et al.* (2012) found that the quality of care provided in the comprehensive community model was superior to the traditional model, based on a number of indicators. For example, waiting times for assessments were considerably lower in the community model and the admission rate and length of stay for in-patient care were much lower in the community model. In addition, service users and their families expressed higher levels of satisfaction with the care in the community model. On the cost side, the cost of the traditional model was 27% higher on a per capita basis than the community model.

A second recent example of an economic evaluation in the mental health area concerned the Suicide Crisis Awareness Nurse (SCAN) service that was introduced in two catchment areas – Cluain Mhuire in Dublin and Wexford (HSE, 2012). The SCAN service is a community-based referral service which provides GPs with an option of specialised nurse-led care when a person presents to the GP clinic exhibiting behaviour symptomatic of suicidal risk. While those deemed at immediate high risk are typically referred directly to in-patient psychiatric hospital services as well as to SCAN, those deemed at lower risk are typically referred initially to the SCAN service. This process involves a referral for an immediate consultation with a specialised nurse, who then determines the next stage of the patient's treatment process. This may involve referral for further care in primary care, community care, hospital out-patient care or in-patient hospital care. The SCAN nurse also facilitates the patient's adherence to their assigned method of care.

The economic analysis focused on comparing the health care costs associated with the SCAN service with an estimate of what these costs would have been had the SCAN service not been in place. The key variable in the analysis was the effect that the SCAN service had on reducing the number of people admitted to in-patient psychiatric care. HSE (2012) found plausible evidence in both Wexford and Cluain Mhuire that the decline in in-patient admissions since 2008 was related to the introduction of the SCAN service. The proportion of the reduction that could be ascribed to the SCAN service was harder to determine. Under reasonable assumptions about the size of the effect, HSE (2012) found that the SCAN service resulted in a reduction of health care costs. Given that survey evidence indicated a high level of satisfaction with the service among service users and providers, there was a high probability that the service was cost-effective.

Cost comparisons and simulations are useful techniques for evaluating particular interventions. For a more reliable analysis of the effectiveness of an intervention, economists would also like to have an estimate of the value of an intervention. Many health services are generally provided by the state, so economists have turned to non-market techniques to estimate the value of interventions. One of these techniques is contingent valuation, and O'Shea et al. (2008) used this technique to elicit preferences for mental health care in Ireland. The intervention that people were asked to consider was one that would have enabled 200 more people with mental illness to be treated in the community rather than in hospitals. The study also asked people about their willingness to pay for, and ranking of, similar interventions in care of the elderly and in cancer care. This was done so that individuals were more likely to think about opportunity costs and scarcity when giving their responses to the questions on a particular intervention.

O'Shea et al. (2008) found that the cancer care programme was generally ranked as more important than the elderly care programme, which was in turn regarded as more important than the mental health care programme. This was true both for people who had personal or close family experience of mental health care and for people who considered themselves at higher risk of needing mental health care services. Given these rankings, it is not surprising that the median willingness-to-pay (WTP) value for the mental health programme was significantly less than for both of the other programmes. One plausible explanation is that the selfish motive for contributing to programmes is stronger for cancer and elderly care than for mental health care. Almost 50% of respondents cited personal reasons when asked why they were willing to contribute to the cancer and elderly care programmes. The corresponding proportion citing these reasons for mental health care valuations was only 33%. Respondents seemed to be motivated more by altruistic reasons when it came to mental health care interventions. Individuals may also have been sceptical that the proposed intervention in mental health would work as outlined in the survey. While health professionals are keen to stress that recovery is possible for mental illness and that effective treatments are available, the general public may be more circumspect in their views of the effectiveness of health care programmes.

The contingent valuation technique continues to be the subject of lively and sometimes acrimonious debate in economics generally (Kling *et al.*, 2012) and in health economics in particular (Baker *et al.*, 2010; Smith and Sach, 2010). One cannot rule out the possibility that the findings in the survey on mental health care in Ireland were affected by general methodological problems associated with using WTP to elicit preferences, despite adherence to best practice in the questionnaire and survey design. Moreover, respondents used to dealing with health care provision in a non-market environment in Ireland may not be able to think about changes to specific health care programmes in a very direct financial way. Consequently, they may be incapable of giving a differentiated response to the question of value.

Conclusions

In some respects the decade since 2004 has seen mental health become more important in global health policy agendas. In May 2012, the World Health Assembly of the WHO adopted a resolution on the global burden of mental disorders and the need for a comprehensive, coordinated response from health and social sectors at the country level. Following this, the WHO has drafted a comprehensive mental health action plan which is currently available as a draft document for consultation and is likely to be ratified at the next World Health Assembly. In Ireland, the publication of *A Vision for Change* marked a significant change in the importance attached to mental health issues in this country.

However, actions, or at least expenditure, speak louder than words and mental health generally did not experience the same kind of increase in expenditure as other health problems during the economic boom of the early 2000s. Total non-capital expenditure on health increased by approximately 173% in nominal terms between 2000 and 2008, as compared to an increase of less than 100% in expenditure on mental health in the same period. The relatively slow progress in implementing many of the recommendations outlined in *A Vision for Change* was particularly unfortunate because, by the end of 2008, it was clear that Ireland was slipping into a serious recession and it has been a major challenge for policymakers in the HSE to simply maintain the current level of mental health services in recent years.

Researchers and policy analysts continue to face major problems in analysing mental health policy and economics. There is no consistent database that brings together economic and social information on mental health. Data on national prevalence rates are limited. Unit cost data are not systematically collected, making it difficult to examine the relative costs of various programmes. Similarly, we know practically nothing about the consequences for Irish society and the economy in relation to the impact that mental health problems can have on many aspects of life, including physical health, family relationships, social networks, employment status, earnings and broader economic status. We also know little about the direct impact that stigma and discrimination have on the lives of people with mental health problems and on their families.

The case for continued investment in mental health remains a strong one, even if the economic analysis underlying that argument is constrained by these information gaps. The reasons that policymakers should invest more in mental health are that the economic cost of poor mental health in Ireland is significant and there is good evidence from outside Ireland, and some evidence from within, that particular interventions have a positive effect on the quality of life of people with mental health problems. In addition, the contingent valuation study in O'Shea *et al.* (2008) found that the Irish public was willing to pay extra taxes for a mental health programme that would enable more people to live in the community, although whether this is still the case in the midst of the current recession is another matter.

One of the problems is that many people have little knowledge about mental health problems, which leads to negative attitudes forming which affect judgements on resource allocation and prioritisation, especially when people are asked to compare mental health problems against more recognisable and socially acceptable illnesses and conditions, such as cancer. Thornicroft (2006) notes that there is no country, society or culture in which people with mental health problems are valued the same as people without mental health problems. This leads to people underestimating their own or their families' use of mental health care services and undervaluing interventions designed to improve care and conditions for people with mental health problems.

Increasing expenditure on mental health care is a necessary but not sufficient condition for realising the potential of people with mental health problems. Expenditure needs to be increased but money needs to be spent wisely. Information is the key to a more efficient and equitable allocation of resources. A community-based analysis of need, linked to local and national psychiatric morbidity studies, should be the first step in setting up new resource allocation structures. A national morbidity survey every five years is necessary to determine the prevalence of mental health problems in the population. We must also generate comprehensive, annual information on existing services by catchment area, including information on unit costs. This would tell us where the gaps are, thereby ensuring greater degrees of equity in the allocation of resources. We already have much of the population-based data on demography, and deprivation could be used to supplement the information on prevalence. Performance indicators should be used to ensure compatibility between need and service delivery, once such information becomes available.

Note

1 Details on how this number was estimated are available upon request.

References

Baker R., Currie G., Donaldson C. (2010) What needs to be done in contingent valuation: Have Smith and Sach missed the boat? *Health Economics, Policy and Law* 5, 113–21.

Barry M.M., Van Lente E., Molcho M., Morgan K., McGee H., Conroy R.M., Watson D., Shelley E., Perry I. (2009) *SLÁN 2007: Survey of Lifestyle, Attitudes and Nutrition in Ireland. Mental Health and Social Well-being Report*, Department of Health and Children, Dublin: The Stationery Office.

Behan C., Kennelly B., O'Callaghan E. (2008) The economic cost of schizophrenia in Ireland: A cost-of-illness study, *Irish Journal of Psychological Medicine* 25, 80–7.

Chisholm D., Stanciole A., Tan Torres Edejer T., Evas D.B. (2010) Economic impact of disease and injury: Counting what matters, *British Medical Journal* 340, 583–6.

Department of Health and Children (2006) *A Vision for Change: Report of the Expert Group on Mental Health Policy*, Dublin: Department of Health and Children.

Department of Health and Children (2007) *Health in Ireland: Key Trends 2007*, Dublin: Department of Health and Children.

Department of Health and Children (2009) *Health in Ireland: Key Trends 2009*, Dublin: Department of Health and Children.

Department of Health and Children (2010) *Health in Ireland: Key Trends 2010*, Dublin: Department of Health and Children.

Department of Public Expenditure and Reform (2012) *Revised Estimates for Public Services 2012*, Dublin: Government Publications Office.

European Commission (2010) *Eurobarometer 73.2 Results for Ireland*, Brussels: European Commission.

Gibbons P., Lee A., Parkes, J., Meaney E. (2012) *Value for Money: A Comparison of Costs and Quality in Two Models of Adult Mental Health Service Provision*, Dublin: Health Service Executive.

HSE (Health Service Executive) (2012) *Research Evaluation of the Suicide Crisis Assessment Nurse (SCAN) Service*, Dublin: Health Service Executive.

Kling C., Phaneuf D., Zhao J. (2012) From Exxon to BP: Has some number become better than no number? *Journal of Economic Perspectives* 26, 3–26.

Knapp M., McDaid D., Medeiros H. (2009) Balance of care (deinstitutionalisation in Europe): results from the Mental Health Economics European Network (MHEEN), *International Journal of Integrated Care* 9: 1–10.

Knapp M., McDaid D., Mossialos E., Thornicroft G. (2007) *Mental Health Policy and Practice Across Europe*, Maidenhead, Berkshire: Open University Press.

Lauriks S., Buster M., de Wit M., Arah O.A., Klazinga N.S. (2012) Performance indicators for public mental healthcare: A systematic international inventory, *BMC Public Health* 12, 214.

Moran V., Jacobs R. (2013) An international comparison of efficiency of inpatient mental health care systems, *Health Policy* 112, 88–99.

OECD (Organisation for Economic Co-operation and Development) (2013a) *Health at a Glance 2013: OECD Indicators*, Paris: OECD Publishing, http://dx.doi.org/10.1787/health_glance-2013-en.

OECD (2013b) *OECD Health Data 2013*, accessed at www.oecd.org/els/health-systems/oecdhealthdata.htm, 3 December 2013.

O'Keane V., Walsh D., Barry S. (2005) *The Black Hole*, Dublin: Irish Psychiatric Association.

O'Shea E., Gannon B., Kennelly B. (2008) Eliciting preferences for resource allocation in mental health care in Ireland, *Health Policy* 88, 359–70.

O'Shea E., Kennelly B. (2008) *The Economics of Mental Health Care in Ireland*, Dublin: Mental Health Commission.

Smith R., Sach T. (2010) Contingent valuation: What needs to be done? *Health Economics, Policy and Law* 5, 91–111.

Staines A., Vega A., O'Shea S., Murrin C. (2010a) *Towards the Development of a Resource Allocation Model for Primary, Continuing and Community Care in the Health Services, Volume 1*, Dublin: Health Research Board.

Staines A., Vega A., O'Shea S., Murrin C. (2010b) *Towards the Development of a Resource Allocation Model for Primary, Continuing and Community Care in the Health Services, Volume 2*, Dublin: Health Research Board.

Tedstone Doherty D., Moran R. (2009) Mental health and associated health service use on the island of Ireland, Health Research Board Research Series 7, Dublin: Health Research Board.

Tedstone Doherty D., Moran R., Kartalova O'Doherty Y. (2007) Psychological distress, mental health problems and use of health services in Ireland, Health Research Board Research Series 5, Dublin: Health Research Board.

Thornicroft G. (2006) *Shunned: Discrimination against People with Mental Illness*, Oxford: Oxford University Press.

WHO (World Health Organisation) (2011) *Mental Health Atlas 2011*, Geneva: World Health Organisation

11

The socioeconomic determinants of mental stress

David Madden

Introduction

This chapter reviews the socioeconomic determinants of mental stress in Ireland. As the title suggests, the focus of the chapter will principally be on those socioeconomic factors which are most closely associated with mental stress, and so the papers reviewed will mainly be from the economics literature. It is also the case that we will take a broad interpretation of mental stress, including in our analysis not just studies of stress, but also other related conditions such as mental illness and suicide. We will also cover socioeconomic determinants of what could be regarded as the complement of mental stress, i.e. subjective well-being.

What evidence exists for Ireland indicates that a link between mental illness and socioeconomic factors has been observed since the 18th and 19th centuries (see Walsh and Daly, 2004). The phenomenon of 'pauper lunacy' was well established in the 19th century and the development of the asylum system was seen in conjunction with the development of indoor poor relief. Walsh and Daly (2004) point out that for much of the 19th century the asylum system was essentially viewed as an element of poor relief and it was not until the end of the century that lay managers were replaced by physicians. This link between poverty and mental illness was echoed by the situation with respect to Irish emigrants in Massachusetts in the mid 19th century, where the links between poverty, intemperance and lunacy were noted. The poverty–mental illness relationship is also reflected in the fact that as the Irish immigrant population in the United States assimilated and gained in prosperity, their rates of hospitalisation for mental illness diminished and they were replaced by newer immigrant groups. To a certain extent this phenomenon was also mirrored in the United Kingdom.

The subsequent sections examine the relationship between social and economic conditions and mental stress (broadly defined) for the more modern era and distinguish between two types of study: cross-section and time-series. Cross-section studies are based on individual-level data and examine, for any given point in time, the degree to which we observe an association between the incidence of mental stress and individual-level socioeconomic factors, such as age, gender, principal economic status (PES), education and income. Time-series studies, on the other hand, look at aggregate historical data for factors such as suicide or hospital admissions and examine the degree to which we observe over time an association between these measures and macroeconomic aggregates such as GDP growth, unemployment, inflation etc.

It is crucial to note that for both types of data it is often the case that the best we can hope for is to observe a degree of association, rather than a direct causal effect. There may be issues with simultaneity (e.g. not having a job contributes to mental stress, but being stressed may also reduce your chances of finding work) and/or unobserved factors. These unobserved factors may simultaneously affect both mental stress and various observed socioeconomic factors, thus producing a correlation in the absence of a causal effect. However, it is also important not to be too pessimistic in this regard. In some cases causality is much more plausible in one direction than in another. In other cases panel data (a combination of time-series and cross-section data) may be available, allowing for more rigorous modelling of causality.

Cross-section studies

We start off by reviewing cross-section studies. As mentioned in the introduction, and as is typical in much of the economics-based literature in this area, we adopt a fairly broad definition of mental stress. We also review studies which examine the cross-section determinants of subjective well-being, as we can regard this as being in some sense the complement of mental stress.

As outlined above, cross-section studies rely upon the availability of nationally representative individual-level datasets that include information on whatever measure of mental stress (or well-being) is in question and also on a variety of individual characteristics such as age, gender, education, income, principal economic status etc. In general, such datasets in Ireland were few and far between before the late 1980s, so this to some degree limits our review. One of the earliest of such studies was that of Whelan (1992), who examined the role of income and life-style deprivation as mediating factors in terms of the impact of unemployment upon psychological stress. Thus, unemployment can affect psychological stress both directly and indirectly via its impact upon poverty and deprivation. Whelan (1992) used the 1987 Survey of Poverty, Income Distribution and Usage of State Services carried out by the Economic and Social Research Institute (ESRI). This was a nationally representative sample of 6,764 individuals. The measure of psychological distress employed was the 12-item version of the General Health Questionnaire (GHQ) developed by Goldberg (1972). As we will encounter this measure a number of times in this review it is worth providing some background.

The GHQ is one of the most commonly employed measures of mental health. The original development of the measure involved a 60-item version (GHQ-60) with the 'best' 30, 20 and 12 of these items being identified for use when the respondent's time was at a premium (giving rise to the GHQ-30, GHQ-20 and GHQ-12 measures, respectively). Items in the GHQ consist of questions asking whether the respondent has recently experienced a particular symptom or item of behaviour, rated on a 4-point scale. For example, a respondent might be asked the question 'have you recently been feeling reasonably happy, all things considered?' The respondent then answers from one of the following four categories: more so than usual, same as usual, less than usual, or much less than usual. The responses are aggregated together to provide the GHQ 'score' and this score can be used as a predictor of an individual being a psychiatric case, as it is highly correlated with results from standardised clinical interviews.

The Whelan (1992) paper concentrates on the impact of unemployment on GHQ score, but crucially also allows for mediating effects via income, financial strain and deprivation (where deprivation is defined via the absence of a number of key goods and life-style factors). His paper shows that the inclusion of these measures reduces the point estimate of the effect of unemployment (on GHQ score) by about a third, with no independent effect for income. An interesting feature of the paper is that he also examines the effect of husband's unemployment on the GHQ score of married women. In this case, the effect operates solely via deprivation and financial strain with no independent effect of its own. The contribution of Whelan's paper is to show that unemployment affects mental stress via a number of channels, including deprivation, financial strain and self-esteem.

Hannan *et al.* (1997) also looked at the relationship between unemployment and psychological distress, in particular concentrating on young people. They used two nationally representative samples, the School Leavers' Survey of 1987 (which interviewed people who left school in 1982) and the 1987 ESRI survey referred to above. Once again, their measure of stress was the GHQ-12. Their cross-tabulations showed that greater stress scores were associated with unemployment amongst young people, but also that, for the young, there did not seem to be a clear relationship between their social class and stress (although there did appear to be some link between stress and their parents' social class). However, when their sample was partitioned into employed and unemployed, a class difference was observed, with higher stress levels amongst those whose father was listed as manual as opposed to non-manual class. Overall, the results here confirm the link between unemployment and stress for young people, but suggest that the relationships are not as strong or clear cut as for older people.

One factor which is worth noting is that the Whelan (1992) and Hannan *et al.* (1997) papers were both analysing data from the 1980s, a time when macroeconomic conditions in Ireland were poor. While we will specifically review evidence concerning the impact of macroeconomic conditions on various indicators of stress in the next section, it is possible that at an individual level the impact of factors such as employment might differ according to the overall macroeconomic background. The remaining individual-level papers that we review all deal with Irish data from the latter part of the 1990s and the first years of the 21st century, a time when macroeconomic conditions were very different.

Continuing with those papers which use the GHQ as a measure of mental stress we review a trio of papers by Madden (2009; 2010; 2011). These papers employed data from the Living in Ireland survey (LII), a survey which in many ways could be seen as the successor to the 1987 ESRI survey. One of the attractive features of the LII data is that it followed people over time and so permitted an addressing, to some degree at least, of both individual-level and time-series issues (although the Madden papers do not specifically exploit the panel nature of the data). Data for this survey were collected on an annual basis from 1994 to 2001 and for two of these papers Madden chose to concentrate on 1994 and 2000. This was partly motivated by the fact that a booster sample was added to the sample in 2000, so these two years were arguably the two years of the survey which suffered least from attrition. Since many accounts of Ireland's Celtic Tiger period date the start of this period as 1995, the choice of years in this paper effectively captured a 'before' and 'during' picture of mental stress in Ireland during an era of economic boom.

The first paper (Madden, 2009) addressed two issues: first of all, what happened to mental stress (as measured by the GHQ) over the 1994–2000 period, and second, what factors were associated with this change. The first of these questions was answered via a stochastic dominance approach which compared the cumulative distribution of GHQ scores for the two years in question and found that first-order stochastic dominance applied. What this essentially means is that for any comparison between 1994 and 2000, on the basis of an objective function whereby less stress is better than more stress, then 2000 dominated. Mental stress fell over the period, regardless of which GHQ score is regarded as the threshold for stress. The second question was addressed via a decomposition technique. The presence of psychological stress (based on a GHQ threshold) was modelled via a probit relationship, with various individual characteristics as explanatory variables. It was then possible to account for part of the change in stress via changes in these characteristics over the 1994–2000 period, without necessarily assigning causality. The results showed that about one quarter of the fall in stress was accounted for by changes in the individual-level characteristics, with the greatest contribution coming from changes in labour force status, including both the fall in unemployment and the rise in employment (not necessarily the same phenomenon at a time of economic boom, when many 'secondary' workers enter the labour force).

In the second paper, Madden (2010) examined the phenomenon whereby women tend to report higher levels of mental stress than men. Using the same years of data and the same measure of mental stress, once again decomposition techniques were applied, this time to the difference in GHQ by gender. The decomposition was carried out for both years and the qualitative results were remarkably similar. Differences in characteristics explained about 65% of the difference in GHQ by gender and the principal contribution once again came from labour force status. Being at work was associated with lower mental stress, and a higher proportion of men were at work than women. Note, however, as explained above, that it is important to be aware of possible simultaneity, especially during a period of near full employment. Thus, being at work is associated with less mental stress, but it may also be the case that those with mental stress find it hardest to obtain a job.

The final paper in this sequence (Madden, 2011) differed from the first two papers in two respects: first, it looked at a variety of measures of well-being apart from just the GHQ, and second, it looked at the distribution of well-being as well as the level. Once again, data from the LII survey were used, as were relatively newly developed techniques specifically designed to deal with ordinal data (Abul Naga and Yalcin, 2008; Allison and Foster, 2004). This paper looked at well-being in a number of different areas (work, leisure, finance and housing), as well as self-assessed health and the GHQ. The results showed that the level of well-being improved in a number of areas (particularly finance and also, to a lesser extent, self-assessed health and mental stress) over the 1994–2001 period. It also showed that inequality in virtually all domains of life satisfaction fell over the period. Unlike the two papers cited above, however, this paper primarily was aimed at characterising the level and distribution of measures of well-being and stress over the period and it did not attempt to find any association with individual-level factors.

The measure of stress we have primarily concentrated upon so far has been the GHQ. It is also possible to analyse mental stress indirectly by looking at what we could loosely regard as the complement of stress, i.e. well-being. There has been a marked increase in the number of papers in economics which look at measures of subjective well-being (SWB) and their determinants (for reviews see Clark et al., 2008 and Stevenson and Wolfers, 2008)). Typically the measure of SWB is based upon answers to a question along the lines of 'taking all aspects of your life into consideration, which of these responses best describes your life as a whole?' Respondents are then given an ordinal categorical scale, where the lowest score counts as the worst possible outcome and the highest point as the best possible outcome. The responses thus obtained can then be used cardinally or ordinally (treating the data as cardinal does not seem to make much difference to the qualitative results). Examples of this in the Irish context are the papers by Brereton *et al.* (2008) and Moro *et al.* (2008).

The Brereton *et al.* (2008) paper continued the theme of looking at the impact of labour force status upon SWB but the innovation of their paper was the use of broader categories of labour force status, including such categories as part-time work etc. They used data from a nationally representative 2001 survey carried out by the Urban Institute of Ireland, with a sample size of about 1,500. The results confirmed again the negative impact of unemployment on SWB and also showed that part-time work can lower SWB, with this effect most prominent for males. Perhaps affected by the macroeconomic conditions in effect at the time of the survey, they found that the negative impact of unemployment on SWB did not apply to first-time job seekers. The Moro *et al.* (2008) paper used the same dataset as that employed by Brereton *et al.* (2008) and concentrated on how SWB measures can be used to construct 'quality of life' indices which take account of variables such as climatic and environmental factors. The paper contained results showing the impact of such variables on SWB and statistically significant effects were found for housing and climate, as well as the expected effects of labour force status.

We conclude our review of cross-section studies by looking at a paper which, once again, does not analyse mental stress per se but, rather, a phenomenon that can be associated with stress: suicide. Corcoran and Arensman (2010) examined suicide and undetermined death rates for different age, gender and employment groups using mortality data supplied by the Irish Central Statistics Office for the 1996–2006 period. Their focus was not on predicting suicide rates per se, but instead on trying to calculate different risk ratios in terms of suicide rates for different demographic groups. Their results once again showed an association with unemployment, with a higher risk ratio for females than males. Their results also showed that for males the effect was greater at times of low unemployment (2001–6), rather than a period when unemployment was falling (1996–2001). This may indicate that by the time full employment is reached, the remaining male unemployed consist of those at highest risk of stress and suicide. They concluded their study by warning that the effect of the economic downturn which began around 2007–8 might have an impact on suicide via increased unemployment. However, as we shall see in the next section, time-series studies which take account of the start of the most recent recession do not completely bear this out.

We now attempt to summarise the results of the cross-section literature on the socioeconomic determinants of mental stress, bearing in mind that we have used a broad set of possible indicators of mental stress and stress-related behaviour. It is also important to reiterate our earlier warnings that, with respect to individual-level studies, there are many unobserved variables which may impact upon stress, and also that what correlations are observed do not necessarily imply causation. Bearing that in mind, probably the most consistent theme arising from the papers cited above is the importance of labour market status, and particularly of being unemployed, to stress. The effect is noticeable at times both of high and of low unemployment and it is also important to note that unemployment can affect stress via a number of channels, such as poverty and deprivation and also self-esteem. Thus, the cross-section studies we have reviewed demonstrate the importance of unemployment at a given point in time. But what about trends over time in overall levels of stress and their relationship to macroeconomic conditions such as unemployment and inflation? To examine this we turn to time-series studies, which are the subject of the next section.

Time-series studies

There are relatively fewer time-series studies on the links between socio-economic factors and mental stress. This reflects the fact that in order to have sufficient observations to provide some statistical significance to findings, it is necessary to wait some time, particularly as data in this area are typically annual rather than quarterly or monthly. Related to this is the fact that each new year brings only one new observation and so papers in this area may be quite sparsely scattered through time as we wait for sufficient new observations to emerge.

Consequently, the first paper we review in this area is that of Lucey *et al.* (2005). They examined time-series data from 1968 to 2000 and looked at the link between male and female suicide rates and seven macro factors: GDP, the unemployment rate, the female labour force participation rate, expenditure on alcohol, the marriage rate, the percentage of births outside of marriage and the indictable crime rate. The data were differenced to account for common trending and the only variable which showed any statistically significant link was indictable crime (for female suicide). However, given that 21 coefficients were examined (three dependent variables and seven independent variables), then on purely statistical grounds alone it is not altogether surprising that only one significant variable was found. However, the authors note that it is possible that age-specific effects might exist, but their data did not permit them to analyse this.

This lack of a link between suicide and macroeconomic variables is also echoed to some degree in a study by Walsh and Walsh (2011). Their study covers the 1968–2009 period and they include only alcohol and the unemployment rate as explanatory variables, though unlike Lucey *et al.* (2005), they were able to examine age-specific suicide rates. From 1988 onwards they were also able to include age-specific unemployment rates. Rather than differencing the data, they include a linear time trend to take account of common trending. They find that their model works better for males than for females and also for younger people rather than for older people. They also find evidence of a structural shift in the relationship between suicide and unemployment after around 1988, with a much stronger relationship to be found, especially for young males. It is also interesting to note that for this demographic group they find a much stronger effect for alcohol use than for unemployment. For females there appears to be little effect of unemployment but some evidence of an alcohol effect, for younger women at least. The results of Walsh and Walsh (2011), in conjunction with those of Lucey et al. (2005), indicate that, where possible, it is vital to analyse age- and demographic-specific suicide rates (and, by extension, other indicators of mental stress). Their results also suggest that an economic recession could have a broadly neutral impact upon suicide, with the effect of rising unemployment offset by decreased alcohol consumption.

The final paper we review is by Walsh (2011) and returns to the use of SWB data, this time in a time-series context. The link between SWB and macroeconomic factors in time-series studies has been an area of controversy for a number of years. Perhaps the most famous finding in this area is the so-called 'Easterlin paradox' (Easterlin, 1974), which claimed that SWB is not higher in richer than in poorer countries at any given point in time, nor does it rise with increasing income over time. Subsequent studies by Stevenson and Wolfers (2008) have challenged this and to some extent the jury is still out on this question. Nevertheless, it is certainly fair to say that conclusive evidence at an aggregate time-series level of a link between GDP and SWB has not been found.

Walsh (2011) revisits this issue for Ireland, using SWB data from the Eurobarometer Survey over the 1975–2010 period, critically including some years' observations from the most recent recession. Respondents aged 18 and over were asked the question 'on the whole are you very satisfied, fairly satisfied, not very satisfied, or not at all satisfied with the life you lead?' and the responses were scored 3, 2, 1 and 0, respectively. He also analysed other measures of stress/well-being such as the rate of admissions to psychiatric hospitals and the birth rate. Walsh (2011) finds that unemployment affects SWB in the first part of this period (1975–93), but has no effect for the 1994–2010 period. It is interesting to note that this is quite a different pattern from that observed in the Walsh and Walsh (2011) study on suicide, indicating that while we have regarded measures such as suicide and SWB as broad correlates of stress, it is dangerous to automatically assume that such measures will always be in concordance. It is also worth noting that the year 2010 showed a sharp drop in the suicide rate, despite unemployment reaching a 20-year high.

In addition, Walsh (2011) finds no effect for inflation and a marginal effect for Gross National Income for the 1975–93 period (interestingly, before the Celtic Tiger boom years), but no effect in subsequent years. There also appears to be no relationship between admissions to psychiatric hospitals and macro-economic conditions. With respect to the birth rate (which could be interpreted as proxying for people's optimism about the future), the most recent recession has had only a marginal downward effect, in contrast to the much sharper reduction observed during the 1980s recession.

To summarise the results from the time-series studies, we have little evidence concerning direct measures of mental stress such as the GHQ, and consequently have looked at studies which have concentrated upon suicide rates and SWB. In this regard, there is still evidence of a link between unemployment and suicide, but the relationship is not clear cut. It appears to be found mostly amongst young males and also appeared to strengthen in the post-1993 period. However, the most recent observations (and it is surely too early to say that this represents another structural shift) seem to indicate a weakening of the relationship. Other macroeconomic factors appear to exert little influence upon suicide or SWB, with the exception of a link between alcohol consumption and suicide.

Conclusions

This chapter has reviewed evidence concerning the link between socioeconomic factors and mental stress. A number of possible indicators of mental stress were covered such as the GHQ score and also suicide and SWB. A clear distinction between individual-based cross-section studies and more aggregate time-series studies was drawn. Probably the clearest message to emerge was the link between unemployment and stress. This was clearly evident in both the cross-section and the time series studies, although with respect to the latter studies the relationship does appear to shift over time. Consistent with the Easterlin paradox, the impact of other macroeconomic factors appears to be marginal, but the link between alcohol consumption and suicide does appear to be quite robust.

References

Abul Naga R., Yalcin T. (2008) Inequality measurement for ordered response health data, *Journal of Health Economics* 27, 1614–25.

Allison R.A., Foster J. (2004) Measuring health inequality using qualitative data, *Journal of Health Economics* 23, 505–24.

Brereton F., Clinch P., Ferreira S. (2008) Employment and life satisfaction: Insights from Ireland, *Economic and Social Review* 39, 207–34.

Clark A., Frijters P., Shields M. (2008) Relative income, happiness and utility: An explanation for the Easterlin paradox and other puzzles, *Journal of Economic Literature* 46, 95–144.

Corcoran P., Arensman E. (2010) Suicide and employment status during Ireland's Celtic Tiger economy, *European Journal of Public Heath* 21, 209–14.

Easterlin R. (1974) Does economic growth improve the human lot? In David P.A., Reder M.W. (Eds) *Nations and Households in Economic Growth: Essays in Honor of Moses Abramovitz*, New York: Academic Press.

Goldberg D. (1972) *The Detection of Psychiatric Illness by Questionnaire*, London: Oxford University Press.

Hannan D., O'Riain S., Whelan C. (1997) Youth unemployment and psychological distress in the Republic of Ireland, *Adolescence* 20, 307–20.

Lucey S., Corcoran P., Keeley H., Brophy J., Arensman E., Perry I.J. (2005) Socioeconomic change and suicide: A time-series study from the Republic of Ireland, *Crisis* 25, 90–4.

Madden D. (2009) Mental stress in Ireland, 1994–2000: A stochastic dominance approach, *Health Economics* 18, 1202–17.

Madden D. (2010) Gender difference in mental well-being: A decomposition analysis, *Social Indicators Research* 99, 101–14.

Madden D. (2011) The impact of an economic boom on the level and distribution of well-being: Ireland 1994–2001, *Journal of Happiness Studies* 12, 667–79.

Moro M., Brereton F., Ferreira S., Clinch P. (2008) Ranking quality of life using subjective well-being data, *Ecological Economics* 65, 448–60.

Stevenson B., Wolfers J. (2008) Economic growth and subjective well-being: Reassessing the Easterlin paradox, *Brookings Papers on Economic Activity*, Spring 2008, 1–87.

Walsh B. (2011) Well-being and economic conditions in Ireland, University College Dublin Centre for Economic Research, Working Paper, WP11/27.

Walsh B., Walsh D. (2011) Suicide in Ireland: The influence of alcohol and unemployment, *Economic and Social Review* 42, 27–47.

Walsh D., Daly A. (2004) *Mental Illness in Ireland, 1750–2002*, Dublin: Health Research Board.

Whelan C.T. (1992) The role of income, life-style deprivation and financial strain in mediating the impact of unemployment on psychological distress: evidence from the Republic of Ireland, *Journal of Occupational and Organisational Psychology* 65, 331–44.

Index

accessibility 2, 19–20, 33, 52–5, 83–4,
115
ageing 3, 11, 66, 110–12, 116–17, 120–1,
124, 137–8, 154
see also policy
and dependency 110, 112, 114–15,
118–20
attitudes 1–2, 53, 113, 118, 120, 174

biopsychosocial model 15, 111

care 42, 81, 111–12, 115–21, 123–38,
143–4, 153–4, 160–1
see also costs
caregivers 3, 87–8, 123, 129, 133, 137,
169
caring *see* care
see also costs
contingent valuation 172–4
cost-effectiveness analysis 170
cost of disability payment 34, 58, 72
cost of illness studies 124–5, 160
dementia 124–32, 138
mental health 160, 169–70
costs
of caring 74, 80–1, 83–9, 123–4,
128–31, 133–6
cost of disability 22, 34, 58–9, 71, 74,
80–1
estimates 62, 63, 68–71
estimation approaches 59–62

budget standards approach 60, 72
direct survey approach 59–60, 62,
72
expenditure diary approach 60,
62, 72
standard of living approach
59–68
of dementia 123–4
estimates 125–35, 138
of intellectual disability and
community living 143–4,
146–7, 150–4
of mental health/illness 169–70

debt 74, 80
dementia 118–19, 123–4
see also cost of illness studies; costs;
policy; prevalence
Dependence Scale (DS) 133–5
Disability Assessment for Dementia
(DAD) 133–5
National Strategy for Dementia 124,
138
resource allocation 136–8
deprivation 23, 28, 34, 78, 89, 114, 178–9,
183
Disability Act (2005) 1, 33, 55, 115, 117
discrimination 38–9, 53–6, 116, 120–1,
174
Americans with Disabilities Act 39
Disability Discrimination Act 39

education
see also policy
and disability 2, 5, 17–22, 34, 53, 79
funding models 93–9, 104–5
general allocation model (GAM)
99–104, 106
input-based model 95–6, 98–9, 104
throughput model 96–9, 101, 104–5
output model 97–8, 105
and inclusion 93, 104–6
parental education 78, 82, 86–9
resource allocation *see* education:
funding models
special education 93, 94, 99–105
employment *see* labour market

health technology assessment 124–5,
136–8

income 5, 14, 22, 27–8, 34, 50–2, 58,
71–2, 74, 78–9, 86, 88–9
see also social protection system:
income support; mental stress
equivilisation 34, 63, 72
informal care 3, 123–4, 126, 128–31,
133–4, 137–8
intellectual disability 18, 30–1, 40, 42, 54,
56, 76–7, 142–4, 153–5
see also costs; policy
community living 142–4, 153–5
deinstitutionalisation 142
Report of the Commission of Inquiry
on Mental Handicap 142
International Classification of
Functioning, Disability and
Health 15, 113

labour market 14–5
see also policy
earnings 38, 50, 51, 52, 55
employment 2, 5, 33–4, 38–9, 41,
43–4, 47–8, 50–2, 54–6, 78, 81,
169–70
labour force participation 22, 38, 40,
43–7, 55, 83–5, 87

barriers to 39, 52–5
and onset of disability 47–50
and persistent disability 49–50
labour force status 40–3
turn down work activities 85, 87
life course 1–2, 4, 11, 17, 19, 79, 111, 116
life cycle 1–2, 10–11

mainstreaming 1–2, 4, 93–4, 117, 120
medical model 111–13, 115–16
mental health 11, 160
see also cost of illness studies; costs;
policy
A Vision for Change 160–1, 166, 173
economic evaluation in 160, 170–3
expenditure on 163–7, 174
outcome measures 168
services 160–1, 173
mental illness 12, 160–1
see also costs; prevalence
admissions 163–4
mental stress 177, 185
and alcohol 183–5
General Health Questionnaire (GHQ)
161–2, 179–81, 185
and income 178–9, 184–5
socioeconomic determinants 178–85
subjective well-being 177, 181–2,
184–5
Easterlin paradox 184–5
and suicide 177, 182–5

National Disability Authority Act, 1999
112
National Disability Strategy 4, 117, 142
needs-based model 2, 96–7

person-centred model 2–3, 116–17, 121,
137, 161
policy 1, 5, 14–15, 33, 38, 58, 72, 111, 117,
120
see also Disability Act (2005); National
Disability Authority Act;
National Disability Strategy;
social protection system

ageing 117–20, 136
  dementia 124, 136–8
  education 93–4, 104–6
    EPSEN Act 94, 105
  implementation 3, 111
  intellectual disability 142–3, 154
  labour market 39, 52, 54–6
  mental health 161, 173–4
  social inclusion 33, 34
poverty 5, 14–15, 22–8, 34, 38, 74, 78,
    80
  at risk of poverty 23–4, 27–8
  consistent poverty 23–6, 28
  economic hardship 78, 88–9
prevalence
  of dementia 118–19, 123–4, 130–2
  of disability 6–8, 16, 75–7, 110
  of mental illness 161–3

residential supports 142–4, 150, 154–5
rights-based approach 33, 112, 117

satisfaction paradox 114
Sen Amartya 10–11, 14, 58–60
social care 111–2, 115–7, 119, 123, 126,
    130, 133–8

social class 87–9
social exclusion 14–15, 38, 58, 112, 116
social inclusion 14–15, 17, 23, 28–9,
    33–4, 58, 153–4
  see also policy
social model 111–18, 120
social participation 15, 29–34, 114
social protection system 14, 34
  disability benefits 5, 6, 15, 38
  income support 15, 33–4, 39
  see also policy
social transfers 14, 33–4, 38
social welfare 5, 26, 33, 63
socioeconomic status 1–2, 74–81, 83,
    89–90, 96, 177–8, 185
supports 19–20, 52–3, 93, 101, 104, 106,
    119
  see also residential supports

technology 136–8
  Connected Health 137
  Technology Research for Independent
    Living project 136
Townsend, Peter 1

unemployment *see* labour market